Trial Consulting

Trial Consulting

Amy J. Posey and Lawrence S. Wrightsman

OXFORD
UNIVERSITY PRESS

2005

OXFORD

UNIVERSITY PRESS

Oxford University Press, Inc., publishes works that further
Oxford University's objective of excellence
in research, scholarship, and education.

Oxford   New York
Auckland   Cape Town   Dar es Salaam   Hong Kong   Karachi
Kuala Lumpur   Madrid   Melbourne   Mexico City   Nairobi
New Delhi   Shanghai   Taipei   Toronto

With offices in
Argentina   Austria   Brazil   Chile   Czech Republic   France   Greece
Guatemala   Hungary   Italy   Japan   Poland   Portugal   Singapore
South Korea   Switzerland   Thailand   Turkey   Ukraine   Vietnam

Published by Oxford University Press, Inc.
198 Madison Avenue, New York, New York 10016

www.oup.com

Oxford is a registered trademark of Oxford University Press

Library of Congress Cataloging-in-Publication Data
Posey, Amy J.
Trial consulting / Amy J. Posey and Lawrence S. Wrightsman.
   p. cm. — (American Psychology-Law Society series)
Includes bibliographical references and index.
ISBN-13 978-0-19-518309-2
ISBN 0-19-518309-6
1. Trial practice—United States.   2. Witnesses—United States.   3. Jury selection—United States.
4. Consultants—United States.   I. Wrightsman, Lawrence S.   II. Title.   III. Series.
KF8915.P67 2005
347.73'75—dc22   2004029052

9 8 7 6 5 4 3 2 1

Printed in the United States of America
on acid-free paper

To Ron and Bea

Series Foreword

Ronald Roesch, Senior Editor

This book series is sponsored by the American Psychology-Law Society (APLS). APLS is an interdisciplinary organization devoted to scholarship, practice, and public service in psychology and law. Its goals include advancing the contributions of psychology to the understanding of law and legal institutions through basic and applied research; promoting the education of psychologists in matters of law and the education of legal personnel in matters of psychology; and informing the psychological and legal communities and the general public of current research, educational, and service activities in the field of psychology and law. APLS membership includes psychologists from the academic research and clinical practice communities as well as members of the legal community. Research and practice are represented in both the civil and criminal legal arenas. APLS has chosen Oxford University Press as a strategic partner because of its commitment to scholarship, quality, and the international dissemination of ideas. These strengths will help APLS reach our goal of educating the psychology and legal professions and the general public about important developments in the fields of psychology and law. The book series will reflect the diversity of the fields of psychology and law by publishing works on a broad range of topics. Books currently in production provide analyses and reviews in the areas of the death penalty, trial consulting, and civil litigation.

Preface

In its roughly 25 years of existence, the trial consulting profession has grown, blossomed, and in some ways sprouted thorns. Membership in the American Society of Trial Consultants (ASTC) numbered about 25 in 1982, when the organization held its first meeting; it now stands near 450. And because membership in ASTC is not required in order to practice as a trial consultant, the actual number of consultants is higher. In the early days, trial consultants were academic social scientists, who offered their services for free and whose activities were limited mainly to assisting with jury selection in criminal trials. Today, trial consultants continue to be primarily social scientists, but there are also many with backgrounds in other disciplines, such as theater and graphics. Although they do occasionally still offer their services for free, salaries in the six figures are not uncommon. Most of their work these days is done in the civil arena, and their activities now include witness preparation, trial graphics, change of venue surveys, focus groups, mock trials, and working with lawyers on their presentation style.

In spite of such enormous growth, the work of trial consultants has gone largely unexamined. In this book, we seek to answer questions about the most common activities of trial consultants. What do they entail? Are they supported empirically? What do they contribute beyond what lawyers do already? What are the relevant ethical issues? We also seek to examine the profession's ongoing struggle to define itself, striking a delicate balance between embracing a diversity of members and practices to placing limits on what can legitimately be called "trial consulting" and the educational and experiential background necessary so that one may be properly referred to as a "trial consultant."

To achieve our objectives, we have drawn upon empirical and other scholarly work in the social sciences, the recommendations of legal scholars gleaned from law journals and other legal periodicals, and the written and spoken recommendations of the trial consultants themselves, which have been published in academic journals and the ASTC publication *Court Call,* presented at annual meetings of the ASTC, and shared in our own conversations with them. Finally, we have drawn on our own experiences doing trial-consulting work. We believe that this book will be of interest to both academic and professional audiences: scientists with an interest in the application of psychology to law; students interested in knowing more about trial consulting as a potential career path; practicing trial consultants; and those with whom they work most closely, the trial lawyers themselves.

Acknowledgments

This book benefited from the contributions of students and guest speakers who participated in a semester-long seminar at the University of Kansas in the fall of 2003. The second author coordinated the seminar, and the first author, who was on sabbatical leave from her institution, participated. We were fortunate to have four of the most distinguished trial consultants in the country come to the seminar and make presentations: Dr. Karen Lisko, Dr. C. K. "Pete" Rowland, Ms. Lisa Dahl, and Dr. Tom Beisecker. We are also grateful to a very experienced trial attorney, Tina Traficanti, who also shared her insights with the class. Dr. George Hunter, a recent graduate and now a trial consultant, also contributed, as did the following students: Vanessa Edkins, Rachel Amo, Ruth Warner, Kevin Boully, Erica de Garmo, Emily MacDonald, and Ryan McNeil.

Permission is granted to reprint Box 7-1, page 161, and Box 7-2, pages 164–165, by Kluwer Academic Publishers and by the authors.

Permission is granted to reprint passages on pages 156, 218, 222, and 227 from *The Majesty of the Law* by Sandra Day O'Connor, copyright © 2003 by Arizona Community Foundation. Used by permission of Random House, Inc.

Permission is granted to reprint passages on pages 138, 139, 140, and 142 from *Punitive Damages: How Juries Decide* by Cass Sunstein et al., published by the University of Chicago Press. Copyright © 2002 by University of Chicago.

Contents

Trial Consulting

1

Trial Consulting
Does It Help to Achieve
the Goal of Justice?

Despite its short history, the term *trial consulting* has developed a distinctly odious connotation. In the eyes of some observers, trial consultants are interlopers who corrupt the fairness of the jury-trial process by identifying and selecting jurors who are biased in one direction, usually that favoring the innocence of a criminal defendant. In fact, several years ago a bill was introduced in the Illinois legislature to prohibit nonlawyers from participating in the jury-selection process (it did not come to a vote). And the first book that systematically examined trial consulting had as its malevolent title *Stack and Sway* (Kressel & Kressel, 2002).

In contrast, many trial lawyers believe that the use of a trial-consulting firm is essential to their success. One Boston lawyer concluded: "No self-respecting trial lawyer will go through the process of jury selection in an important case without the assistance of highly paid trial consultants" (Walker, 1995, p. 34). A New York City attorney also conceded, "It's gotten to the point where if the case is large enough, it's almost malpractice not to use them" (quoted by Adler, 1989, p. 1). In O. J. Simpson's criminal trial, both sides—initially, at least—used litigation consultants, and when Martha Stewart was scheduled for trial early in 2004, her attorneys hired a highly successful consultant, Julie Blackman. In highly publicized trials in the mid-2000s, it seemingly had become the norm for each side to hire a trial consultant; this was true for Stewart's trial in early 2004, and also for Scott Peterson's, which stretched through the middle of that year.

It is claimed that trial consulting is now a $400 million industry (Gordon, 1995); the number of practitioners, while not easy to pinpoint, has been estimated to include 700 individuals and more than 400 firms (Gallagher, 1995; Lassiter, 1996). Likewise, it is difficult to determine the number of cases a year in which they participate, although figures between 6,000 and 10,000 per year have been offered (Kressel & Kressel, 2002). Regardless, the field is booming and is likely to expand. Ann Harriet Cole, a recent president of the American Society of Trial Consultants (ASTC), told a gathering of new members: "Business is burgeoning. Most people are turning away work, referring it to colleagues. We're not seen [by attorneys] as some weird thing, but as something they need to do or they may not be doing all they can for their clients. It is a growing field, not a profession with finite opportunities. The more people, the more opportunity" (Kressel & Kressel, 2002, p. 74). Elsewhere, Cole wrote:

> Our profession has finally arrived. I know this is true because
> when I tell folks that I meet socially, not just high stakes civil and
> criminal attorneys, that I'm one of those people who work with
> lawyers to define trial strategy, find the "story" in every case,
> prepare witnesses to testify and . . . help select juries—that in short,
> I'm a litigation consultant, a trial consultant or a jury consultant
> (whichever one falls out of my mouth depends on whim and mood
> of the moment), most of them have a sense of what I mean and also
> know that I'm not some shady kind of private investigator who
> attempts to tamper with an actual jury. Ten years ago . . . that
> mostly wasn't the case. Sixteen years ago, when I first paid my dues
> and showed up at the 1983 ASTC Conference in Chicago that surely
> wasn't the case. (Cole, 1999, p. 10)

But what do trial consultants really do? Is their only vital function to assist in selecting the jury? And how good are they at that? The purposes of this book are to explore the multitude of roles for trial consultants, to describe the major activities they do (not just the misnamed "jury selection"), and to evaluate both their effectiveness and their ethics. Our basic viewpoint is that trial consultants do a number of things that extend beyond the public's casual awareness. Assisting attorneys in the identification of undesirable jurors propelled the field into a solid existence, but trial consultants place less emphasis on jury selection than they did earlier (Kressel & Kressel, 2002). As Florence Keller has said, "Selecting a jury is in many ways the least important thing we do" (Kressel & Kressel, 2002, p. 87).

We also propose that it is difficult to provide an all-encompassing evaluation of trial consultants because some of their activities are more beneficial to the achievement of justice than are others. In this chapter, we will describe examples of several activities which, we believe, differ with respect to their aiding in the cause of justice. Then we consider the general criticisms of the field and its responses to these criticisms. Our intended stance, throughout the book, is neither a broadside attack nor an unqualified endorsement of what trial consultants do. Instead, the fundamental questions we seek to answer are: Does what they do make any difference in outcomes? Does what they do serve the cause of justice?

Terminology: A "Trial Consultant" or a "Litigation Consultant"?

First, let us address the matter of terminology: we use the terms *trial consultant*, *legal consultant*, and *litigation consultant* interchangeably. The latter term is probably most descriptive, as *litigation* is a broader term than *trial*, and many cases are resolved before a trial is held (trial consultants, by conducting focus groups of mock jurors, may produce sample awards in civil cases, causing their clients to settle prior to a trial). But the term *trial consultant* appears in the literature more often than does *litigation consultant*, and thus we will use it predominantly. Another term, *jury consultant*, is also used. We avoid this term because it implies a narrower scope; trial consultants work with attorneys to develop their theory of the case and with witnesses to make effective presentations. These are done in order to achieve success for their clients, whether the outcome is decided by a jury or by a judge, or even settled before trial.

The Field of Trial Consulting

Who are trial consultants and what kind of training do they receive? No simple answers are available for these questions, for several reasons. The occupation of *trial consultant* is not licensed or otherwise regulated in any state; hence, anyone can call him- or herself a trial consultant. The official organization, the American Society of Trial Consultants, is currently composed of about 450 members, but membership in this organization is not required in order to hang out a shingle, and the organization is still in the process of developing standards for what is acceptable behavior by its members.

In keeping with the lack of training requirements, not all of those who call themselves trial consultants have had any graduate training; while many have a Ph.D. or law degree and some a master's degree, for others, who entered trial consulting from a theater or graphics background, a bachelor's degree is sufficient. The field of specialization is quite varied; most typically it is psychology or speech communication, but some trial consultants are also lawyers or have done their graduate work in political science or sociology. The membership in ASTC cannot be used as a firm estimate of the number of consultants in the field; some of the most prominent consultants are not members of ASTC. Furthermore, while for many consultants, this is a full-time activity, others are college professors or psychotherapists who consult on a part-time basis. And, rarely, a part-time trial consultant and part-time psychotherapist becomes a media celebrity, as "Dr. Phil" (Phil McGraw) did, after assisting Oprah Winfrey when she was a defendant in a civil suit. (McGraw was, until recently, a member of the American Society of Trial Consultants; its 2002–2003 membership directory identified him as the president of Courtroom Sciences, Incorporated, of Irving, Texas.)

The ASTC has organizational memberships as well as individual ones, although not all of the large consulting organizations participate. Some trial-consulting firms, such as Forensic Technologies International and DecisionQuest, have offices in a number of cities throughout the United States and employ a hundred or so consultants, although the number of consultants in each of their branch offices is usually small. Other firms have only one office, with perhaps three, four, or five practitioners. Many consultants exist as one-person operations, with a bare-bones support staff.

The History of Trial Consulting

The history of trial consulting is a brief one. If one beginning date could be specified for scientific jury selection, it would be the year 1972, when a group of sociologists and social psychologists assisted in the defense of the "Harrisburg Seven," a group of priests and nuns who had been charged with conspiring to raid draft boards, blow up steam tunnels under Washington, DC, and plot other anti–Vietnam War activities. (The procedures used by the consultants in this case are described in detail in chapter 8.) The social scientists received no pay for their work; they did it because of their uncompromising commitment to the antiwar movement. Some of their activities remain staples of the business, but consultants have broadened their efforts to other topics, such as the use of focus groups and witness preparation.

Trial consulting "has come a long way from its origins in political activism" (Kressel & Kressel, 2002, p. 65). Perhaps the major difference between the field in 1972 and now is in the nature of the clients. Encouraged by their success in the Harrisburg Seven trial, consultants assisted the defense in a number of other highly publicized trials of war protesters and civil-rights activists in the 1970s and 1980s. More recently, however, public attention has been directed toward consultants' contributions to the defense of celebrities such as O. J. Simpson and William Kennedy Smith, Senator Ted Kennedy's nephew who was charged with rape. In 2004, several highly publicized cases, those of Michael Jackson, Scott Peterson, and Kobe Bryant, as well as the aforementioned Martha Stewart, intensified the public's curiosity about trial consultants.

But the public's focus on consulting in criminal trials is misleading; currently more consulting activities involve civil litigation rather than criminal. For this book, we did a survey of ASTC members and found that, on the average, only 5% of their time was spent working on criminal cases, while nearly 80% of their time was spent representing clients who were involved in civil cases. (The remainder of consultants' practice was dedicated to activities they listed under the category "other," including congressional testimony, international arbitrations, patent hearings, and continuing legal education.) Today the typical client is a large organization that is a defendant in a product-liability case or even a wrongful-death civil suit; it may be the maker of automobile seat belts or a drug manufacturer. Mass torts—such as asbestos cases, breast-implant suits, or Fen-Phen lawsuits—are now common examples of cases in which defendants hire consultants for assistance. One firm, Trial Behavior Consulting Inc., assisted the defense in 150 asbestos-related trials in the 1980s, and David Island, TBCI's founder, has estimated that he has picked between 300 and 400 juries and prepared between 1,000 and 1,500 witnesses in such cases (Kressel & Kressel, 2002). Strier (1999) comments on this shift:

> One inescapable irony marks the evolution of trial consulting. The first beneficiaries of trial consulting were indigent criminal defendants tried in the crucible of the antiwar protest[s] and other political involvements of the later 1970s. Protest sympathizers . . . assembled teams to counteract the overwhelming advantage of the state against poor political dissidents. In contrast, today's typical clienteles are the wealthy and the privileged—corporations and well-heeled, prominent individuals, often celebrities, engaged in civil litigation. (p. 95)

If we date the beginning of systematic jury selection from 1972, the field reflects a history of a little more than 30 years. The formal organization, the American Society of Trial Consultants, was formed in October 1982, with only a couple of dozen members present at the initial meeting in Phoenix, Arizona (Matlon, 1998). (At this meeting, the organization was named "Association of Trial Behavior Consultants"; the name was changed in 1985.) The organization's purposes are "to foster communication among its members, provide a forum for development of trial practice methods, and promote knowledge of effective and ethical use of trial consulting techniques" ("About Court Call," 2001, p. 2). The organization maintains a central office headed by its executive director, Dr. Ronald J. Matlon, in Timonium, Maryland, and has an e-mail address, ASTCOffice@aol.com, and a Web page, www.astcweb.org. (It also has a listserv available only to ASTC members.) It publishes a combined journal-newsletter on-line, titled Court Call.

It is difficult to determine the typical fees and income of trial consultants. A decade ago, one report stated that consultants charged $75 to $300 an hour (Torry, 1994). Recently, a participant on the ASTC listserv sought to determine the current range of hourly fees; the general reaction was not only rejection of this inquiry, but also a concern that a quasi-public discussion of fee structures would risk a challenge of restraint of trade.

The reactions to this innocent inquiry reflect one of the dilemmas of the field. Trial consultants fill two roles: as practitioners, they are applied researchers, but they are also entrepreneurs. They constantly seek to determine what works, and they attend conventions and peruse journals in order to discover new techniques and instruments that improve their craft. But as entrepreneurs, they are in competition with each other. They must sell their product to trial attorneys, by offering cheaper rates, or a better likelihood of success, or some other incentive. It is not surprising that inflated claims about their effectiveness are sometimes made.

Scientists, even applied scientists, are expected to share their findings with others, as scientific knowledge is cumulative and constantly changing in response to new and recent research. But what if a consultant develops a surefire method of identifying probusiness jurors in, for example, product-liability suits? Does the consultant publish his or her findings and report them at professional meetings? Some do, and some don't. The central office of ASTC periodically offers a list of contributions sent in by members; some of these make the work of their competitors easier—a motion for an expanded voir dire or an example of a supplemental juror questionnaire. But there is a certain defensiveness about sharing "trade secrets"; some ASTC members have told us that consultants shouldn't disseminate instruments that they have developed because competitors might benefit from using them. Kressel and Kressel (2002) quote two prominent trial consultants:

> Explained David Island[,] . . . "trial consultants, by and large, are loathe to share with each other anything substantive about what they know." Harold Varinsky . . . agrees: "We don't really share knowledge the way other professions share knowledge. We try to protect our little insights and methodologies, more often than not. . . . What you find at conferences is geared toward the beginner . . . basic . . . platitudinal. . . . Knowledge is protected by each firm." Most consultants are very tight-lipped about what they do on the job, in part to protect client interests and confidentiality, but also because, as several concede privately, this is a somewhat paranoid field. In this business, many of the firms refer to much of what they do as "trade secrets." (p. 76)

Thus, a certain identity struggle characterizes the field. Other professions have struggled with this; consider, for example the legal profession and the debate over the propriety of lawyers' advertising. But these other professions have been able to come to terms over the conflict between competing values.

What Do Trial Consultants Do?

The task of the trial consultant is to be just that—a "consultant" to the attorney. Training in psychology, communications studies, and other social sciences gives the trial consultant a knowledge base that the lawyer usually does not have. The empirical study of jury behavior has been ongoing for 30 years now, beginning with the study of jurors' reactions in criminal trials and more recently moving to an investigation of reactions in civil cases. (These findings are summarized in chapter 6.) Some of the empirical findings are consistent with trial attorneys' expectations and stereotypes, but many are not. The knowledge possessed by the typical trial consultant can benefit the attorney, not just in selecting a "winning jury" but in deciding what aspects of the evidence to emphasize, which witness to present first, what type of closing argument to give, and other ways to make a more effective trial presentation.

Trial Consultants and Change-of-Venue Surveys

Trial consultants do much more than assist in the selection of jurors. Our survey found that they spend almost one third of their professional time in conducting focus groups and mock trials, about 10% of their time in preparation of witnesses for trial, and a similar amount of time working with attorneys in the preparation of case strategies, opening statements, and closing arguments. Only 12% of the time was spent in jury selection. One activity, not well known by the public, is determining if a criminal defendant can get a fair trial in a local jurisdiction. If the crime was a particularly heinous one, or if its alleged perpetrator or victim was widely known, the publicity in the local media may be so extensive (and, characteristically, so one-sided) as to prevent the defendant from receiving a fair trial in that locale. For example, early in 2004, a judge agreed to move Scott Peterson's trial away from Peterson's home town of Modesto, California, because of excessive publicity.

Trial consultants may design and execute surveys of samples of the jury pool to determine the extent of knowledge of the case and the likelihood of forming a verdict prior to the trial. Ideally, these responses are compared with those of prospective jurors in another jurisdiction that is distant but demographically similar to the local jurisdiction. (Chapter 3 describes this procedure in detail.) If the percentage of prospective jurors in the local jurisdiction who have already formed an opinion of guilt is high, the defendant's attorney may request a change of venue. The trial consultant prepares an affidavit and may testify in support of this appeal.

The Sixth Amendment of the U.S. Constitution guarantees criminal defendants a fair trial, and even if the evidence prior to trial appears to be overwhelmingly against the defendant, it is unfair to have a defendant's fate decided by a group of jurors who have firmly made up their minds before hearing all of the evidence at trial.

So, trial consultants engage in activities that are in support of the goals of the criminal justice system. An example is provided by the work of Lisa Dahl of Litigation Consultants, a small trial consulting firm in Lawrence, Kansas. In March 1996, Gary Kleypas was charged with the murder of Carrie

Williams, a young woman who lived only two doors from him in Pittsburg, Kansas. Not only was this a heinous crime, but it was the second time in 3 years that a female student at Pittsburg State University had been murdered by someone whom she knew and trusted.

Pittsburg, Kansas, is a town of fewer than 20,000, in Crawford County (population around 38,000). The local newspaper and regional television stations devoted extensive coverage to the crime; people learned that Kleypas was a parolee with a record of violent crimes; coverage focused on similarities to the other murder 3 years before. In the 9 months between the murder and the trial, publicity about the case included the following (derived from an analysis of 146 articles in 11 newspapers):

> Readers learned that Kleypas was arrested on an unrelated rape charge two days after the murder, following a suicide attempt in which he injected himself with cocaine and slit his wrists. They also learned that Kleypas admitted three times to murdering Williams: once in the police car following his arrest, once on videotape during interrogation, and a third time during the preliminary hearing. The videotaped confession was aired repeatedly on television in Crawford County. The media also revealed that Kleypas had served half of a 30-year sentence for the sexual assault of a 78-year-old woman who had been his neighbor. Sensational details of that crime, such as the presence of his pubic hair and teeth marks about her breast and body, were disclosed. Finally, the newspapers made reference to Kleypas' "criminal habit," and relayed his admission that alcohol leaves him powerless against his violent impulses. (Posey & Dahl, 2002, p. 108)

After being contacted by Kleypas's defense attorney, the trial consultant designed a telephone survey to elicit the knowledge possessed by persons in the countywide jury pool. Of 300 Crawford County respondents, 294, or 98%, recognized the case based on a very brief description. Of these, 87% believed that Kleypas was guilty (Posey & Dahl, 2002). On the basis of the findings from this survey, the presiding judge in Crawford County accepted the request of a change of venue and moved the trial to another county in a different part of the state. The jury there found Gary Kleypas guilty of murder and sentenced him to death. While it is probably small consolation to him, the legal system was responsive to the data provided by a trial consultant.

Did the trial consultant do "the right thing" in this case? We believe she did. First, she followed the guidelines of good question construction; she identified a comparison county; she interviewed adequate numbers of respondents in each county; she reported the results accurately; and she drew fair conclusions. (Had the results been similar in the two counties, or had the sample in Crawford County not reflected a pretrial bias, she would have so reported.) While judges may have legitimate reasons for refusing to move a trial to another jurisdiction, we believe that anyone broadly concerned with justice would not find fault with the trial consultant's activities in this example.

Trial Consultants and Trial Strategy

But are there examples of trial consultants going beyond their designated role? Do trial consultants sometimes exceed what the public might think is appropriate? Consider the following case. (Our description is based on the interviews and extensive review of the case by Adler, 1994.)

Bruce Bochini, a 17-year-old boy, had been riding his bicycle around twilight when he was hit by a drunk driver. The result was a smashed foot, a fractured collarbone, some broken vertebrae—and, most important—some brain damage that affected his mental abilities. Examining physicians predicted that "he would have trouble holding down a job and even greater difficulty in personal relationships" (Adler, 1994, p. 91). The medical bills his family accrued and the losses he had sustained could be justification for a million-dollar award in a lawsuit. Marty Cohen, an Easton, Pennsylvania, lawyer, brought suit against the driver, Cindy Yerkes, but he soon encountered a problem: the defendant didn't have much money. Her insurance limit was only $100,000. Cohen asked a prominent trial consultant, Arthur Patterson, whom he had employed before, to conduct a focus group of mock jurors and to advise him after studying their reactions. Adler (1994) gives a concise description of the procedure:

> At a focus group conducted by Patterson in June 1991 Cohen learned a great deal about the challenge before him. In typical fashion the focus group had been selected meticulously. Patterson had started with the lists the county used to call residents for jury duty, then factored in the no-show rate for different ethnic groups. In addition, he had accounted for the likelihood that individuals in certain professions, such as law office employees or journalists, would be eliminated in a real case through peremptory challenges. On the basis of these calculations, he had determined that the jury that would hear the case would probably include at most five white-collar workers, among them two professionals; four housewives; two unemployed people; and two or three retirees. Within this group at least three would be unmarried or divorced. Five, at most, would have college degrees. The pre-trial focus group would reflect these calculations in the belief that it would presage the actual jury's attitudes and concerns. In voir dire, of course, Cohen would seek to use his peremptory challenges to control the shape of the jury that would hear his case. (p. 92)

The focus group, acting as a mock jury, heard a streamlined presentation of the trial, with one of Cohen's partners acting as the plaintiff's attorney. He attempted to focus responsibility not only on Mrs. Yerkes, but on Pizza Hut, because she had reported that she had been drinking that afternoon at the local Pizza Hut (although she consistently claimed that she couldn't remember who her drinking companion was). Marty Cohen chose to represent Pizza Hut in this mock trial, and he ridiculed the plaintiff for bringing suit against a major, "deep-pockets" firm. Apparently he was quite effective; 9 of the 12 in the focus group, acting as mock jurors, found that Cindy Yerkes had been negligent, but only one believed that Pizza Hut was also liable. While individual mock jurors made awards as high as $4 million, the $100,000 ceiling on Mrs. Yerkes's insurance stood as a barrier.

At this point, Arthur Patterson, the trial consultant, devised an alternative opening statement for attorney Cohen, which focused on the responsibility of Pizza Hut to regulate those customers who showed signs of getting drunk. (The law in Pennsylvania requires that servers refuse to provide drinks to anyone who is visibly intoxicated.) "We need to stress that the restaurant's profit margin on alcohol is higher than it is on food," Patterson noted. "[T]he restaurant is there to make money; they have a motive. Jurors love motives" (Adler, 1994, p. 98). Blaming Pizza Hut became the focus: "Aim the blame at managers. It's the executives, the people above," Patterson told Cohen (Adler, 1994, p. 99).

Cohen was able, at the actual trial, to implement Patterson's suggestions, not only emphasizing Pizza Hut's negligence but noting the fact that Mrs. Yerkes had spent 3 hours there, drinking with an unnamed person. But the jury didn't get to decide the case; in the middle of the testimony, a mistrial was declared by the judge because an expert witness had made an inadmissible claim. Just as a new panel of jurors was called in and a second trial was to start, Pizza Hut's lawyers offered to settle the case for $350,000; this, along with Mrs. Yerkes's insurance limit of $100,000, meant an award of $450,000 to Bruce Bochini. Cohen and his client accepted the offer.

It seems clear that Patterson's advice to Cohen had affected the outcome of the lawsuit and the size of the award. Was justice done? Did the trial consultant intrude improperly on the trial process? The goal of attorneys is to "zealously" represent their clients, and it is appropriate for an attorney to ask a trial consultant: "What is the best way to maximize my client receiving benefits?" The trial consultant who accepts the ethical standards of the legal profession as his or her own would consider what Arthur Patterson did as not just acceptable, but required. And a further defense that is offered here is that, if the jury thought that Pizza Hut was not liable, the jury could so rule.

Criticisms of Trial Consulting

Concerns with the field of trial consulting center around its efficacy, the fairness of its procedures, and its ethics (Strier, 2001). We will consider its efficacy when we review the specific kinds of activities in subsequent chapters; we focus here on its fairness and its ethics. The following are among the major criticisms of trial consulting:

1. Trial consultants intrude on the trial process, usurp the functions of lawyers, and have a disproportionate effect on the outcome of jury trials.
2. Trial consultants make unwarranted or unverifiable claims about their effectiveness.
3. Trial consultants favor the rich.
4. Trial consultants are not regulated and hence are uncontrolled.

We consider each of these criticisms in turn.

Intruding on the Trial Process

Strier (1999) has observed that criticism of trial consulting is now more salient because of the unpopular jury decisions in cases that utilized trial consultants:

> Consultants were heralded as winning or helping gain a favorable outcome in the O. J. Simpson criminal trial, . . . the first [so-called] Rodney King trial, the first Menendez brothers' trial, the trial of the individuals who beat trucker Reginald Denny during the Los Angeles riots, the trial of New York "subway vigilante" Bernhard Goetz, and the William Kennedy Smith rape trial. Included on the civil side would be the recent jury award in excess of $1 million to compensate a McDonald's customer for injuries attributable to coffee that was "too hot." (pp. 93–94)

The trial of John Mitchell and Maurice Stans has been nominated as an example of the worst fears of those critics of trial consulting who claim that "jury rigging" is easily accomplished. Yet, in truth, the defense attorneys and the consultants they hired succeeded despite themselves.

In the spring of 1974, at the height of the publicity over the break-in at Democratic Party headquarters at the Watergate Hotel in Washington, DC, John Mitchell and Maurice Stans were brought to trial in federal court in New York City, charged with perjury, obstruction of justice, and conspiracy to impede a Securities and Exchange Commission investigation of Robert L. Vesco, a financier and fugitive from justice. It was claimed that Mitchell, who had chaired President Richard Nixon's reelection campaign in 1972, and Stans, the campaign treasurer, had received a $200,000 contribution from Vesco, targeted for use in the campaign, in return for promised assistance to Vesco, who was being investigated by the government commission. Mitchell and Stans also had played prominent roles in Nixon's administration, serving as attorney general and secretary of the Treasury, respectively; in fact, the trial was the first in American history in which two of the president's Cabinet members were tried jointly on criminal charges.

Rumor has it that, before the trial, Stans and Mitchell told their defense attorneys to approach a group of social scientists for help in selecting their jury. The procedure, which came to be called *scientific jury selection*, had only come to light a few years before, when Jay Schulman, Richard Christie, and other social scientists had assisted the Harrisburg Seven defendants. But these social scientists were willing to offer their free services only to those activists and protest groups who were considered to be the targets of a government that sought to stifle dissent. They decidedly had no interest in furthering the cause of President Nixon's cronies.

Having been rebuffed by the social scientists, Mitchell and Stans hired a public relations firm to conduct a survey, in order to give their attorneys guidance in selecting their jury. Jury "selection," is of course, a misnomer; no attorney can guarantee that a desirable prospective juror will end up on the jury. The goal is to dismiss from jury service those persons who are predicted to be biased against their side, and that is what the public relations firm attempted to do. Its profile of "the worst possible juror" included the following characteristics: a liberal Democrat, Jewish, someone who read the *New York Times* or the *New York Post*, someone who watched the TV news with Walter Cronkite (then the most influential of television news anchorpersons), someone who was interested in political issues, and someone who was well informed about Watergate.

This would appear to be a daunting task: to try to compose a jury of 12 residents of New York City who were not well educated, who were not Jewish, and who—in 1974—had never heard of Watergate. Thanks to the detailed analysis of this case's jury-selection procedures by social scientists Hans Zeisel and Shari Seidman Diamond (1976), on whose report we have heavily relied, an evaluation can be made of the defense team's success.

The jury selection process begins with the drawing of a panel, or venire, of prospective jurors. In the Mitchell/Stans trial, an abnormally large number—196 persons—was included. The presiding judge promptly excluded 85 of these potential jurors for "hardship" reasons, including childcare responsibilities, poor health, or work demands. After questioning of the panel, 38 more were excused because they had a possible conflict of interest or bias. Then the judge excused 21 more, leaving a net pool of 52, a figure he considered sufficient to cover the number of peremptory challenges he had granted to each side.

The prosecuting attorneys, representing the federal government, were apparently not especially concerned about making dismissals from within this group; they used only 6 of their allotted 8 peremptory challenges. In contrast, the Mitchell/Stans defense team capitalized on every opportunity, using all 20 of its peremptory challenges for the 12-person jury and its 3 for the 6 alternate jurors. And it was highly successful: of the original 196 members of the venire, 45% had some college education, while only 1 (or

8%) of the actual jurors did—and only 1 year of college at that. Thirty-two percent of the original pool described themselves as "well informed" about Watergate; only 1 of the 12 eventual jurors did. None of the jurors or alternates had an apparently Jewish name. The jury was composed mostly of clerical and blue-collar workers with high-school educations, who seemingly were unconcerned about the Watergate break-in. The foreperson was a 21-year-old woman who was a bank teller.

If a jury-selection strategy ever had a good chance of being successful, this one did. Not only was representativeness severely eroded, but the actual jurors were almost handpicked to avoid the defense team's "worst-possible" label. So how well did this strategy work? One of the delicious ironies of this case is that it would not have worked, except for an accidental happening that the defense team even tried to prevent.

Newspaper reporters covering the case and local court observers figured that Mitchell and Stans would surely be found guilty. Although conspiracy is a hard charge to prove, the government had accumulated some impressive evidence regarding the charges of perjury and obstruction of justice. And despite the one-sidedness of the jury's composition, the inclination of most jurors, once they began their deliberations, was to find the defendants guilty. A *New York Times* reporter, Martin Arnold (1974), interviewed some of the jurors after the verdict was announced and reconstructed the process of the deliberations. He learned that the initial, informal vote by the jurors was 8 for conviction and 4 for acquittal. Even given the stringent requirement of a unanimous verdict, it is very likely that this jury would have eventually found Mitchell and Stans guilty—unless special circumstances intervened. We can draw this conclusion based on an extensive survey of actual juries done by Kalven and Zeisel (1966), which examined the first ballot and final verdict in 225 jury trials that used 12-person juries. They found that when the number of votes for conviction on the first ballot was between 7 and 11—recall that here it was 8—the final result was a unanimous verdict of guilty in 86% of the trials.

In only 1 trial out of every 20 does an initial vote split like this one lead to an eventual acquittal. But such a turnaround *did* happen in the Mitchell/Stans trial, because a special circumstance intervened in the person of Andrew Choa, an alternate juror. He and he alone appears to have been the cause for the shift of the majority from conviction to acquittal—for despite its original vote leaning toward a vote of guilty, the jury eventually, and unanimously, acquitted the defendants. (Both Mitchell and Stans were later found guilty of other Watergate-related crimes, however.)

Among the ironies surrounding this special circumstance, one is that Choa would not have been serving on this jury had not one of the jurors become ill a few weeks into the 10-week trial. And most certainly he was not what the defense team wanted on the jury. Andrew Choa was a vice president of the First National City Bank (then the second largest in the United States); he was a college graduate; he most certainly read the *New York Times* every day; and he probably knew as much about the Watergate issue as anyone in the original venire of 196 persons. In fact, the defense team had even tried to have him removed for cause (that is, for prejudice) on the grounds that he was "too" well informed about Watergate, but the judge had rejected their request (however, Maurice Stans's account of the trial claims that he and Mitchell had wished to have a "businessman or person of money sophistication" on the jury [Stans, 1978, p. 320]).

What the defense team did not know was that Choa was a dedicated supporter of President Nixon. Although he did not reveal his allegiances to his fellow jurors at the beginning of the deliberations, he gradually became an open advocate for the defense of Stans and Mitchell. He also ingratiated himself with the other jurors by breaking the monotony of the long evenings during sequestration (because of the publicity accorded this case before and during the trial, the judge had decided to isolate the jurors in a local hotel to shield them from outside influences in the evenings after they had heard the evidence or deliberated). Choa controlled a bunch of privileges that impressed and benefited the other jurors. For example, when the jurors wanted to see the St. Patrick's Day parade but were not allowed to mingle with the street crowds, Choa arranged for them to watch the festivities from one of the branch offices of his bank. Occasionally he took the other jurors to movies in the private auditorium of the bank. Choa served as a kind of social director for the group; he also paid some minor expenses of some of the other jurors. Observers have asked if the other jurors could have resisted being appreciative toward the man who used his high social position to make their 10 long weeks of sequestration more bearable (Zeisel & Diamond, 1976). How could they resist being influenced by him?

Not only was Choa ingratiating, but he also seemed to be aware of the tactics necessary to influence others. During the deliberations, he was initially circumspect. He later told the *New York Times* reporter that he had purposely chosen a seat that would ensure his being called on last. Even while declaring, "I did not want to influence my fellow jurors," he may have known that the person who speaks last carries an extra measure of influence. All of these actions swung the tide. Zeisel and Diamond (1976) wrote:

> We know that Choa was one of the four jurors who from the outset voted for acquittal and, we must presume, began the arduous task of converting the majority to his view. We know no details, but are told that he persuaded the jury at several points to have testimony as well as the judge's instructions reread. We do not know what testimony, but are told that these requests were drafted by Choa for the forelady's signature. When it came to the jury's appraisal of the memorandum written by Vesco (or an associate) to Nixon's brother, in which Vesco threatened to disclose his secret $200,000 cash contribution unless the SEC dropped his case, Choa

said he considered it "trash"—and the jury seemed to have agreed.
(p. 166)

Put yourself in the other jurors' shoes. Choa was rich and successful; he
was well informed on financial and governmental matters; and he seemed to
be a very helpful person. Whether he intended to or not, it would have been
difficult for Andrew Choa not to have been influential with his juror colleagues. And simply because of his accidental inclusion on the jury, the
defense team triumphed.

This trial is not typical, but it does serve as an example of the possible
impact of an intensive attempt to create a sympathetic jury. The eventual
success of the defense team was facilitated by the fact that they were given a
large number of peremptory challenges by the judge, a matter to which we
will return in the last chapter of this book. While the activities during voir
dire here may be considered unsavory, they were not illegal. We believe that
the primary fault lies in a system that provides opportunities to dismiss so
many "bad" jurors.

As we consider the criticism that the use of trial consultants is unfair, it
is important to distinguish between a perception of unfairness and actual
unfairness. The latter concern is dependent upon the effectiveness of scientific jury selection, a topic explored in great detail in chapters 7, 8, and 9.
But regardless of the actual effectiveness—a question that leads to complex
answers—if the public's perception is that consultants are rigging juries or
otherwise violating the goal of fairness, we need to be concerned (Etzioni,
1974a, 1974b). Periodically, such criticisms emerge in the popular media
and in law journals. For example, Gold (1987) feared that consultants'
application of persuasion techniques and analyses of jury decision making
would increase the likelihood of extraneous influences affecting verdicts.
Armed with such knowledge, "lawyers can induce jurors to make judgments
about the credibility of a speaker through manipulations of the 'power-
fulness' of the speaker's language" (Gold, 1987, p. 484).

The largest antitrust judgment of all time, $1.8 billion, was awarded to
MCI in its suit against AT&T in 1980. MCI's attorneys hired trial consultants who did a thorough survey of residents in that locale to identify
demographic characteristics that were related to support or rejection of
MCI's claims. Then the consultants had mock juries listen to presentations
from both sides, thus identifying which types of arguments were effective for
different types of jurors (Hans & Vidmar, 1986). They even tried out different award amounts with different mock juries (Kressel & Kressel, 2002).

Was this large award the result of consultants' intervention, or would it
have occurred regardless? We cannot say. However, instances exist in which
the actions of a trial consultant were designed deliberately to lead to a
mistrial or to subvert or at least delay the goals of the legal system. Strier
(1999) offers the example of trial consultant and psychologist Amy Singer,
who used a "poison pill" strategy to elicit a mistrial in the so-called Miami

River Cops trial in 1987. For defense lawyers, a mistrial may be just as useful as an acquittal, because the prosecutor might decide not to retry the case. According to newspaper reports of this case, Dr. Singer deliberately facilitated the inclusion of jurors "who would explode, would hate each other. That's what you want to do in a criminal case when it is obvious that people are guilty. You go for personalities [and then] you hope the personalities will combust" (Evans & Van Natta, 1993, p. A24).

Responses to this criticism of trial consultants usually reflect a claim that jury selection is nothing new, that lawyers have always acknowledged that, in the words of Clarence Darrow, "Never forget, almost every case has been won or lost when the jury is sworn" (quoted by Strier, 1999, p. 93). The late Judge Harold Rothwax cynically observed that a defense attorney would seek "jurors who will not or cannot intelligently evaluate evidence. He [sic] will want gullible, manipulatable, emotional, suggestible jurors— and through our system of selection he will get them" (1996, pp. 200–201). There is nothing to prevent lawyers from doing what trial consultants do during voir dire, observing the answers of prospective jurors and rating each with regard to his or her sympathy with the lawyer's client. This position views the activities of the consultant—witness preparation, use of focus groups, preparation of questions for voir dire—as things attorneys would do, if they had the time, and often do, regardless. But the trial consultant usually has skills in relation to these activities that are not possessed by most trial attorneys.

Taking the broad view, we ask: just because attorneys *may*, in the course of preparing for a trial, do all of the things that trial consultants are hired to do, should psychologists and other social scientists be involved in such activities? Trial lawyers inevitably must accept the adversary system, and their professional success is defined by how often they win cases. But social scientists operate from an ethic of concern for the betterment of human welfare. Some trial consultants would propose that their activities here fall squarely under the rubric of the betterment of human welfare; potential jurors who have their minds made up are difficult to detect, and trial consultants—they would claim—can make "a constructive contribution to the objectivity of American juries by increasing the accuracy by which unfair jurors are rooted out" (Kressel & Kressel, 2002, p. 15). The temptation is for the social scientist who has already forsaken scientific neutrality to accept the ethics of the adversary system.

Exaggerated Claims of Success

A second criticism focuses on the claims made by trial consultants. The entrepreneurial nature of the trial-consulting business has, on occasion, tempted firms to offer—or at least suggest—a level of effectiveness that challenges credulity. Litigation Sciences, one of the earliest and largest of the trial-consulting firms, in its brochure, has claimed an impressive record of success: "We have been involved in more than 900 cases, and our research findings have been consistent with the actual outcome in more than 95% of the matters that have gone to trial" (Litigation Sciences, 1988, p. 3). This rather vague boast generates great optimism for any law firm that hires Litigation Sciences. Is a 95% success rate consistent with the degree to which social scientists can predict outcomes in real-life situations? In actuality, the outcome of a trial—especially a jury trial—is dependent upon so many factors, some discernible, some capricious, that success rates of this magnitude are quite unlikely. Furthermore, the American Society of Trial Consultants does not approve of reporting win-loss records, stating, "The trial consultant may advertise services. Such advertisement avoids material misrepresentation of qualifications, experience, research, or trial outcomes. . . . The trial consultant does not publish a claim to a win-loss record" (American Society of Trial Consultants, 2003, p. 6).

Attempts by the ASTC to provide more detailed ethical guidelines reflect the diversity of its membership and the strong realization of the competitive environment in which they operate. In May 2002, guidelines for small-group research were drafted (American Society of Trial Consultants, 2002). Among them was the following: "Recognizing that factors like the inability to replicate all of the evidence that will be presented at trial inhibit SGR's [small-group research] ability to predict litigation outcomes, inform clients that SGR cannot predict litigation outcomes" (American Society of Trial Consultants, 2002, p. 2). Some ASTC members reacted negatively to this wording, suggesting that they are able, on the basis of the use of focus groups and related procedures, to predict litigation outcomes with some accuracy, and to be required to suggest otherwise would diminish their appeal to clients. A poll of ASTC members found that only 63% felt that "claims of success in jury selection" should be a topic addressed in the developing ASTC standards on that topic (Frederick, 2003). We will discuss these guidelines further in chapter 4, but will note at this point that the guidelines have been changed.

Many trial lawyers lack the training or inclination to critically examine such claims of success. In seeking to attain their goal of "zealously" representing their client, they grab whatever resources are available, especially if their client is willing to pay for them. In the words of trial consultant Gary Moran (2001), "Too often, lawyers suspend the evidence of their experience and accept nonsense because they think psychologists [and other trial consultants] have training allowing them to do what lawyers know others cannot do" (p. 78).

So, excessive claims aside, how effective are consultants? The reliance on consultants is, in the eyes of some, itself an indication of their effectiveness. Stolle, Robbennolt, and Wiener (1996) observed:

> The fact that trial consultants have been able to thrive in the marketplace serves as a somewhat compelling indication that trial

consulting is effective.... Lawyers from the most prestigious firms in the world are increasingly relying on the success of trial consultants, with some firms even bringing consulting services in-house. It seems quite unlikely that lawyers in control of high-stakes litigation would repeatedly pay the often high cost of scientific trial consulting services if such services were ineffective.... Over time the free market should weed out the less effective consultants leaving attorneys with the product of increasingly high quality. (p. 102)

As noted, we believe that effectiveness has to be considered separately for each of the types of activities of the trial consultant. Often, clear evidence is limited, but we consider effectiveness in chapter 2 (on witness preparation), chapter 4 (on focus groups), and chapters 7, 8, and 9 (on jury selection).

Favoring the Rich

The criticism that trial consultants favor the rich is especially challenging for the profession. Sociologist Amitai Etzioni, a persistent critic, stated in an interview: "The affluent people and the corporations can buy it, the poor radicals get it free, and everybody in between is at a disadvantage" (Adler, 1994, p. 114). As noted, trial consultants have come a long way from their work in the Harrisburg Seven trial, for which all the labor was voluntary and the total cost of their contributions to the defense was only about $400. One Los Angeles attorney has stated, "Very few trial consultants can come in and do any meaningful work for less than $50,000 or $100,000" (Lambert, 1994, p. B7). Kressel and Kressel (2002) claim that "trial consultants often come with six-figure price tags and seven figures are not unheard of" (p. 7). In civil trials it is much more likely that a corporate defendant, rather than a private-citizen plaintiff, will have a trial consultant, and in criminal trials, wealthy defendants are obviously more able to hire consultants than are indigent ones. Some would dismiss this concern, by saying it is inevitable; wealthy defendants such as Martha Stewart or Kobe Bryant can afford higher-priced attorneys, investigators, and expert witnesses. For example, consultant Lucy Keele has stated: "Money affects everything in our society.... We are an extension, obviously; if you have the money and can afford these services, it will go better for you" (Kressel & Kressel, 2002, p. 80). Of course, the fact remains that if at any time one side has resources that the other lacks, the achievement of justice is in jeopardy.

Traditionally, the courts have seemed to overlook imbalances in trial representation. The Virginia judge who presided over the trial of the alleged Washington, DC, serial sniper, John Muhammad, refused his lawyer's request for a trial consultant to be paid by the state. The adversary system is committed to the idea that each side is fully capable of carrying out the activities that benefit its side, from jury selection to cross-examination of witnesses to providing effective arguments. Jury experts Valerie Hans and Neil Vidmar (1986) have challenged this assumption:

> The viability of the adversary system to ensure a fair and impartial jury and trial, in jury selection as well as in other stages of the trial, is sorely tested when the adversaries possess unequal resources. In this light, the major ethical problem with social science in the courtroom is not the techniques themselves but rather the fact that in our society the condition for equality of resources is most often not met. Jury experts may exacerbate the impact of such disparities. (p. 94)

In criminal trials, if a consultant is used, typically it is by the defense and not by the prosecution (one exception is detailed in chapter 8, in the description of the Byron de la Beckwith retrial). Why do prosecutors not often use trial consultants? As in all criminal cases, there are budgetary constraints, but prosecutors may also have biases against consultants. Marcia Clark, who was deputy district attorney of Los Angeles County when she was chosen to try O. J. Simpson, may reflect the general attitude of prosecutors toward trial consultants.

Donald Vinson, who founded the trial-consulting firm Litigation Sciences, offered his services pro bono to the prosecution, and for a while Marcia Clark accepted them. Trial consultants on both sides conducted separate focus groups; each concluded that African American women, as a group, were sympathetic to the defense, so Vinson strongly urged Clark and her staff to use some of their peremptory challenges to dismiss them from the jury pool. But Clark refused. She was fully convinced that she could persuade African American women that Simpson was guilty; she had a gut feeling that Black women, if on the jury, would sympathize with the victim and accept the prosecution's theory of the case—that the murder of Nicole Brown Simpson was an outgrowth of the pattern of domestic violence she had experienced while she had been married to O. J. Simpson. As the lead attorney, Clark prevailed; for example, the prosecution did not even use all 20 of its peremptory challenges (Toobin, 1996). Vinson came to have, in Clark's words, "zero credibility" (Clark, 1997, p. 118), and she abruptly dismissed him after only a day and a half of jury selection (Toobin, 1996). The 12-person jury that quickly found Simpson not guilty included 8 African American women and 1 African American man.

Why was the trial consultant's advice summarily dismissed? In her very candid book about the trial, Marcia Clark (1997) explicitly states that she did not like Donald Vinson from their first meeting. She had been urged by her boss, District Attorney Gil Garcetti, to accept Vinson's pro bono offer. This is how she described their initial encounter (which took place, based on Vinson's arrangements, at a private dining room of a very exclusive club): "We found Vinson, a heavy, florid man with huge jowls. Thin wisps of white hair had been combed into submission across his pate. [His greeting was] in a drawl that suggested an *haut bourgeois* pedigree. When he rose to shake my hand, I caught the flash of gold cuff links" (Clark, 1997, p. 138).

Furthermore, Clark does not like trial consultants in general: "As far as I'm concerned they are creatures of the defense. They charge a lot, so the only people who can afford them are wealthy defendants in a criminal trial or fat cat corporations defending against class-action suits" (1997, p. 138). (This despite the fact that Vinson had offered his services gratis to the prosecution.) She only agreed to the trial consultant's participation in deference to her boss's insistence and against her own judgment. Additionally, Clark revealed that she is opposed to many of the staples of trial consultants' practices: "I don't feel that the government should be in the position of market-testing its arguments" (1997, p. 138). She also rejected the solid conclusions from psychological research that jurors who are death-qualified (i.e., not strongly opposed to the death penalty) are more likely to convict defendants. She wrote:

> I know there is a school of thought that in a capital case, the district attorney should ask for the death penalty as a tactical ploy. If you asked for the death penalty, every juror empaneled must be "death certified"—in other words, willing in principle to vote for death. And so, the reasoning goes, if you pack the jury with law-and-order types, they will be more willing to convict. I never believed that. What you're likely to get, in my view, is a panel of tough talkers who, when push comes to verdict, can't bring themselves to convict. Why? Because it has only just dawned on them that their actions may result in a person's death. (p. 144)

Lack of Regulation

The last criticism of trial consultants is related to their lack of regulation. Should they be licensed? The call for regulation of trial consultants reflects the practice of almost every profession (medicine, law, clinical psychology) to be regulated by the state as a means of protecting consumers against ineffective or unethical practitioners. As Strier (2001) noted, this is especially important in a new field, such as trial consulting: "practitioners need guidelines with which to navigate ethically nebulous terrain; the public needs assurance that practitioners sincerely intend to abide by some sort of moral compass" (p. 71).

The ASTC does provide a set of general ethical principles for its members to follow, as well as principles on particular topics, including witness preparation and small-group research. The following are the general principles:

Principle A: Trial consultants strive to maintain high standards of competence in their work. They recognize the boundaries of their particular competencies and the limitations of their expertise.... Trial consultants provide only those services and use only those techniques for which they are qualified by education, training, or experience.

Principle B: Trial consultants...do not make statements that are false, misleading, or deceptive.

Principle C: Trial consultants uphold professional standards of conduct and clarify their professional roles and obligations.

Principle D: Trial consultants comply with the law and encourage the development of law and social policy that serve the interests of their clients and the public generally. (American Society of Trial Consultants, 2003, p. 4)

Furthermore, the ASTC is currently developing guidelines for its members on specific activities, including use of focus groups and jury selection. These will be described in subsequent chapters.

As we pointed out earlier, the trial-consulting field is only approaching the kind of regulation expected in other professions. Furthermore, there is no continuing education requirement. While the American Society of Trial Consultants holds an annual convention, attendance is not mandatory, and the organization's Code of Professional Standards does not include any punishments for malpractice or unethical acts, in contrast to those of other professional organizations, such as the American Psychological Association (Strier, 2001). Licensing would seem to lead to the following benefits:

1. Establishment of minimum requirements for practice, such as experience, education, or completion of examinations, thus demonstrating an understanding of the law and legal procedures.
2. Reporting of unethical conduct by other trial consultants.
3. A vehicle for reviewing complaints from clients.
4. The establishment of training programs and the emergence of a generally agreed-upon curriculum for the training of trial consultants.
5. An increase in the amount of pro bono activity by trial consultants. The current ASTC Code of Professional Standards merely encourages such activity by its members; while we have no general indication of the extent of pro bono work currently, we doubt that it is very extensive, given the highly competitive nature of trial-consulting firms.

Strier (2001) polled 377 consultants listed in the 1996–1997 edition of the ASTC membership directory, to determine their attitudes toward licensing. Two thirds of those who expressed an opinion were opposed to licensing; most of these respondents (68%) "strongly disagreed" with the proposal, rather than "moderately" or "slightly" disagreeing.

The Remainder of This Book

This book is organized around the activities that trial consultants do. For each, the procedure is described, its effectiveness is evaluated, and the ethical issues are discussed.

Chapter 2 describes the procedures in the preparation of witnesses. Lawyers may lack the time—and, more important, the skills—to determine how effective their witnesses will be before the jury. Witness preparation is clearly a topic fraught with temptations to exceed what is ethical and legal; the chapter provides a framework for distinguishing among various actions in this gray area.

Chapter 3 reviews the issue of pretrial publicity's possible biasing effect and the use of community surveys to determine the extent of bias, especially bias against criminal defendants prior to their jury trials.

As attorneys prepare for trial, consultants can be of assistance in a number of ways beyond the preparation of witnesses. In actuality, trial consultants can be of help long before the trial begins. Does the attorney have an effective theory of the case? Do focus groups, composed of members of the community similar to the actual jurors, see the issues in the case in the same way that attorneys do? Trial consultant Amy Singer (1996a) has stated, "Attorneys often assume that they are in touch with the key issues of the case, only to learn through jury simulations that what they considered important is not important to jurors" (p. 28). The goal of trial simulations is "to learn everything you can about what sells your case and what sells your opponent's case" (Kressel & Kressel, 2002, p. 5). Chapter 4 reviews the use of pretrial focus groups and evaluates whether trial simulations can represent the actual trial jury's experience.

Related to issues in chapter 4 are trial strategic decisions, for example, what to include in the opening statement, what should be the proper order of witnesses, what should be the nature of the closing argument. Research findings from communication studies, psychology, and other social sciences are relevant to decisions here and are evaluated in chapter 5.

In advising attorneys, trial consultants need to have a sense of how jurors think and why they decide as they do. The structure and process of jury deliberations need to be understood. Chapter 6 describes what social scientists have learned about jury deliberations.

Three chapters are devoted to jury selection. Chapter 7 reviews instruments devised by psychologists to measure general attitudes of jurors—for example, if they have any biases favoring or doubting criminal defendants, doctors on trial for medical malpractice, or corporations. Chapter 8 describes more case-specific approaches, by providing case histories of two trials, one of which is the 1972 Harrisburg Seven trial, in which scientific jury selection had its initial highly publicized impact. The effectiveness of these various jury-selection procedures is evaluated in chapter 9. One of the strongest criticisms of the trial-consulting field stems from the belief that, to use the title and theme of Kressel and Kressel's (2002) book, consultants can "stack and sway the jury, promising to take much of the guesswork out of voir dire" (p. 14). Chapter 9 concludes that matters are not that simple.

The final chapter is our assessment of the current state of trial consulting and the needed reforms. In our assessment, we cannot avoid also evaluating the operation of the jury system in the United States. We consider possible changes and discuss the ethics of the various activities of trial consultants described in the previous chapters. Finally, we discuss the challenges in developing an identity for the profession.

2

Witness Preparation

When NFL football player Rae Carruth was tried for plotting the murder of his pregnant girlfriend, his defense attorneys put on the stand Van Brett Watkins. They confidently expected that Watkins would strengthen Carruth's claim of innocence, specifically that he would repeat his own jailhouse statement that he had shot Cherica Adams because he was angry at Carruth for backing out of a drug deal. Instead, on the stand, Watkins testified that Carruth had planned the attack and paid him to carry it out: "I was very afraid of Rae Carruth; he made me do it" (Associated Press, 2000, p. C26). Carruth was convicted of conspiracy to commit murder and sentenced to 18 to 24 years in prison.

When an attorney puts his or her "star witness" on the stand to testify, the attorney may feel something like a football coach whose first-string quarterback runs the risk of fumbling, thus possibly costing the team a victory and the coach a job. Despite the best plans and preparations, witnesses may—through their testimony in depositions or at trial—weaken or even lose their side's case.

Thus, most trial attorneys—prosecutors and defense attorneys alike—seek to determine, prior to the trial, what their witnesses (and in the case of defense attorneys, what their clients) are going to say. *Witness preparation*, as the process has come to be called, is a vital aspect of trial preparation, but it is largely an unknown process. Witnesses are prepared in private; no taping of the exchange is done or even a record kept, and the participants do not publicly discuss the procedure (Gershman, 2002).

Although trial attorneys have traditionally supervised witness preparation, some of them are turning the responsibility over to litigation consultants. The purposes of this chapter are to examine what occurs during the preparation of witnesses and to indicate some of the contributions that can be uniquely made by trial consultants.

President Clinton's Deposition

Even talented and high-priced lawyers sometimes cannot keep their own clients from becoming too exuberant or voluble witnesses. You would think that President Bill Clinton would have been an ideal witness in his own behalf; as one commentator noted, "Bill Clinton seems the kind of witness who would strike fear in the hearts of opposing lawyers: he is charismatic, confident, and used to pressure situations; he looks good in a dark suit; and he is well-educated in the law" (Craig, 1998, p. 48). But in his deposition as a part of the sexual-harassment suit against him by Paula Jones, he was ineffective and even self-defeating.

In preparing a witness who is a defendant in a civil suit and who is being deposed by the opposition, lawyers need to counsel their client (among other matters) to give away only as much or as little as the law requires. Certainly William Bennett, President Clinton's attorney, briefed him on how to proceed. But a variety of observers concluded that Clinton, at least part of the time, failed to follow the advice. One reviewer wrote: "Although Clinton was at times a model witness, answering questions succinctly and directly, at other times he clean forgot some of the 'do's and don'ts'" (Stewart, 1998, p. 43). Another observed: "Bill Clinton, surprisingly, came off as an unsophisticated witness, revealing a desire to please the opposing lawyer, and telling prepared stories that suggested that he had lots to hide" (Craig, 1998, p. 48).

Among the do's and don'ts that Clinton violated are the following:

1. If the answer calls for a yes-or-no response, answer yes or no, period.
2. Don't speculate. If you don't know or don't remember, say so.
3. Avoid phrases like "to the best of my recollection," "as memory serves me," or "I'm trying to be accurate."
4. Speak clearly and audibly.
5. Be consistent. Don't change stories in mid-deposition. (Stewart, 1998, p. 43)

For example, regarding an encounter between President Clinton and Kathleen Willey on November 29, 1993, an opposing attorney asked him: "What, if anything, do you recall being said in that meeting?" Alert witnesses would have restricted their answers to what they knew and would have kept their responses brief. Instead, Clinton gave a long-winded answer that gratuitously included, "But she was, she was very upset that day, I remember this very well, and she didn't stay long, but she was quite agitated" (quoted by Craig, 1998, p. 48). The follow-up question asked if this conversation occurred in the Oval Office; the answer should have simply been yes or no, but Clinton rambled on: "I think it was partly in the Oval Office and partly in the dining room I have in back, which is—my memory is she was quite upset; I asked her if she wanted something to drink, she said she did, we went back there" (quoted by Craig, 1998, p. 48).

Observers of Clinton's deposition noted that he was so soft-spoken that his attorney had to remind him on at least six occasions to speak up in order to be heard. Furthermore, Clinton became rattled several times during the deposition. When asked if he had ever been alone with Monica Lewinsky in the private kitchen adjacent to the Oval Office, he gave a wandering, seemingly irrelevant answer, which included: "I was, after I went through a presidential campaign in which the far right tried to convince the American people that I had committed murder, run drugs, slept in my mother's bed with four prostitutes and done numerous other things, I had a high level of paranoia" (quoted by Craig, 1998, p. 50).

Effective Testimony by a Different Politician, John Connally

In contrast, another politician's seemingly forthright testimony played a major role in the jury's verdict that he was not guilty of taking a bribe. John Connally, originally a Democrat, had served as governor of Texas and was one of America's leading politicians in the 1970s. He switched allegiance to the Republican party and was appointed secretary of the Treasury by President Nixon, who was so impressed with Connally that he considered choosing him as the vice-presidential nominee for his second-term campaign. While secretary of the Treasury, Connally was charged with taking a $10,000 bribe from a group of milk producers and lying to a grand jury; he was put on trial in the spring of 1975. The conventional wisdom was that he would be found guilty; the reporters covering his trial had to abandon their usual practice of assembling a betting pool when it was discovered that every one of them expected a conviction (Thomas, 1991). Connally's attorney, Edward Bennett Williams, called him to the stand and bluntly asked him if the accusations were true. "No, sir!" was Connally's answer, almost shouting, and communicating righteous indignation and strong determination.

"Did you conspire to conceal the bribe?"

"I did not! No such conversation ever took place!"

This answer was also delivered unhesitatingly and authoritatively, leading court watchers to conclude that Connally was telling the truth and leading jurors to find him not guilty. But the jurors were unaware of the hours and hours of witness preparation, during which Williams and his associates sought to curb Connally's arrogance while maintaining his self-confidence.

The Impact of the Defendant's Demeanor

In a criminal trial, the defendant's demeanor, when he or she testifies, may influence the jury as much as what is said. Rightly or wrongly, jurors make assumptions about guilt or innocence based on the level of emotion displayed by the defendant. When Pamela Smart, a New Hampshire high-school administrator, was tried for coercing her 15-year-old lover and his friends to murder her husband, she acknowledged the relationship with the student but denied that she had conspired to have her husband killed. But the style of her testimony—uninflected, without any intensity or emotion—contributed to the eventual verdict; she was "guilty as sin. . . . She's just too cool" (Larrabee, 1991, p. 3A). William Flynn, her high school–aged lover, testified—"between sobs and tears" (Abell, 1991, p. 6)—that he killed Smart's husband because she threatened to end their affair if he refused. His testimony influenced the jury to find Smart guilty; she received a sentence of life in prison without parole (*State v. Smart*, 1991/1993).

Jurors, after the verdict has been announced, will sometimes acknowledge that the defendant's level of emotion affected their decision. After Ronald Cotton was convicted of raping Jennifer Thompson—a verdict that was overturned 11 years later because of DNA testing—one juror noted that Cotton had "no change of emotion for eight days. He never changed his facial expression. This was extremely strange to me. And as time went by, I expected to see him react and he never did. And so he seemed more guilty and guiltier as time went by" (Loeterman, 1997).

This juror's response is not unique. When 28 jurors who had served on Florida capital murder cases were interviewed, 32% mentioned the defendant's demeanor—including a lack of concern or remorse—as a contributing factor in their decision to recommend the death penalty (Geimer & Amsterdam, 1988). The style of witnesses' and defendants' testimony appears to be especially influential when jurors are faced with a "Who do you believe?" type of case, one in which the jurors must decide which is telling the truth, a prosecution witness or the defendant. Stephen Adler (1994), a journalist for the *Wall Street Journal*, observed a number of trials and sought out information from jurors afterward about the bases for their decisions. In one of these, a murder trial, the critical witness who accused the defendant was seen as cold, unfriendly, and possessing an "unpleasant toughness" (Adler, 1994, p. 185). After fewer than 3 hours of deliberations, the jury found the defendant not guilty.

But can the style of the witness overcome the weight of evidence favoring the other side? Psychological researchers have sought to determine the limits of the impact of the defendant's emotional level on mock jurors' verdicts, specifically whether jurors use the defendant's level of emotion as an indicator that he or she is guilty. In one such study (Heath, Grannemann, & Peacock, 2004), college-student respondents viewed one of three versions of the defendant's testimony in a murder trial. On each tape, the defendant described the night she came home and found her husband dead. The words on each tape were exactly the same, but the level of emotion was varied. In a low-emotion condition, the defendant displayed flat affect, testifying with almost no emotion in her facial expression or her voice. In a condition designed to reflect moderate affect, the defendant's voice and expression were shown manifesting verbal and nonverbal behavior previously identified in research studies as indicating sadness, while in the condition designed to reflect a high degree of emotion, the defendant's voice and expression reflected an even greater level of emotion, as her voice cracked and she cried and wiped away her tears. Each tape was 3 to 4 minutes long.

The strength of the evidence against the defendant was also varied. Half of the respondents, in a weak-evidence condition, were told that results of a paraffin test indicated a "very small possibility" that the defendant had fired a gun during the day that the victim was killed, and a fingerprint expert testified that the probability was "extremely low" that the partial prints found on the gun belonged to the defendant. Respondents in a strong-evidence condition were told that the paraffin test indicated a "very strong possibility" that the defendant had fired a gun and the fingerprint testimony reflected "an extremely high probability" that her fingerprints were on the gun.

The defendant's emotional level had a notable effect on verdicts and sentences, under certain circumstances. When the evidence against the defendant was weak, mock jurors were more likely to find the defendant guilty when she displayed little emotion, and less likely to find her guilty when she displayed a high degree of emotion. When the evidence against her was weak, the defendant was also seen as less honest when she showed little emotion. But when the evidence against the defendant was strong, the level of emotion in her testimony had no effect on the verdicts (Heath et al., 2004).

Two points seem important here. First, when evidence against the defendant is strong, variations in the style of the defendant's testimony have no appreciable effect on jurors' judgments of guilt; this conclusion is in keeping with research findings that the strength of the evidence is the most important determinant of jurors' verdicts (Visher, 1987). Second, when evidence against the defendant is weak, the emotion displayed in the defendant's testimony liberates the jurors to reflect their feelings and biases; in the words of Kalven and Zeisel (1966), "doubts about the evidence free the jury to follow sentiment" (p. 166).

In the latter situation, jurors feel free to consider factors other than the evidence in arriving at their verdict. Some empirical support exists for what Kalven and Zeisel called a "liberation hypothesis"; for example, jurors have been found to ignore extralegal characteristics of the defendant and accuser (such as their physical appearance) when relatively strong evidence for guilt was presented. But in the face of relatively weak prosecutorial evidence, verdicts were influenced by the jurors' attitudes toward crime and by the characteristics of the defendant and those of the accuser (Reskin & Visher, 1986). We will return to this point when we consider jury deliberations in chapter 6.

What Lawyers Do to Prepare Witnesses

Witness preparation is largely an American phenomenon; it traces back 150 years and is mentioned in several of the novels of James Fenimore Cooper (Boccaccini, 2002). In contrast, it is improper for English barristers to speak directly to clients or witnesses under most circumstances (McElhaney, 1987). Similarly, in Germany, attorneys are not permitted to contact witnesses; in France, judges determine who serve as witnesses. But trial attorneys certainly know that they want their witnesses to be persuasive and credible when they testify at the trial or give a deposition, and in the United States they are permitted to "prepare" them in advance. Hence, a credo has developed that witness preparation is proper and necessary to do, whether the attorney or someone else does it.

As we will detail later in this chapter, legal consultants do many of the same things with witnesses that lawyers do, but more literature is directed toward preparation by lawyers. One extensive review, by Boccaccini (2002), proposes that three basic components are typical of witness preparation activities: to educate witnesses, both about courtroom procedure and about inconsistencies or gaps in their testimony, to educate the attorney about what the witnesses will say on the stand, so there are no surprises (Aron & Rosner, 1998), and to suggest modifications in the testimony. Educating the witness includes orienting novice witnesses to the courtroom layout and trial processes, in order to reduce their nervousness and confusion about appearing in court (Brodsky, 1991). Educating the attorney refers to the process by which the attorney learns, in detail, just what the witness's testimony will be. The third component, modification of the delivery of the testimony, is considered by many experts to be the most important component of witness preparation (Aron & Rosner, 1998; Follingstad, 1984), and we will devote most of this chapter to this activity.

In the best of worlds, preparation of a witness begins early in the case. As noted above, performance of a witness in a deposition can be as influential as performance in a trial; in many civil suits, "the deposition *is* the trial" (McElhaney, 1987, p. 80), as most civil suits are settled before a trial begins.

When trial attorneys meet with their clients prior to depositions or trial, they usually have several goals. One is to let the client vent his or her concerns. The lawyer explains the format of the testimony and reviews specific topics for the examination. The rules of testifying are usually reviewed. Trial lawyers even have available a number of lists of procedures to follow or avoid when preparing witnesses; for example, most law-school textbooks for trial advocacy courses devote a chapter or section to witness preparation, and several trial practice manuals deal with witness preparation procedures (Aron & Rosner, 1998; Finlay & Cromwell, 1999; Small, 1998). Thomas Mauet's (1996) trial advocacy text, in its fourth edition, offers the following propositions:

1. The attorney who will be doing the direct examination of the witness should be the one who works with this witness prior to trial. "Having an 'associate' prepare witnesses rarely works well," concludes Mauet (1996, p. 475).
2. Prior to trial, the attorney should review with the witness everything that is "down on paper," including depositions, other sworn testimony, and interrogatory answers. It is essential to determine if the witness's current memory differs from any of these statements.
3. The lawyer needs to review with the witness the probable testimony of other witnesses to see if any inconsistencies exist.
4. An explicit expression of the direct examination is essential. Mauet emphasizes:

   > Once the general outline of the direct examination is clear, go over the actual questions you intend to ask on direct. Above all, *practice the actual examination with the witness!* Do it in your office. Do it in an empty courtroom. Do it as though the jury were watching. Do it repeatedly until both you and the witness are comfortable with the examination (but stop if the examination begins to sound rehearsed). (Mauet, 1996, p. 475; italics in original)

5. Similarly, the attorney needs to prepare the witness for cross-examination, by reviewing topics that the cross-examination might cover. Mauet recommends also practicing the cross-examination with the witness.

Additionally, some law firms develop printed guidelines for witnesses. The firm of Winthrop, Stimson, Putnam, and Roberts (1990) has provided a list of 56 admonitions to witnesses, covering their answers to direct and cross-examination, their demeanor, and documents that they might be shown and about which they might be questioned while testifying. Some of these admonitions, beyond the previously cited "do's and don'ts," include:

> Pause after each question to formulate the main points to your answer.
> Do not try to be funny or sarcastic, or say something that depends on the tone of your voice for its meaning.
> Be sure that opposing counsel has completed his or her question before you begin your reply to it.
> Do not assume that a question introduced casually during your cross examination should be answered casually. (Winthrop et al., 1990)

Perhaps the most explicit set of instructions in this vein was a 20-page guide to its clients—plaintiffs in asbestos-injury lawsuits—prepared by Baron and Budd, a Dallas law firm. Over the last 25 years, this firm has represented more than 20,000 clients in asbestos litigation. Directed toward blue-collar workers who are usually inexperienced in the legal world, the document begins:

> Your deposition is probably the single most important part of your lawsuit. It is an opportunity for the lawyers representing the asbestos manufacturers whom you are suing to ask you questions, under oath, about their product. The burden of proof is on you, the plaintiff, to show how you *know* it was *their* product you were exposed to. How well you know the name of each product and the details of your exposure to it will determine whether the defendant will want to offer you a settlement.
>
> At the deposition, it might help to pretend that you are a "prisoner of war" in an enemy camp where you must give only your "name, rank, and serial number." The defense attorneys may try to make you lose your temper or feel stupid because you have less education than they do. But answer ONLY the question asked and DO NOT VOLUNTEER any information! (Anonymous, 1998, p. 20; italics and capitalization in original)

The Baron and Budd document went on to warn the client of "things to watch out for," including implications that "you are not telling the truth or are mistaken" and that "you had no idea that asbestos was dangerous" (p. 20). Regarding the latter, the document instructed as follows:

> You will be asked if you ever saw any WARNING labels on containers of asbestos. It is important to maintain that you NEVER saw any labels on asbestos products that said WARNING or DANGER. You might even be asked to spell "warning" or "danger" to prove that you knew what these words meant if you saw them. (pp. 20–21)

The document even made gratuitous comments about the opposing attorneys:

> They will try to confuse you and make you think *they* know something different from what you recall and that what you are saying cannot be true. Keep in mind that these attorneys are very young and WERE NOT PRESENT at the job sites where you worked. They have NO RECORDS to tell them what products were used on a particular job, even if they act like they do. (p. 20)

What Lawyers Cannot Do

The above set of instructions seems quite heavy-handed. It even told witnesses what to say. Interestingly, it only became public knowledge when, at a routine deposition in one of Baron and Budd's asbestos-liability cases, a defense attorney asked to see a stack of documents on the table in front of the young Baron and Budd attorney who was representing the plaintiff. The attorney, who had been with Baron and Budd only a month, handed over the documents, one of which was the 20-page "Preparing for Your Deposition" (Van Voris, 1997).

Witness Preparation Versus Coaching

Is such a set of instructions permissible? How far may an attorney go in "preparing" a witness? What is the difference between "preparing" and "coaching"? (In this chapter, we will use the term *coaching* as shorthand for practices that go past the acceptable limits.) Attorneys representing the defendant companies in the asbestos suits complained to the judge that the document encouraged plaintiffs to lie and to do it with confidence. At a hearing in Dallas, a state court judge who had reviewed the memorandum wondered, "How much more ink would it have taken to say, 'Tell the truth'?" but then he referred the matter to the local ethics committee (Van Voris, 1997, p. A30). A named partner of the firm (whose wife was a trial consultant) stated that none of his eight partners approved or even saw the document before the depositions and that the firm had determined that the document had been written by a paralegal (Van Voris, 1997).

Examples of questionable practices abound, both in real life and in literature. During a CNN program on the trial of a battered woman who killed her husband, the reporter overheard the woman's attorney explicitly tell her how to answer a question on cross-examination. In John Grisham's novel *The Testament* (1999), a 78-year-old man—a very, very rich man—has suddenly committed suicide and has left a handwritten will that freezes out all of his legitimate children and leaves his multibillion-dollar estate to an unknown, illegitimate child. The legitimate children, each now in adulthood, decide to contest the will and each hires a high-priced lawyer from a different law firm. An employee of the deceased man, a kind of manservant, offers to testify that his employer was not competent at the time of his death, as long as he is paid an exorbitant amount to do so. The lawyers discuss the possibility. "We don't know if he's lying," one says. Another replies, "No one knows. He was alone with Mr. Phelan. There are no witnesses. The truth will be whatever Mr. Snead wants it to be" (Grisham, 1999, p. 265). They decide to join in; one says, "His version needs some work. That's the beauty of the deal. Once we pay him, he's ours. We get to shape his testimony, to structure it to suit ourselves. Keep in mind there are no other witnesses." But one lawyer is cautious: "We could all be disbarred. Suborning perjury is a felony." Another responds: "You're missing the point; there can be no perjury. The truth is defined by Snead and Snead alone. If he says he helped write the will, and at the time the old man was nuts, then who in the world can dispute it?" (Grisham, 1999, pp. 266–267). Is this the way lawyers usually operate, or is it simply fictional license? It is hard to say. As noted earlier, witness preparation is done behind closed doors, and lawyers are not required to reveal to the opposition their preparations with their witnesses, as this information is protected by the attorney-client privilege (Davis & Beisecker, 1994). Law professor Richard Wydick (1995) concludes that the conventional wisdom about the distinction between witness preparation and witness coaching is the following:

> First, a lawyer may discuss a case with the witnesses before they testify. A lawyer in our common-law adversary system has an ethical and legal duty to investigate the facts of the case, and the investigation typically requires the lawyer to talk to the witnesses— the people who know what happened on the occasion in question.... Second, when a lawyer discusses the case with a witness, the lawyer must not try to bend the witness's story or put words in the witness's mouth.... Third, a lawyer can be disciplined by the bar for counseling or assisting a witness to testify falsely or for knowingly offering testimony that the lawyer knows is false. (pp. 1–2)

Furthermore, lawyers can be charged with suborning perjury if they put witnesses on the stand knowing that they are going to lie (Salmi, 1999). However, in real life—and even in some fiction—things are not so simple. In Grisham's novel, the attorneys for the offspring of the deceased man agree to hire Mr. Snead; at a preliminary meeting with him, they tell him: "Look, Mr. Snead, this is what we want. We need the quirks, the little oddities, the glaring lapses, the strange things he said and did when taken as a whole will convince anyone he was not of sound mind" (Grisham, 1999, p. 285). Then they rehearse his deposition testimony. But one of the problems arises from the fact that right before his death, Mr. Phelan had been examined by three psychiatrists, each of whom concluded that he was mentally competent. At the rehearsal, one of the attorneys asks Mr. Snead, "Then how did he perform so well for the three psychiatrists?" Snead is at a loss for an answer; he asks, "What would you guess?" And the lawyer replies:

> I would guess that Mr. Phelan knew the examination would be difficult because he knew he was slipping, and so he asked you to prepare lists of anticipated questions, and that you and Mr. Phelan spent that morning reviewing such simple matters as today's date, he couldn't keep it straight, and the names of his children, names he'd virtually forgotten, where they went to college, whom they were married to, et cetera, then you covered questions about his health. I would guess that after you drilled him on these basics, you spent at least two hours prompting him on his holdings, the structure of the Phelan Group, the companies he owned, the

acquisitions he'd made, the closing prices of certain stocks. He relied on you more and more for financial news, and so this came easy to you. It was tedious for the old man, but you were determined to keep him sharp just before you wheeled him in for the exam. Does this sound familiar? (p. 286)

Levels of Coaching

Does this represent a common practice of lawyers in preparing for depositions and trial? Do lawyers talk more than they listen? When does preparation move into the category of unethical and illegal behavior? Answers are not simple or easy; when coaching occurs, it may be subtle rather than blatant. Wydick (1995) divides coaching into three grades.

Grade One occurs when "the lawyer knowingly and overtly induces a witness to testify to something the lawyer knows is false" (p. 3). "Overtly" means that the lawyer's conduct is, on its face, an inducement to testify falsely. Consider the following: suppose that an attorney is representing Porter, a plaintiff, in a suit against Dempsey, the defendant. It is important to know how far apart Porter and Dempsey were standing at the time in question. The plaintiff's lawyer knows that the distance was about 150 yards. The lawyer interviews an eyewitness, Edgar, who is the plaintiff's best friend and therefore quite cooperative:

Q. At the time in question, were you standing where you could see both Porter and Dempsey?

A. Yes.

Q. Let me be frank. In this lawsuit it would be very helpful to Porter if the distance between Porter and Dempsey was less than 50 yards. Could you help us out on that?

A. Oh, I'm quite sure it was less than 50 yards. (adapted from Wydick, 1995, pp. 19–20)

This is overt, or Grade One, because the lawyer is offering the witness a way to benefit his friend by giving testimony that the lawyer knows to be false, and the inducement is obvious enough to be called apparent. Cooperative witnesses—friends and family members of the defendant, on the one hand, or police informants, on the other—may be quite susceptible to such suggestions. As Wydick observes, "Grade One witness coaching obviously interferes with the court's truth-seeking function and corrodes the morals of both the witness and the lawyer" (p. 3).

Grade Two witness coaching has the same intention as Grade One except that the attorney acts *covertly*; that is, the inducement is masked, and it is transmitted only by implication. Wydick uses as an example of Grade Two coaching "the Lecture scene" from the novel *Anatomy of a Murder* (Traver, 1958). An attorney named Biegler is defending a client named Manion against a charge of murdering a man who allegedly raped

Manion's wife. At their first meeting, Manion tells the attorney that he killed the man about an hour after learning of the rape. When the lawyer hears about the time lapse, he stops this first interview, realizing that "a few wrong answers to a few right questions" could mean a first-degree murder conviction and life in prison for his client (Traver, 1958, p. 32). When they meet a second time, the lawyer gives his client "the Lecture," or a step-by-step explanation of the law regarding murder and the possible defenses. The client begins to understand that his only possibly successful defense is a type of insanity defense, and he comes to describe his mental state at the time of the act in a way that permits the attorney to invoke the insanity defense. Just to make it clear, the author has the attorney explain to the reader:

> The Lecture is an ancient device that lawyers use to coach their clients so that the client won't quite know he has been coached and his lawyer can still preserve the face-saving illusion that he hasn't done any coaching. For coaching clients, like robbing them, is not only frowned upon, it is downright unethical. . . . Hence the Lecture, an artful device as old as the law itself, and one used constantly by some of the nicest and most ethical lawyers in the land. "Who, me? I didn't tell him what to say," the lawyer can later comfort himself. "I merely explained the law, see." It is a good practice to scowl and shrug here and add virtuously: "That's my duty, isn't it?" (Traver, 1958, p. 35)

(Incidentally, the author of this novel, "Robert Traver," is a pen name used by John D. Voelker, who was a justice on the Michigan Supreme Court.)

Why would a lawyer encourage false testimony covertly rather than overtly? Wydick (1995) suggests two reasons: first, to save face; lawyers do not want to be perceived by others as dishonest. If the witness refuses to acquiesce, the lawyer can claim that the inducement was not that, but instead an explanation of the law. The second reason is the lower risk of an inducement being reported and punished, because covert inducement is not so apparent. But Wydick concludes that Grade Two witness coaching is "no less harmful than Grade One to the court's truth-seeking function, nor to the morals of the lawyer and witness, nor is it any less serious a violation of disciplinary rules or subornation of perjury statutes" (p. 27).

In Grade Three coaching, the lawyer's intent is less explicit. "The lawyer does not knowingly induce the witness to testify to something the lawyer knows is false, but the lawyer's conversation with the witness nonetheless alters the witness's story" (Wydick, 1995, p. 4). Like the others, it interferes with the court's truth-seeking function, intended or not; equally important, it is very hard to avoid altering the witness's memory. The questions that the lawyer chooses to ask the witness during the preparation period can convey to the witness implications that are never made explicit, but that still influence what the witness later says.

Coaching and the Alteration of Memories

Psychologists have frequently shown that memory is malleable and that questions addressed to witnesses after an event can change the content of their memories. When information is retrieved from memory, the wording of the questions can affect the responses. Even the simple manipulation of the question: "Did you see a broken headlight?" versus "Did you see the broken headlight?" led to an increase in "yes" answers from 7% to 18% (Loftus & Zanni, 1975). (There was no broken headlight in the film that the respondents had viewed.) Furthermore, the verb that is used to describe the action in a retrieval question can influence factual reports. Researchers asked, "How fast were the cars going when they smashed?" Or "...when they collided," or "...when they bumped" or "hit" or "contacted." The average report of how fast the car was going was 40.8 miles per hour for "smashed," 39.3 mph for "collided," 38.1 mph for "bumped," 34 mph for "hit," and 31.8 mph for "contacted" (Loftus & Palmer, 1974).

Even ethical and well-intentioned lawyers can ask suggestive questions, and psychologists agree that respondents "can be easily led to report misinformation that has been suggested to them" (Zaragoza & Lane, 1994, p. 934). Additionally, most witnesses only perceive a part of the events at question; the gaps in memory are filled in with conjecture and inference. Questioning may lead to an inaccurate filling of these gaps. And as witnesses rehearse their memory of events—at least in their minds if not out loud—a version of the events can "harden" and become "the truth" for that witness. As Judge Jerome Frank (1949) wrote many years ago, "Telling and re-telling it to the lawyer, he will honestly believe that his story, as he narrates it in court, is true, although it importantly deviates from what he originally believed" (p. 86).

As Judge Frank observed, the line between intentional and inadvertent grooming of witnesses cannot always be drawn clearly. And what about a lawyer seeking to alter the witness's style, rather than the content of the testimony? What if an attorney is rehearsing his client, and in response to his question, "Mr. Innis, did you commit this crime?" his client responds meekly with a barely audible one-word answer of "no." One of us witnessed such an exchange in a trial rehearsal; the attorney then responded by screaming at his client about the unconvincing style of his response. Doubtless when it came to the actual trial, the witness was more outgoing and eloquent. Note that in this example, the lawyer was not trying to get his client to lie; yet some would argue that the truth-seeking function of the court may have been jeopardized.

What Can Trial Consultants Do?

As the above indicates, trial attorneys are concerned with the preparation of their witnesses. They don't want to be surprised by what their clients or supporting witnesses say on the stand. A primary purpose of an attorney meeting with a client or other witness prior to trial is to learn what the person will say. The ensuing discovery process often leads to efforts by the attorney to "improve" the testimony.

The activities of the trial consultant expand upon the above goals of the attorney. The task of trial consultants is to make the client the most effective witness that he or she can be. The brochure from Litigation Sciences (1983) states:

> Our communication professionals work very closely with witnesses in the preparation of credible courtroom testimony on both direct and cross examination. Juries evaluate witnesses on many dimensions. Hence, we devote considerable attention to not only *what* a witness will say, but also to his or her *total* communication impact. We are concerned about such factors as non-verbal communication, appearance, general demeanor, voice pitch, response style and a host of other communication variables which are frequently as important as what the witness actually says. (p. 6; italics in original)

Some attorneys do a superb job of questioning their witnesses prior to trial and preparing them for their court appearances. But some do not: they may not have the patience, the skills, or the time to do an acceptable job. Sometimes the attorney may only have a few hours available to prepare a witness. When psychiatrist Jeffrey Masson filed a libel suit against writer Janet Malcolm for her series of articles about him, jurors reacted negatively to her testimony; they perceived her to be arrogant and defensive. However, the jury could not agree on a verdict, and a second trial was held. Janet Malcolm's defense attorney hired a trial consultant, who spent several hours a week for 8 months working with Malcolm, especially to improve her demeanor and appearance. In the second trial, the jury found for the defense.

Lawyers are not usually trained in interviewing or achieving behavior change. Furthermore, during practice sessions, some lawyers are more intent on learning what their clients are going to say than in making sure that clients understand the questions. It has also been suggested that preparation conducted by the lawyer is more effective for direct examination than for cross-examination; even though the client's attorney may role-play a cross-examination of his or her client, the lawyer is perceived by the client as supportive and the client is frequently not ready for the emotion present in the actual court proceedings (Follingstad, 1984).

Another problem is that lawyers are often untrained in dealing with the challenge of working with clients or witnesses who are resistant to feedback about the limitations in their presentation style or appearance. A trial consultant may observe the attorney question his or her client and be useful in several ways. First, being unfamiliar with the witness, the trial consultant can describe how the witness appears to a stranger. Inconsistencies and gaps in the testimony are not "filled in" in the mind of the consultant, as they are in the mind of the client's lawyer, who has familiarity and a fund of information (Krauss & Bonora, 1983). A second focus is the relationship between the attorney and the witness. As Krauss and Bonora note, "Often attorneys are unaware of the interpersonal dynamic that develops between themselves and a witness because they are too involved in directing the witness's testimony" (p. 33).

Witnesses' Anxiety

The courtroom is an austere setting that reflects authority and tradition. The judge, seated at a raised podium and cloaked in a black robe, may be intimidating. Witnesses may also experience anxiety over the uncertainty of a novel situation, especially one in which they know they run the risk of being discredited upon cross-examination (Follingstad, 1984). Some common fears about testifying are reflected in the following statements:

> I'll be embarrassed, humiliated, or ashamed.
> I'm not going to remember what I'm supposed to do on the stand.
> I won't be believed.
> I'll make a fool of myself. (from Krauss & Bonora, 1983, p. 26)

Furthermore, witnesses may possess other negative attitudes about testifying; they may be angry about even being questioned, or they may feel that testifying is a waste of time. The behavior that results from these negative attitudes and feelings may be very influential to jurors; in the formation of impressions, observers are influenced more by negative information about the person than by positive information (Leathers, 1997), and jurors' ratings of witnesses' nervousness are negatively related to their ratings of those same witnesses' levels of confidence (Bothwell & Jalil, 1992). Trial consultants possess ways of exploring and possibly reducing such anxieties and negative attitudes about testifying. For example, Krauss and Bonora (1983) suggest the following questions:

> What is your worst nightmare about testifying?
> Has that ever happened to you before?
> If so, what happened then? How did you handle it?
> How likely is it to happen on the witness stand?
> How bad would it be if it did happen?
> How would you handle the situation? (p. 28)

These trial consultants propose responding to such fears by empowering the witness, especially by replacing a negative statement about oneself with a positive one that is incompatible. They write:

> For example, suppose the witness is paralyzed and testifying in an
> overly-cautious, halting fashion because he is afraid that he will say

the wrong thing. First validate his fears as real. It's important not to dismiss them without recognition. Acknowledge that anxiety about testifying is normal because few people have ever had this unusual and unfamiliar experience. Most people are concerned that they don't know what the rules are or how to do a good job. Reassure him that your job is to help him learn the rules of testimony and to explain how the courtroom situation works.

Then say something like, "I want you to think of it this way. This is my chance to tell my story. Nobody can tell my story but me. I'm glad I have an opportunity to tell the jury what I know so they can see it my way."

One of the most important things you can do with witnesses is give them a sense of control. Most often, they feel helpless and vulnerable. If you can present them with the means to take charge of the situation, they can relax and become an active participant in their testimony rather than a passive victim or an angry combatant. (Krauss & Bonora, 1983, p. 30)

Let us now reconsider the above example of Mr. Innis, who responded with a very meek "no" when asked if he had committed the crime. Do the brevity and tentativeness of this response reflect his attempt to deceive, or his nervousness about being questioned? That is the problem. If the latter, the actions of trial consultants seem to us as justifiable, because they are facilitating a truthful expression and serving the cause of justice.

Speech Style

On the witness stand, a speaker may be either emphatic or hesitant, rambling or coherent, mumbling or shouting. One of the variables apparently most influential in jurors' evaluations of testimony is what O'Barr (1982) has called *powerful* versus *powerless speech*. The latter is characterized by the following:

1. Hesitations, or frequent use of "uh," "well . . . uh," "you know," and similar expressions.
2. Hedges and equivocations, such as "I guess . . ." or "I would say that . . ."; these reduce the force of the statement.
3. Responding to a question with an answer that contains a rising inflection, as if it too were a question.
4. Overly polite speech, including excessive use of "please," "Sir," or "Madam."

In contrast, a powerful or persuasive speech style includes a conversational delivery, a lowered pitch (but at varying levels), and fluency of expression (Krauss & Bonora, 1983). Speech style (separated from content) has been found to influence the credibility of witnesses. O'Barr (1982) taped segments of testimony that reflected types of powerless speech; he then had actors read these statements in two ways, either replicating as closely as possible the speech characteristics of the original testimony, or reading the same testimony but omitting the aspects of powerless speech. (The taped testimony lasted 15 to 20 minutes.) Mock jurors' ratings of the taped testimony indicated clearly significant differences between that with and without the powerless speech; presence of a powerless speech style made the witness appear to be less convincing and less believable. In fact, the powerless speech had generalized effects, leading those witnesses to be seen as less competent, trustworthy, and intelligent. These effects are found regardless of whether the mode of communication is audiotaped testimony (Johnson & Vinson, 1987), videotaped testimony (Lisko, 1992), or a written trial transcript (Bradac, Hemphill, & Tardy, 1981). Clearly, it is advantageous for witnesses and their attorneys to be seen as forthright, confident, and unequivocal. Boccaccini (2002) summarizes as follows:

> Findings from studies of courtroom testimony suggest that effective witnesses use a powerful speaking style, express confidence in themselves when asked to do so, provide descriptive answers to attorneys' questions, and avoid hyper correct speech. However, because most of these studies used all-or-nothing manipulations of speech variables, relatively little is known about how moderate levels of these variables affect perceptions of credibility and persuasiveness. (pp. 173–174)

Sometimes, if witnesses are shown two videotapes of two speakers—one reflecting powerless speech and one reflecting powerful speech—they will recognize the differences and try to amend their own speaking style. Questioning by a trial consultant can help witnesses to understand their own limitations and encourage them to change.

Appearance of Lying on the Stand

People in general do a poor job of detecting deception in others (Zuckerman, DePaulo, & Rosenthal, 1981). Even more disturbing is the finding that many people have unrealistically high levels of confidence about their own ability to detect deception from the cues they use (Hocking, Miller, & Fontes, 1978). A meta-analysis of studies relating the levels of confidence that people had about their judgments and the actual degree of accuracy in their judgments of deception by others found the average correlation to be only .04 (DePaulo, Charlton, Cooper, Lindsay, & Muhlenbruck, 1997). Even those persons whose jobs rely on their ability to tell whether someone is lying—polygraphers, psychiatrists, police investigators—often make mistakes (Ekman, 1989; Ekman & O'Sullivan, 1991). In a clever study, Kassin, Meissner, and Norwick (2003) found that on a task of distinguishing between false and true confessions (generated by convicts in a state prison), police detectives did a significantly poorer job than did college students; the police officers were actually correct less often than chance.

But what is relevant to witness preparation is the fact that people—including jurors—believe they can tell when someone else is not being honest, and they rely upon some stereotypical characteristics to make such determinations. Rightly or wrongly, "the shifty-eyed, perspiring, lip-licking, nail-biting, ill-at-ease, fidgety witness" is seen as less credible than the calm, collected, straight-in-the eye one (Lykken, 1998, p. 102). Thus, the issue of the *appearance of truthfulness* needs to be given special attention in witness preparation. The following have been identified as the nonverbal characteristics upon which people rely when detecting lying among strangers:

1. Poor eye contact
2. Rapid blinking
3. What Paul Ekman (1992) calls "manipulators": fidgeting, scratching, rubbing, grooming, or other distracting movements
4. Shifting positions frequently
5. Squelching emotions
6. Mixed facial messages, including a half smile that does not involve the whole face (Krauss & Bonora, 1983, p. 13)

Of related concern is the appearance that a witness is being defensive; a defensive posture can lead jurors to conclude that the witness is worried about his or her testimony and may be trying to conceal an important fact (Krauss & Bonora, 1983). For example, crossed arms or crossed legs by a witness are often interpreted as meaning that the witness has placed barriers against questioning. Hand-wringing may be seen as a sign of nervousness.

General Demeanor

Black's Law Dictionary defines *demeanor* as including

> [s]uch facts as the tone of voice in which a witness's statement is made, the hesitation or readiness with which his answers are given, the look of the witness, his carriage, his evidences of surprise, his gestures, his zeal, his bearing, his expression, his yawns, the use of his eyes, his furtive or meaning glances, or his shrugs, the pitch of his voice, his self-possession or embarrassment, his air of candor, or seeming levity. (quoted by Piorkowski, 1987, p. 406)

Jurors, as fact finders, are permitted to use the demeanor of witnesses as a consideration in their verdicts; for example, the Federal Rules of Evidence state that "the demeanor of the witness traditionally has been believed to furnish trier and opponent with valuable clues" (quoted by Piorkowski, 1987, p. 405). The Supreme Court has also upheld this procedure; in *Universal Camera Corp. v. N.L.R.B.* (1951), the majority opinion stated that "material facts in any case depend on the determination of credibility of witnesses as shown by their demeanor or conduct at hearings" (p. 496).

As far as the court is concerned, demeanor of witnesses should be a consideration *only when they are testifying*, but realistically jurors have an opportunity to observe defendants (and plaintiffs in civil trials) as they sit with their attorneys while others testify or while other aspects of the trial occur. And it is impossible for jurors to separate their impressions of the witness in the two different settings. A story attributed to Chief Judge Howard T. Markey of the federal Circuit Court illustrates the problem:

> An attorney, preparing for his closing argument, was faced with overwhelming evidence that his client was guilty of murder. Because the victim's body had never been recovered, the attorney considered this to be his one opportunity to create a reasonable doubt. In closing argument, he asserted that in three minutes the alleged victim would walk into the courtroom. The jurors watched the door eagerly but, of course, no one entered after three minutes. The attorney argued, however, that the jurors' anticipation demonstrated that they had reasonable doubt. After a guilty verdict was returned, the attorney asked the foreman, "How could the jury have found the defendant guilty beyond a reasonable doubt when every head in the courtroom was turned toward the door?" The foreman responded, "Correction, sir; every head in the courtroom except one—the defendant never looked at the door." (quoted by Piorkowski, 1987, p. 407)

Diane Follingstad (1984), a forensic and clinical psychologist, has offered a detailed program for preparing witnesses which includes questions that "require the witnesses to consider the impression they initially make on others and induce an awareness of their manner of dress, demeanor, posture, and facial expressions that affect impressions prior to talking with others" (p. 52). Witnesses are asked:

1. What are you like as a person? What are your most favorable characteristics? Why would someone not like you as an individual?
2. What do your close friends/relatives think of you? If this picture is different from the way a stranger would perceive you, why do you think that is so?
3. What might strangers think about you if they were not able to interact with you? What might they think if they only had a short period of time with you? (Follingstad, 1984, pp. 52–53)

If witnesses only mention positive qualities about themselves, they are specifically asked which negative qualities a stranger might notice. In contrast, witnesses who focus only on their faults are asked to look at the possible positive characteristics that could be noted by a stranger. Questioning should be patient, giving the witness ample time to respond. At the same time, the attorney and the trial consultant should record verbal and nonverbal characteristics that create problems, such as rigid or slumped body posture, weak voice quality, tense or angry facial expressions, inappropriate vocabulary, flippant or condescending style of communicating, and ineffective reactions to stress.

Videotaping the witness's responses and replaying them may aid in communicating to the witness that his or her fidgeting, grimacing, speaking too quickly, or lack of eye contact negatively affect effectiveness on the stand.

Follingstad believes that anxiety and anger are the two greatest causes of witnesses' difficulty in testifying. Telling witnesses that they need to appear less defensive and angry is rarely successful. Instead, she proposes an intervention procedure that includes techniques that help the witness to "identify the source of and recognize early stages of problem behaviors, handle the emotional aspects of the situation, cognitively handle the stress, and rethink beliefs about the situation" (Follingstad, 1984, p. 54), and as a result, to learn new behaviors to replace the negative ones.

Preparing for Cross-Examination

Preparing for a cross-examination is especially challenging to attorneys because they may believe so strongly in their own case that they cannot see the other side's position in detail. And witnesses' anxieties are heightened over the thought of having their statements intensively questioned or even ridiculed. Krauss and Bonora (1983) suggest an intensive cross-examination as part of the practice session, but they believe it is best for the trial consultant not to play the role of the opposing attorney: "You want to protect your relationship with the witness, so don't risk alienating the witness by playing the devil's advocate. Instead, observe the witness and suggest strategies for responding to hostile questioning" (pp. 35–36). These strategies include:

> If the questioning comes too fast, the witness can always ask that a question be repeated.
>
> Witnesses should remember that the opposing attorney is attacking issues, not the person. If the questioning takes the form of a browbeating, the witness should imagine himself or herself "gently but firmly pushing the lawyer back" (p. 36). The witness should take a deep breath and regain composure.
>
> Also, a witness should remember that if the attack is a personal one, it means the witness is doing a good job of testifying because there are no facts to question.

Preparing Children for Testifying

When a child is called upon to testify, the problems of adult witnesses—especially anxiety and uncertainty—are compounded by the child's relative lack of understanding of courtroom procedures (Perry & Wrightsman, 1991). Trial consultants can help to relieve uncertainty by introducing the child to the courtroom prior to the trial and explaining the functions of the different officers of the court. A careful rehearsal in a vacant courtroom is essential. In cases of alleged sexual abuse of a child, the child may experience fear in anticipation of once more seeing his or her attacker in the courtroom. Some states have adopted alternative procedures for testifying that permit the child to testify and be cross-examined while in a separate room from the defendant; for example, in Maryland, closed-circuit television is permitted. However, many states require the judge to conclude that the child would suffer from additional trauma if he or she testified in the presence of the defendant before such an alternative may be instituted. The trial consultant can assist in making such an assessment.

Does Witness Preparation "Work"?

The effectiveness of witness preparation varies, of course, depending on the goals, skills, and ethics of the attorney and trial consultant, the nature of the witness, and the relevance of the testimony. The sparse empirical literature directed specifically to this question, reviewed by Boccaccini (2002), indicates a qualified yes to the question of whether witness preparation works.

Two studies are most relevant. In the first, experimental social psychologist Gary Wells and his colleagues (Wells, Ferguson, & Lindsay, 1981) arranged a situation in which the research participants saw a confederate steal a calculator; subsequently, they were asked to identify the perpetrator in a photo lineup. Then the experimenters divided the participants into two groups: one half of the respondents were briefed by someone playing the role of a prosecutor; they were told that they were going to be "cross-examined" about their identification and were given the kinds of questions that a defense attorney might ask them. These briefed respondents were given 18 minutes to think about, and rehearse, their answers to the questions. In contrast, respondents in the nonbriefed condition waited 25 minutes before being cross-examined. Respondents in both conditions were individually questioned, and their responses were videotaped. Mock jurors watched these tapes and rated each respondent with respect to the witness's confidence and accuracy, as well as the defendant's guilt. Witnesses who had been briefed prior to the cross-examination had higher levels of confidence in their testimony, and this contributed to the mock jurors being more likely to find the defendant guilty when the witness had been briefed.

A study by Nicholas Spanos and his colleagues (Spanos, Quigley, Gwynn, Glatt, & Perlini, 1991) led to generally similar conclusions. Again, the participants were eyewitnesses (in this study, they watched a 60-second videotape of a shooting) who were asked to identify the perpetrator in a lineup. Half of the respondents later received witness-preparation training; included in this were instructions to speak in complete sentences, answer questions fully, and present themselves with confidence. Similar to the Wells et al. study above, observers rated the witnesses' testimony; it was found that the prepared respondents maintained the certainty of their identifications better during cross-examination than did the unprepared respondents.

These studies have their limitations, as noted in the review by Boccaccini (2002); only one type of witness was studied, the eyewitness; the witness-preparation sessions were brief; the testimony sessions were also brief and questions were restricted; and there was no evaluation of the witnesses' testimony prior to any briefing that took place. But their results and conclusions certainly are "consistent with attorneys' assumptions about the impact of testimony delivery skills on perceptions of credibility and persuasiveness" (Boccaccini, 2002, p. 169).

Can a Witness Be Overprepared?

A client or witness may be so rehearsed that his or her appearance and testimony take on unrealistic or even suspicious qualities. McElhaney (1987) advises:

> The most fundamental rule about dress is that the witness should
> be clean and well groomed. But be careful. It is a mistake to dress
> people up beyond their ability to handle it. While dark business
> suits with neckties and white or light blue shirts can create a nice
> impression, some men cannot wear those clothes without looking
> stiff and uncomfortable. (p. 80)

If an attorney structures the response for the witness, as was illustrated in John Grisham's novel described earlier, the greatest risk is that when attacked on cross-examination, the witness is likely to blurt out, "That's what the lawyer told me to say" (McElhaney, 1987, p. 84). The effects of overpreparation may be subtle, but equally damaging. On March 25, 1911, a fire swept through a ten-story building in Greenwich Village, and more than 100 young women who worked in the Triangle Shirtwaist Factory were killed. One of the survivors, a young immigrant woman named Kate Alterman, testified for the prosecution and was cross-examined. But her testimony had a mechanical and hence a suspicious quality; "the words she used when testifying, the dramatic images, and her development of the facts did not go with the grammar and accent of a barely literate young immigrant" (McElhaney, 1987, p. 84). The attorney who cross-examined her asked her to repeat her story over and over again; always, it was exactly the same, even though she insisted that she had not discussed her testimony with anyone. What could have been highly influential testimony came to be ridiculed.

Trial Consultants and the Difference Between Witness Preparation and Coaching

Trial consultants have ethical standards that prohibit them from coaching witnesses; the American Society of Trial Consultants has developed a set of guidelines for its members. Krauss and Bonora (1983) state:

> The goal of witness preparation is to facilitate the telling of a witness's story. Needless to say, it is *not* aimed at tampering with or altering what the witness has to say. In fact, just the opposite; preparation enhances the witness's ability to speak clearly and honestly so that the story unfolds in a way that is understandable to the jury. (p. 18)

Experienced forensic psychologists Michael Nietzel and Ronald Dillehay (1986) agree: "the consultant is not present to alter the facts" (p. 121). But in their very next sentence, they reflect the challenge: "Presentational style is fair game for intervention, however" (p. 121).

But what *are* the limits of preparation? One of us posed this question to several experienced trial consultants when they were attending the meeting of the Executive Committee of the American Society of Trial Consultants in 1992. Their reactions were so varied that it is difficult to give a consistent answer to the question. One responded: "What are the boundaries? I don't like: 'I'll work on the credibility but not change the fact pattern,' because once you work on the credibility you affect the fact pattern." Some consultants accepted the attorney's goals without question. One said, "The trial is a justice-seeking event, not a truth-seeking event," emphasizing that the goal was to increase the witness's persuasiveness. One felt that the witness's testimony was more "valid" if he or she had been prepared. Another consultant posed the dilemma succinctly: "I don't 'fix' a witness's testimony but I can enhance it." There was a sense that it is irresponsible if you don't ensure that the witness is as clear as possible. One consultant said: "I ask: 'What's the most colorful way you can express this?' I don't tell them what to say." But they did agree that the dividing line is not a clear one.

Even the lawyers' code is not that clear. Suborning perjury is clearly wrong, but where is the line drawn? Historically, only the most extreme violations by attorneys have caused them to be disciplined or punished (Piorkowski, 1987). Suggested alterations of speech style, as noted above, appear to be within the limits of acceptability. When the witness, during a rehearsal, uses loose language, such as referring to a small van as a "car," an attorney can recommend the use of a more precise term (Piorkowski, 1987). Even colorful language that affects the witness's credibility may be altered. Piorkowski writes:

> For example, a witness who refers to a handgun as a "piece" or refers to a lawyer as a "mouthpiece" is likely to give the jury the

impression that he is associated with a criminal activity. Under these circumstances, an attorney cannot be characterized as having falsified or misrepresented the witness's intended meaning by recommending a substitute word. (1987, p. 400)

But if an attorney recommends that a witness modify his or her intended meaning, it is clearly prohibited conduct. In the case of *Geders v. United States* (1976), the Supreme Court addressed the problem of coaching witnesses and concluded that "an attorney must respect the important ethical distinction between discussing testimony and seeking improperly to influence it" (p. 90), but the Court did not articulate what constitutes improper influence. Recall that psychologists have shown that the verb used to describe a car crash can affect a memory of the speed of the cars. Consider a situation in which a witness states that the attorney's client "beat" another person; the attorney suggests that the witness use the word "hit" instead. The latter verb weakens the emotional impact; we find this unacceptable. We agree with Piorkowski (1987): "where the factual meaning of testimony has been altered, one may characterize the attorney as inducing a misrepresentation of the actual facts that transpired" (p. 402).

In the *Geders* decision, the Supreme Court noted that a skillful cross-examination could uncover the coaching of a witness. The Court proposed that the line between ethical pretrial preparation and coaching was easily defined (*Geders v. United States*, 1976, pp. 89, 90). We are not so sanguine. What can a cross-examiner do if a witness has been coached to say, "I don't remember"?

Attempts to alter the demeanor of clients—a staple of the trial consultant's contributions—also raise ethical considerations. One legal expert has written:

It is at least arguable that when an attorney encourages a witness to appear confident, and during testimony the witness displays a sense of confidence while making an assertion about which he is in fact not confident, the attorney has encouraged the witness to testify "falsely" or to engage in "misrepresentation." (Piorkowski, 1987, p. 404)

Not all attempts to alter demeanor should be considered unethical, however. What if a client is of an ethnic minority and speaks with a thick dialect? If jurors, who, like all of us, have some biases, conclude that this witness is not credible because of his or her dialect, is it proper to try to improve the client's speaking skills? The goals of witness preparation should include trying to prevent jurors from drawing prejudicial and erroneous conclusions from the witness's testimony.

Yet the problem remains. In a law review article titled "Witness Coaching by Prosecutors," Gershman (2002) makes the statement that "it is indisputable that some prosecutors coach witnesses with the deliberate objective of promoting false or misleading testimony" (p. 833), in clear violation of the principle that both attorneys and trial consultants should follow in witness preparation: to avoid any actions that are likely to induce a witness to misrepresent or falsify facts that are of relevance at the trial.

Conclusions

As we described in the introductory chapter, the public's main awareness of trial consultants focuses on their role in jury selection. We believe that trial consultants can play a useful role in witness preparation, as they possess skills and an awareness that many lawyers do not have. For example, many attorneys "do not appreciate the dangers associated with retrieving a memory of an event" (Gershman, 2002, p. 839), and thus reflect what Wydick called Grade Three coaching.

But there are limits on what consultants should do. Manipulation of a witness's emotions—for example, urging a defendant to cry during his or her testimony—deals directly with the truth-determining function of the trial. What research is available indicates that it works and that jurors are not very able to distinguish genuine emotion and false emotion in witnesses. We acknowledge that when a legal consultant—or a lawyer—is working with a witness prior to the trial, it is difficult to draw the line between legitimate feedback, which has the effect of producing testimony that reflects the facts of the situation, and inducing behavior on the witness stand that is fake and disingenuous. The consultant must take extra care not to encourage the latter.

3

—

Change of Venue

Under the Sixth Amendment to the U.S. Constitution, criminal defendants are guaranteed, among other things, the right to a fair trial by an impartial jury. At the same time, the First Amendment to the Constitution protects the freedom of the press. In high-profile cases, such as those involving public figures, children, or particularly heinous crimes, the Sixth Amendment rights of the defendant and the First Amendment rights of the media are often at odds (Linz & Penrod, 1992). This conflict creates a dilemma for the courts, which are faced with the task of determining whether it is possible to seat an impartial jury in the jurisdiction in which the alleged crime was committed and, if deemed impossible (or highly unlikely), what to do about it. In such cases, the trial consultant can provide an invaluable service to the court by examining the content and extent of media coverage and by surveying prospective jurors in order to measure the degree of knowledge (both factual and erroneous) about the case and the amount of bias present against the defendant. In this chapter, we will discuss the research on the effects of pretrial publicity on jurors' decisions, evaluate methods commonly used by the courts in an attempt to alleviate such effects, review several highly publicized cases, and examine the role that the consultant plays in the change-of-venue motion, a request to the court that the trial be moved to a different location. Before we proceed, however, it is important to note that although change-of-venue surveys are conducted for both civil and criminal cases, most of the research has focused on criminal cases, motions for change of venue are more frequently filed in criminal cases, and therefore we will focus primarily on them.

Publicity Effects: Laying the Foundation for Bias

Of course, not all cases receive extensive media coverage. Especially in large, urban jurisdictions, coverage of most criminal cases is limited to a brief mention of the case in the newspaper, if that. However, when the case involves elements that make it distinctive due to the severity of the crime or the unusual status of the victim or the accused, coverage is likely to be extensive, and often is not limited to a presentation of factual information. Consider the following editorial, which appeared in *Sports Illustrated* about 4 months prior to Mike Tyson's 1992 rape trial:

> Tyson's sexual aggressiveness has led him down some disturbing paths before. This is a man who two years ago, upon being awarded an honorary doctorate of humanities at Central State University, stood at the podium and said, "I don't know what kind of doctor I am but watching all these beautiful sisters here, I'm debating whether I should be a gynecologist"; who, according to published reports, was thrown out of a department store in 1986 for making "lewd and obscene" comments to female customers; who once told his biographer that "the best punch I ever threw" was one that connected with his former wife, Robin Givens; who two years ago allegedly tried to kiss a parking lot attendant against her will and then hit the man who came to the woman's aid; who settled a civil suit by paying damages to a woman who said he fondled her as she danced with another man; who was found by a New York jury to have committed battery on a woman who charged him with grabbing her buttocks and breasts at a nightclub; who in a pending suit has been accused by a former assistant to Givens of assault and sexual harassment; and who *Newsday*'s Wallace Matthews reported earlier this month, took off his pants at a party and began rubbing himself against women. (Reilly, 1991, p. 36)

How might this editorial influence the prospective juror? Is it possible for someone to read this and remain impartial regarding the defendant's character and, more important, the likelihood that he committed rape? Although there are some variations in the strength of the effect and the circumstances under which it is strongest, the gist of the psychological research findings is that pretrial publicity *does* influence judgments of guilt. And because most of the information provided to the press prior to the trial comes from the prosecution (Imrich, Mullin, & Linz, 1995), the effect of pretrial publicity is almost always to increase perceptions that the defendant is guilty

(Costantini & King, 1980; Moran & Cutler, 1991; Steblay, Besirevic, Fulero, & Jimenez-Lorente, 1999).[1]

Nancy Mehrkens Steblay and her colleagues (1999) conducted a meta-analysis of 44 studies that tested the hypothesis that negative pretrial publicity increases judgments of the defendant's guilt. Some of the studies included in the analysis relied on mock jurors and publicity materials created by the researchers; others obtained feedback from prospective jurors who had been exposed to publicity surrounding an actual case. Research participants who were exposed to pretrial publicity were significantly more likely to judge the defendant guilty (percentage of guilty verdicts averaged 59%) than were those exposed to little or no publicity (guilty verdicts averaged 45%). The strongest effects occurred in studies that utilized a survey method, such as those conducted by Costantini and King (1980) and Moran and Cutler (1991). These researchers conducted surveys of jury-eligible citizens' familiarity with an actual case and judgments of the defendant's culpability in that case. In each study, the degree of familiarity with pretrial publicity was directly related to perceptions of the defendant's guilt.

Given that the majority of those surveyed from the original venue are generally familiar with the case (in five venue surveys, Nietzel and Dillehay [1983] found that an average of 80% of respondents from the original venue were familiar with the case) and that increased familiarity corresponds to increased perceptions of the defendant's guilt (Costantini & King, 1980; Moran & Cutler, 1991), it is clear that highly publicized cases pose a very real threat to the Sixth Amendment right to an impartial jury. Fortunately, the courts have several remedies available to them to counteract the negative effects of pretrial publicity. Unfortunately, research suggests that most of those remedies are largely ineffective.

Judicial Remedies: A False Sense of Security?

In spite of research findings demonstrating that pretrial publicity does bias jurors in favor of the prosecution, some evidence exists that trial judges are not particularly concerned, believing that the publicity has no significant effect on actual jury behavior (Carroll et al., 1986). Their apparent lack of concern probably stems from the belief that judicial remedies (especially the jury-selection phase, or voir dire) are effective in weeding out those

---

1. Most of the pretrial publicity research has focused on criminal cases; however, there have been a few studies that examined the effects of publicity in civil cases (e.g., Bornstein, Whisenhunt, Nemeth, & Dunaway, 2002; Kline & Jess, 1966; Robbennolt & Studebaker, 2003; Tanford & Cox, 1988). The antidefense bias that is typically present in criminal cases is not as likely to be present in civil cases, where negative publicity is often aimed at the plaintiff, as well.

prospective jurors who are hopelessly biased and counteracting the effects of publicity in the other jurors (Seibert, 1970). However, a review of the existing research suggests that the judges are overconfident with regard to at least some of the remedies.

Gag Orders

Although the First Amendment protects freedom of the press in the United States, the Supreme Court has upheld a ban on coverage of pretrial hearings and gag orders which restrict the discussion of case facts prior to the trial, as well as bans on press coverage of pretrial hearings (*Gannett Co., Inc., v. DePasquale,* 1979). In some countries, such as Canada, media restrictions are more common. However, the restrictions do not always have the intended effect. Vidmar (2002) describes an Ontario case in which a husband and wife were charged in the kidnapping, sexual assault, and murder of two young women. The wife pleaded guilty. Although media representatives were permitted to attend her sentencing hearing, they were banned from releasing details until after the husband's trial. In spite of compliance by Canada's media, detailed coverage was provided in the *New York Times* and the *Washington Post,* which were available for purchase by prospective Ontario jurors. Details additionally became available through U.S.-based television stations and from fliers distributed in Canada by an organization based in Buffalo, New York. In spite of the Canadian court's best efforts, a poll revealed that 26% of Ontario residents obtained information about the case (Vidmar, 2002).

More recently, in the United States, a gag order was issued by the judge presiding over the case against NBA basketball star Kobe Bryant, who was charged with raping a 19-year-old woman in Eagle, Colorado. In addition to ordering trial participants to avoid discussing topics that were likely to be prejudicial, including issues related to the character and credibility of the parties and witnesses in the case, the judge sealed the case file, barring public access to both sides' statements about the alleged rape and any evidence seized by police. But the gag order applied only to trial participants and law-enforcement personnel and could not stop the steady stream of speculation and insinuation available on the Internet, including character attacks aimed primarily at the alleged victim. The name, address, phone number, and photos of the alleged victim were also posted on various Internet sites, and her name was announced by a nationally syndicated radio talk-show host (Whitcomb, 2003). Criminal charges against Bryant were eventually dropped when the alleged victim decided that she did not want to testify in the case.

Similar problems exist in small communities where information is spread by word-of-mouth, against which the courts have no restrictive measures. Posey and Dahl (2002) describe a multiple-murder case in which 63% of survey respondents indicated that they initially learned about the crimes through a friend, family member, or coworker, rather than the media.

In such cases, a gag order would be futile. And, as noted by Vidmar (2002), when case-relevant information is spread by rumors and gossip, the consequence is often a perception within the community that there is a consensus as to the defendant's guilt, and we would add that the feeling of consensus often extends to beliefs about the appropriate punishment, as well.

Continuances

Another measure available to the courts as a safeguard against pretrial publicity effects is trial continuance, in which the judge delays the trial, assuming that the effects of the media coverage will dissipate over time. The possibility that continuance will be effective only exists in cases for which publicity does die down after a period of time; for some high-profile cases, delaying the trial merely provides greater opportunity for the media to seek out and introduce additional hype. However, for most cases, media coverage of the case does fade with the passage of time. Do the effects of the publicity also fade?

Research on the effectiveness of trial continuance has yielded mixed results. In one study (Kramer, Kerr, & Carroll, 1990), mock jurors were exposed to publicity that was characterized as either emotional (i.e., the defendant was identified as a suspect in an unrelated case involving the injury of a child) or factual (i.e., information regarding prior convictions and physical evidence that was not admissible at trial). Some of the jurors were exposed to the publicity 12 days before the trial; others learned of it the day before the trial. Results revealed that the 12-day delay ameliorated the effects of the factual, but not the emotional, publicity. Conversely, in an earlier study conducted by Davis (1986), participants who were exposed to prejudicial publicity followed by a 1-week continuance were somewhat *more* likely to convict than those exposed to the prejudicial publicity immediately prior to the trial. The author suggests that this might be the result of a "sleeper effect," whereby information gleaned from a low-credibility source becomes more persuasive over time, as the source characteristics dissipate (Kelman & Hovland, 1953; Pratkanis, Greenwald, Leippe, & Baumgardner, 1988). In any event, delays of just 1 week, or even 12 days, do not correspond to the length of delay likely to be imposed in an actual case, and neither study involved repeated exposure to publicity as occurs in actual cases. Therefore, further research is needed, especially to determine whether the effects of emotional evidence remain potent after several months, or even a year, time frames which more realistically correspond with the length of delay one might see for a highly publicized case.

Voir Dire

Many judges believe that a properly conducted voir dire will lead to the identification and elimination of jurors whose impartiality has been irreversibly damaged by their exposure to pretrial publicity. Generally, prospective jurors are questioned about the extent of their exposure to the publicity and are asked whether they are capable of putting that information aside to evaluate the evidence in an unbiased fashion. Those who respond in the negative will be eliminated for cause, resulting in what is believed to be an unbiased jury. The belief that a properly conducted voir dire will remedy the effects of pretrial publicity is evident in Supreme Court decisions (e.g., *Irvin v. Dowd*, 1961; *Mu'Min v. Virginia*, 1991; *Patton v. Yount*, 1984).

In the most recent of those cases, David Mu'Min was convicted of murdering a woman while he was out of prison on work detail in Prince William County, Virginia, and was sentenced to death (*Mu'Min v. Virginia*, 1991). At the time, Mu'Min was serving a 48-year sentence for a murder he had committed 15 years earlier, in 1973. There was a swell of publicity surrounding the second murder, in part because it was committed during the 1988 presidential election campaigns. The reader may recall that a hot-button issue in that election was prison work-release, and crimes committed by inmates participating in such programs, especially Willie Horton, were in the national spotlight. In addition to media attacks on officials viewed as responsible for Mu'Min's access to his victim, headlines and articles that focused specifically on Mu'Min's case declared that he had confessed to the murder, detailed his prior criminal record, and informed the reader that Mu'Min had been rejected for parole six times due to bad behavior in prison.

The trial court rejected Mu'Min's requests for individual voir dire and that jurors be questioned about the specific content of the publicity to which they had been exposed. Instead the judge questioned jurors first en masse, and then in groups of four, as to whether they had acquired information about the offense from the media. He followed up with four questions asking whether jurors who had been exposed to publicity could be impartial, keep an open mind, and suspend judgment. In the end, 8 of 12 seated jurors had been exposed to pretrial publicity, and all indicated that they could be impartial. The jury convicted Mu'Min of capital murder.

On appeal, the U.S. Supreme Court upheld the conviction. Writing for the majority, Chief Justice William Rehnquist wrote that questions about the content of publicity to which jurors were exposed are not constitutionally required. Furthermore, he noted the fact that none of the eight jurors who had been exposed to publicity indicated that they had formed an opinion as to Mu'Min's guilt and, consistent with the Court's ruling in *Patton v. Yount* (1984), deferred to the discretion of the trial court judge to determine the appropriate depth of inquiry during voir dire.

As noted by Carroll et al. (1986), the belief that voir dire is an effective remedy for the effects of pretrial publicity assumes that prospective jurors are capable of assessing their own biases and that they are willing to admit to such biases during the jury selection process. It also requires that judges and attorneys be able to identify those who should appropriately be challenged for cause. Research suggests that none of these is a safe assumption (Dexter, Cutler, & Moran, 1992; Kerr, Kramer, Carroll, & Alfini, 1991; Mize, 1999;

Seltzer, Venuti, & Lopes, 1991; Sue, Smith, & Pedroza, 1975; Vidmar, 2002). Mock jurors who have been exposed to negative publicity, and who consequently claim that they can disregard that publicity and base their decisions solely on the evidence, are consistently more likely to convict than those who have not been exposed to pretrial publicity.

Often, jurors are either unaware of their biases or are hesitant to admit to them in court, and judges are inclined to have faith in jurors' promises of impartiality. Posey (2002) conducted an archival study of all Kansas Supreme Court cases involving a change-of-venue appeal from 1992 to 2001. The search yielded 18 criminal cases; in all cases, the Supreme Court upheld the trial court's decision to deny the motion for change of venue. In six cases in this sample, the defense presented survey evidence in support of its change-of-venue motion. Case recognition rates ranged from 90% to 98%, indicating that there was substantial familiarity with the case among residents of the community in which the offense had occurred. Guilt ratings ranged from 56% to 71%, indicating that a majority of respondents believed the defendant to be guilty of the offense. In all cases in which a survey was conducted, and in 12 cases overall, the Court specifically cited seated jurors' reported ability to remain impartial or the apparent ease of finding an impartial jury as justification for upholding the denial of the change-of-venue motion.

Deliberations

Even if some biased jurors slip through the voir dire cracks, an additional safeguard is believed to emerge during deliberations. According to this belief, should an issue arise during deliberations that was present in the pretrial publicity but not introduced as evidence during the trial, at least one member of the jury will admonish the others and they will disregard the irrelevant issue. Of course, it is difficult to know whether this occurs in actual trials, as jury deliberations are not accessible to anyone outside the jury. The results of simulation research suggest that, rather than reduce the effects of pretrial publicity, deliberations actually serve to enhance those effects. In the Kramer et al. (1990) study discussed above, the predeliberation judgments of those exposed to emotionally biasing publicity differed from those not exposed to such publicity by just 5.9%. Following deliberations, the two groups differed by 43.3%, indicating that deliberations served to exacerbate, rather than ameliorate, the biasing effects of the publicity. This is an example of what social psychologists refer to as "group polarization" (Moscovici & Zavalloni, 1969; Myers & Lamm, 1976), whereby attitudes among like-minded individuals become more extreme after discussion. It is interesting to note that videotapes of deliberations in this study revealed that jurors *did* admonish one another against discussion of pretrial publicity when such information arose. Thus, in spite of jurors' own attempts to police themselves, they were affected by the inadmissible pretrial publicity.

Changes of Venue and Imported Venire

In light of research demonstrating that voir dire and deliberations, the remedies most often relied upon by judges, are not effective in reducing the biasing effects of pretrial publicity, it is important to examine more drastic, and less frequently relied upon, remedies, including the use of an imported venire and change of venue. For example, in the Byron de la Beckwith retrial discussed in chapter 8, jurors were selected and imported to Jackson, Mississippi, from Panola County, which is about 140 miles north of Jackson. The rationale behind both is that, due to the extent and nature of the media coverage, it will be difficult, if not impossible, to seat an impartial jury in the jurisdiction in which the crime was committed or where the lawsuit has been filed. Assuming that the jurors from the alternate jurisdiction have been exposed to little or no publicity or discussions regarding the case and that they are not familiar with or have no vested interest in the parties involved in a civil suit, each of these should be effective in reducing, if not eliminating, the effects of pretrial bias. However, for a number of reasons, judges are often reluctant to take these more drastic measures.

In the remainder of this chapter, we will examine the role that trial consultants play in the change-of-venue motion. First, we review two Supreme Court cases in which defendants filed motions for change of venue due to excessive media coverage and discuss problems associated with nationally publicized cases. Next, we describe the contributions that trial consultants make to the examination of the effects of media surrounding a particular case in a specific venue. Finally, we will discuss standards and guidelines established by the ASTC for conducting change-of-venue surveys.

High-Profile Cases and Supreme Court Rationale

We have chosen two highly publicized cases for review. The first, *Patton v. Yount* (1984), was chosen because the U.S. Supreme Court based its ruling in this case on assumptions that run contrary to psychological research findings. In addition, this case represents a good example of the type of case for which social science research methods could have been used to assist the court in assessing bias among prospective jurors. The second case, *United States v. McVeigh and Nichols* (1996), was chosen because social scientists were utilized as consultants to examine the effects of pretrial publicity, and a change of venue was ultimately granted. At the same time, the McVeigh case exemplifies those cases for which it is becoming increasingly difficult, due to public interest and substantial national media coverage, to find an impartial jury anywhere in the country.

The Jon Yount Case

On April 28, 1966, the body of Pamela Rimer, an 18-year-old high school student, was found in a wooded area near her home in Luthersburg,

Clearfield County, Pennsylvania. There were numerous wounds about her head and cuts on her throat and neck. The victim had been left in the woods to drown in her own blood; an autopsy revealed that she died of strangulation when blood from her wounds was drawn into her lungs. At about 5:45 the following morning, Jon Yount, who had been Pamela Rimer's high school math teacher, entered a police station in nearby DuBois and made oral and written confessions to the murder. His confessions were published in two local papers and were admitted into evidence at his trial.

In spite of his plea of temporary insanity, Yount was convicted of rape and first-degree murder in 1966. His conviction was later overturned because his confession had been obtained in violation of his Miranda rights, and he was retried, in the same county and before the same judge, in 1970. Prior to and during voir dire for the second trial, Yount requested a change of venue because of the continued publicity surrounding his case, which included mention of his confession, his testimony regarding his temporary insanity during the first trial, and his prior rape conviction, none of which would be admissible in his second trial (prosecutors had dismissed the rape charge and were seeking only a first-degree murder conviction). The motions for change of venue were denied, and Yount was convicted of first-degree murder and sentenced to life in prison.

Clearfield County, where both Yount and the victim lived, is a rural county whose population was about 70,000 at the time of the crime. Of 163 prospective jurors who had been questioned by the judge prior to the second trial, all but two reported that they had heard about the case, and 77% admitted to having formed an opinion about Yount's guilt. Eight of those who ultimately served as jurors admitted that at some time they had formed an opinion regarding his guilt. Yount appealed his conviction, claiming that his Sixth Amendment right to an impartial jury had been denied. The Supreme Court, by a 6–2 majority (Justice Thurgood Marshall did not participate), ruled that the passage of time between the two trials had cured the prejudice that existed at the first trial and that there was not a "wave of public passion" that made a fair trial unlikely by the second jury. The Court went on to state that a "presumption of correctness" should be given to the trial judge's opinion because, having been present in the courtroom, he was in a better position to evaluate the demeanor, credibility, and competence of the prospective jurors.

In this case, the Supreme Court made two assumptions for which there are relevant psychological research findings. First, the Court assumed that the passage of time weakens the effects of publicity. As discussed above, research findings suggest that this is not necessarily the case, especially when the publicity contains emotional content, such as that relating to the murder of a child (Davis, 1986; Kramer et al., 1990; Steblay et al., 1999). Clearfield County, Pennsylvania, was served primarily by two newspapers. Both papers gave front-page coverage to the murder, the pretrial proceedings, and Yount's first trial. In numerous editions, the *DuBois Courier Express* carried banner headlines, news stories, and feature articles. The *Clearfield Progress* named the trial as the "top news story of 1966," thus placing it ahead of the Watts riots, the mass murder of eight Chicago nursing students by Richard Speck, the shooting deaths of 15 people by sniper Charles Whitman at the University of Texas, Austin, and events surrounding the Vietnam War. Both papers reported that public interest in the case was unprecedented. Of course, the case also received television coverage.

As noted by Supreme Court justice John Paul Stevens in his dissenting opinion, articles covering the case were extremely detailed and were often accompanied by photos of the victim's body on the front page of the paper. When the Pennsylvania Supreme Court reversed Yount's initial conviction in 1969 on the grounds that his confession had been illegally obtained, the reversal was headline news, and the local press reprinted the entire dissenting opinion. Many listeners called in to a local radio program in order to express their hostility toward Yount. Justice Stevens argued that because emotional response was so strong 3 years after the first trial, the passage of time had done little to decrease public sentiment surrounding the case. However, in its majority decision in the Yount case, written by Justice Lewis Powell, the Supreme Court assumed that trial court judges are capable of assessing jurors' ability to set aside their prior judgments of the defendant, that, in spite of their exposure to information regarding the defendant's confession, for example, they could act as impartial jurors.

The problem is that judges must base such an assessment largely on jurors' own self-reported ability to be an "unbiased" juror, and there are a number of reasons to question the validity of such reports. First, there are significant demand characteristics associated with the voir dire process. Even when prospective jurors are questioned individually, they are aware that a "good juror" is an unbiased, objective juror, and they are therefore likely to respond in such a way as to appear "good" to the judge and attorneys. Furthermore, as discussed above, research has shown no relationship between jurors' self-reported ability to be impartial and their pretrial perceptions of the defendant's guilt (e.g., Costantini & King, 1980; Kerr et al., 1991; Sue et al., 1975). In their description of two community surveys they had conducted regarding specific highly publicized cases, Moran and Cutler (1991) reported no relationship between respondents' own assessments of their ability to be impartial and their degree of knowledge about the case or their assessments of the strength of the evidence against the defendant. Intentionally or not, prospective jurors inaccurately assess their own ability to be unbiased if called to jury duty.

A community survey such as those used by Moran and Cutler (1991) might have provided the trial judge in the Yount case with valuable information regarding the extent of prejudgment of Jon Yount, the continuing effects of the pretrial publicity on prospective jurors' attitudes, and the degree of difficulty in identifying jurors through voir dire who had not formed an opinion regarding the defendant's guilt. Such an instrument was used in the other case we discuss, *United States v. McVeigh and Nichols* (1996).

The Timothy McVeigh Case

On April 19, 1995, a bomb exploded outside the Murrah Federal Building in Oklahoma City, resulting in the deaths of 168 persons, 19 of them children. Hundreds of others were injured. Not surprisingly, the media coverage of the bombing was extensive, providing round-the-clock coverage of the carnage, eyewitness reports, the search for victims, and the hunt for the person or persons responsible. Two days later, authorities arrested Timothy McVeigh in Perry, Oklahoma. He was later charged in federal court with the bombing of the Murrah Federal Building and with the first-degree murder of eight federal law enforcement officers. Authorities also named Terry Nichols as an accomplice who had helped McVeigh to plan the bombing.

Because of extensive media coverage, attorneys for the defendants filed a motion for a change of venue, requesting that the trials be moved from Oklahoma City, where the bombing had occurred. But to where? Media coverage of the bombing, the arrest of the defendants, and the government's case against them had been extensive on a national level. Network and cable television stations had sent news crews to Oklahoma City in order to provide the entire country with a view of the destruction, interviews with the victims and their families, and each development in the case against McVeigh and Nichols. After his arrest, viewers across the country were presented with video footage of McVeigh, clad in orange jail clothing, being led into a van while surrounded by a vocal and angry crowd. Where, in the United States, could there be found 12 jury-eligible adults who had not formed an opinion about the bombing of the Murrah Federal Building and the men charged with its commission?

According to Judge Richard Matsch's opinion on the change-of-venue motion, there was "no disagreement among the parties...about a trial in Oklahoma City" (*United States v. McVeigh and Nichols*, 1996). "The effects of the explosion on that community [were] so profound and pervasive that no detailed discussion of the evidence [was] necessary" (p. 1470). The focus of inquiry became a determination of whether the defendants could receive a fair trial anywhere in the state of Oklahoma. To buttress its argument that the trial should be moved from Oklahoma, the defense sought the assistance of social scientists, who conducted media analyses and public opinion surveys (Studebaker & Penrod, 1997). Christina Studebaker and her colleagues conducted a content analysis of newspaper articles published in the *Daily Oklahoman* (Oklahoma City), the *Lawton Constitution* (Lawton, Oklahoma, about 90 miles from Oklahoma City), the *Tulsa World* (Tulsa, Oklahoma), and the *Denver Post* (Denver, Colorado). The analysis revealed that, from the day after the bombing to the time that coding of articles began approximately 9 months later, there were 939 articles published in the

Oklahoma City paper related to the bombing. This compares with 251, 235, and 174 in the other newspapers, respectively. Further, the Oklahoma City paper contained much more content that would be characterized as emotional publicity (e.g., statements related to emotional suffering, the goriness of the crime scene, profiles of victims and their families, and helping/togetherness themes) than did the other papers.

Both the prosecution and the defense employed consultants who conducted public opinion surveys to assess the extent of knowledge regarding the case and opinions regarding the defendants' culpability. However, it appears from Judge Matsch's opinion that he all but dismissed the results of the surveys as being of no use in his decision. For example, he stated:

> The possible prejudicial impact of this type of publicity is not something measurable by any objective standards. The parties have submitted data from opinion surveys done by qualified experts who have given their opinions about the results and their meaning.... Such surveys are but crude measures of opinion at the time of the interviews. Human behavior is far less knowable and predictable than chemical reactions or other subjects of study by scientific methodology. (p. 1473)

Judge Matsch went on to state:

> The opinion surveys done for this hearing attempted to test the ability of the persons questioned to be fair and impartial jurors.... The commonly used phrase "presumption of innocence" is not an appropriate or even apt description of the position of an accused in this court. What is more descriptive is whether a juror is ready, willing and able to give a defendant the benefit of a reasonable doubt after careful consideration of all of the evidence admitted at a trial. (p. 1473)

Here again, we see a court official endorsing the belief that jurors are capable of simply setting aside their prior knowledge and opinions.

Judge Matsch expressed further dissatisfaction with the surveys' ability to assess the death penalty issue in the case and relied instead on television interviews in which citizens of Oklahoma expressed the sentiment that it is important to ensure conviction of McVeigh so that he could then be put to death. It appears that the decision to move the trial to Denver was based in large part on Matsch's belief that this sentiment was pervasive in Oklahoma, but not so in Colorado. This judge's apparent rejection of social science research findings as a reliable source of information upon which to base judicial decisions is not unique (e.g., see opinions of Supreme Court justices Powell [*Ballew v. Georgia*, 1978], Antonin Scalia [*Stanford v. Kentucky*, 1989], and Rehnquist [*Lockhart v. McCree*, 1986]).

In the end, Judge Richard Matsch cited the following reasons for his decision to grant the venue change, moving the trials of McVeigh and Nichols out of the state of Oklahoma: the development of differences over time in both the volume and focus of media coverage in Oklahoma versus local coverage outside Oklahoma and national coverage; the ratio of demonization of the defendants to humanization of the victims in the local pretrial publicity; and the frequency of televised interviews with Oklahoma citizens emphasizing the importance of ensuring a conviction, with an evident implication that death would be the appropriate punishment (Studebaker & Penrod, 1997). While Judge Matsch appears to have dismissed survey evidence as important to his decision, he did rely on social scientists' reviews and interpretations of the effects of media coverage. These reviews demonstrated that, while it may have been difficult to find a jury with no knowledge of the case anywhere in the country, there existed a substantial difference by locale in the nature and extent of coverage of the case, thus enabling the court to move the trial to a location that had been exposed to significantly less emotional coverage of the case (*United States v. McVeigh and Nichols*, 1996). In the much-delayed state trial of Terry Nichols, an Oklahoma district judge—in September 2003— approved moving his trial from Oklahoma City to another city in Oklahoma.

National Publicity

Although few cases will reach the degree of media coverage received by the Oklahoma City bombing case, national coverage of crimes, especially, it seems, those involving children or celebrities as victims or defendants, continues to increase. Twenty-four-hour cable news networks are often desperate for news to fill air time; Court TV broadcasts and provides analyses of criminal trials; and programs such as "America's Most Wanted" introduce the country to cases, and many times to specific suspects, that would otherwise be limited to local news coverage. Add to that the as-yet unmeasured coverage and commentary available on the Internet, and more and more cases are becoming national news.

As this occurs, an ever-higher hurdle is presented to the defendant who seeks to move his or her trial, as the defense carries the burden to prove that a fair trial cannot be had in the local jurisdiction. It proves this in part by pointing to the contrast in coverage given to its case versus that given to others and by demonstrating that such coverage is more emotional, more extensive, and generally "over the top" than the media coverage allotted to other news stories. In three separate cases involving pretrial publicity (*Rideau v. Louisiana*, 1963; *Estes v. Texas*, 1965; and *Sheppard v. Maxwell*, 1966), the Supreme Court ruled for the defendants, noting that publicity surrounding those cases had far exceeded community standards for reporting. However, as community standards for reporting shift in the direction of greater intensity (emotional and otherwise), the task for the defense becomes more difficult. According to Beisecker (1995): "proving that sensational, inflammatory publicity has permeated a community and necessarily will affect jurors' decisions becomes more difficult as the norm of reporting in the community itself becomes increasingly sensational" (p. 85).

Rideau v. Louisiana (1963) is the only Supreme Court decision in which prejudice was presumed from pretrial publicity alone. In that case, the defendant had confessed to robbing a bank, kidnapping three of the bank's employees, and killing one of them. The 20-minute confession was videotaped and broadcast three times on local television. In the view of the author of the Supreme Court opinion—again, Justice Powell—the televised confession "*was* Rideau's trial" (p. 665), and any subsequent proceedings in the community "so pervasively exposed to such a spectacle could be but a hollow formality" (p. 665). However, the Court has noted that the presumptive prejudice standard recognized in *Rideau* is rarely applicable and is reserved for extreme situations (*Coleman v. Kemp*, 1985). Additionally, some legal scholars have argued that exposure to a barrage of media coverage actually enhances the likelihood that jurors will be impartial, because it provides them the opportunity to hone their skills in evaluating the nature and quality of reports to which they are exposed (see Minow & Cate, 1991).

Trial judges have generally been reluctant to grant a venue change based solely on media content. As normative media coverage is increasingly characterized by sensationalism, the minimum standard for what is considered extreme will rise, and the reluctance on the part of judges is likely to increase, especially when the defendant presents nothing but a compilation of the media reports as evidence of prejudice. Beisecker (1995) predicts that, at the very least, defendants will need expert evaluation and interpretation of the media, as was provided in the McVeigh/Nichols case, to explain how it is distinctive and how it has probably affected prospective jurors. However, courts will increasingly also require data from venue surveys explicitly demonstrating that a high percentage of jury-eligible citizens have been influenced by the publicity. Trial consultants are in a position to provide both of these services. In the remainder of this chapter, we will focus on the role of the trial consultant in the change-of-venue motion.

Role of the Trial Consultant

The most significant role played by the trial consultant in the change-of-venue motion is to construct and administer a survey designed to assess prospective jurors' attitudes and knowledge regarding a specific case. However, data from such change-of-venue surveys have not always been allowed as evidence in court.

Change-of-Venue Surveys: Historical Perspective

Historically, two kinds of information were presented to the court in support of the motion to change venue (Hans & Vidmar, 1982). One of these consisted of sworn affidavits from citizens who were believed to "have their finger on the pulse" of the community. These individuals would attest to the general opinions of the venue as a whole regarding a specific case. The second type of information was a compilation of media coverage of the case, especially newspaper articles, sometimes accompanied by affidavits regarding the likely effects of such coverage on public opinion. As Hans and Vidmar (1982) point out, neither of these has much scientific merit. The former suffers from sampling bias and is really nothing more than conjecture, and the latter falls short of establishing that the media have even been attended to, much less tainted the jury pool. Neither provides definitive evidence regarding the actual opinions of prospective jurors regarding the case.

Some of the earliest attempts to introduce survey evidence in support of the change-of-venue motion occurred in the 1950s. One attempt was made in the trial of Alger Hiss, for which the defense submitted survey results in support of its claim that prospective jurors in Vermont had less bias regarding Hiss's degree of guilt than did prospective jurors in New York City, where the trial was to be held. At the hearing on the motion, the prosecution successfully argued that the results of surveys constituted hearsay, one person's statements about a second person's remarks, and were therefore not admissible as evidence (see Pollock, 1977). In another early case, *Irvin v. State* (1953), the defense introduced the results of a four-county survey conducted in Florida. In that case, which involved a Black defendant on trial for rape, social scientists surveyed prospective jurors in the county in which the offense was allegedly committed, a neighboring county, and two additional counties located some distance away. Results revealed that a greater number of respondents in the first two counties believed that the defendant was guilty than did those in the more distant counties (see Woodward, 1952). Although the researchers were allowed to testify regarding methodological issues during the hearing on the motion, they were not allowed to present their findings because, once again, the court ruled that they were hearsay because the interviews were anonymous, the respondents had not testified under oath, and they could not be cross-examined.

Few attempts were made to introduce venue surveys as evidence during the next decade (Pollock, 1977), but things changed in the late 1960s and early 1970s. The courts began to recognize the scientific legitimacy of survey research, and the hearsay argument was partially eroded by the admission of survey evidence in other types of cases, such as those involving copyright infringement. In addition, the Supreme Court in *Sheppard v. Maxwell* (1966) ruled that grounds for a change of venue do not require the demonstration of actual prejudice among seated jurors, but that a reasonable likelihood of prejudice is sufficient. This opened the door for survey evidence that speaks to the *probability of prejudice* in a given community (Hans & Vidmar, 1982). Finally, the Federal Rules of Evidence include two rules that allow a survey to be introduced into evidence. Rule 803 allows the admission of data or materials that are compiled in the course of the regular activities of a particular occupation or profession (Saltzburg, Martin, & Capra, 1998a). Therefore, the survey researcher is allowed to submit his or her data as one of the "tools of the trade." Survey evidence is also admissible under Rule 705, which allows experts to testify by disclosing the foundations for their views (Saltzburg, Martin, & Capra, 1998b). Thus, the expert may refer to the survey data as the foundation for his or her conclusions about community sentiment and the probability of prejudice in the community. These changes paved the way for the increased involvement of social scientists in the change-of-venue motion.

Professional Standards

When Stephen Schoenthaler, a criminal justice professor at California State University, Stanislaus, conducted the change-of-venue survey in the Scott Peterson case, he provided a good example of how things should *not* be done. Peterson, who was charged in Stanislaus County, California, with the murders of his pregnant wife and their unborn child, filed a motion for change of venue due to extensive publicity surrounding his case. In a hearing on January 8, 2004, Judge Al Girolami ruled that the trial would be moved, citing Stanislaus County residents' emotional involvement in the case, the magnitude of media coverage of the case, and the results of Schoenthaler's survey, which showed that 70% of residents in Stanislaus County had formed an opinion of Peterson's guilt (Ryan, 2004).

However, shortly after Girolami's ruling, it was reported that some of the survey results had been fabricated. It seems that Schoenthaler required that students in one of his classes conduct the surveys to earn credit for an assignment worth 20% of their course grade (Jardine, 2004). Each student was required to complete 20 telephone surveys, many with respondents outside Stanislaus County (Stapley, 2004). The survey was assigned 2 days before Thanksgiving break, and 1 week before the start of final exams (Stapley & Cote, 2004). Prior to the administration of the survey, Schoenthaler reportedly told his students to expect that respondents who lived far from Stanislaus County would know less about the case than those living in or near the county. Students made the calls from their own telephones, outside Schoenthaler's supervision. At least 9 of the 65 students in the class admitted to fabricating at least some of the survey results that they submitted. Although Judge Girolami did not change his decision to move the case, an investigation led by the university resulted in disciplinary action against 25 of 58 students enrolled in the class, and Schoenthaler was removed from the classroom and placed on paid administrative leave until the university could determine whether he had engaged in scientific misconduct (Turner, 2004).

As noted in chapter 1, one of the primary criticisms of trial consulting as a profession is its lack of any certification or licensure requirements. However, the American Society of Trial Consultants (ASTC), through its

Subcommittee on Certification and Education, has sought to establish professional guidelines for the activities in which consultants are likely to engage. In 1998, work began to establish such guidelines for the use of surveys in connection with change-of-venue motions (American Society of Trial Consultants, 1998). In its final report, the task force delineated specific guidelines regarding (1) questionnaire design, including the basic components of a venue survey, appropriate question style and content, length of the questionnaire, appropriate questionnaire introduction, context and order effects, and the importance of pretesting the survey instrument; (2) survey procedure, including respondent selection, sampling issues, correct reporting of completion rates, handling of call-backs and refusals, training and supervision of callers, respondent confidentiality, and availability of original data to opposing counsel; and (3) data analysis issues, including appropriate analyses and validity measures (American Society of Trial Consultants, 2003). The guidelines also include a summary of items that should be included in a report presenting survey results to the court. Task force members (Susan Macpherson, Elissa Krauss, Ronald Dillehay, and Ed Bronson) had extensive experience in venue work, and their recommendations are consistent with those published elsewhere (e.g., Diamond, 1995; Krauss & Bonora, 1983; Morgan, 1990; Nietzel & Dillehay, 1983).

The consultant's involvement in the change-of-venue motion generally begins with contact from the defense attorney who is concerned about the ability of his or her client to receive a fair trial due to pretrial publicity. Following a discussion with the defense attorney regarding case issues, media content, and admissibility of items released in the media, the consultant generally conducts a thorough review of all coverage of the case, including primarily newspaper articles and editorials, but also television, radio, and Internet coverage. A survey is constructed for administration in the venue in which the crime occurred and, ideally, at least one other venue outside the media circle, for comparison purposes. Most often, the venue will consist of a county, and the alternate venue will be a different county in the same state. For federal trials, the alternate venue will usually be within the same circuit. The alternate venue is generally chosen by the consultant, along with the defense attorney, based on the degree of exposure to the case and its demographic and numerical similarity to the venue in which the crime was committed (see Santivasci, 1993, for a discussion of the consideration of demographic factors when choosing an alternate venue).

The survey is often administered by callers who are employed by a market research firm and have been trained by the consultant to administer venue surveys. The trial consultant also monitors the calls to ensure that interviews are being conducted appropriately. Ideally, the callers will not be aware that the survey is being conducted on behalf of the defense, in order to minimize biased administration. Once an adequate sample of respondents has been obtained, the consultant conducts the appropriate data analyses (most often, these are limited to descriptive statistics) and prepares a report to be submitted to the court in support of the motion for a venue change. Of course, if the data do not appear to warrant a change of venue, the defense may simply choose not to file a motion. An experienced consultant can be quite helpful in providing guidance at this point. Finally, the consultant is often called to testify at the change-of-venue hearing regarding the survey design and analyses. All told, trial consultants will typically work about 40 hours on the change-of-venue survey and its related tasks, and the total cost is often in the range of $40,000. Costs can be reduced somewhat by cutting corners here and there, but because this work product must be able to withstand the scrutiny of cross-examination, sticking with best practices is advisable.

Ethical Issues

Along the way, the consultant encounters a number of ethical issues associated with conducting the change-of-venue survey. Among those are the conflicting roles of advocate for the defense versus objective researcher, the danger of tainting the jury pool due to the administration of the survey, and problems associated with conducting surveys in small jurisdictions.

Advocate Versus Researcher

Because consultants doing venue work are almost always hired by the defense,[2] they are particularly at risk for being described as "hired guns" working to "get criminals off." In reality, however, the consultant working in this context is an expert witness: hired by one side but expected to present the facts as supported by the research. It is therefore crucial that the consultant educate the defense attorney about the limits of the consultant's role in the report writing and in testifying. Some suggest that the consultant's reports and testimony should be limited to a discussion of the methods and results associated with the development and administration of the survey and should not include a statement as to the ultimate issue of whether the survey results warrant a venue change (Kinch, 1991; Posey & Dahl, 2002). If one is concerned that the data may be misinterpreted by the court, a second expert can be utilized who can testify regarding the total body of information relevant to the issue of venue change, including the survey results. If such an expert is used, the venue consultant makes available the raw survey data, including open-ended comments from respondents, so that they may

---

2. Although the defense always initiates the change-of-venue motion and creation of the survey, there have been occasions in which social scientists have been hired by the prosecution to critique change-of-venue surveys or to conduct their own survey to contradict the findings of the defense survey. In addition, defendants in these cases are often indigent, in which case the consultant's payment comes from state defense funds.

be reanalyzed. This expert might also discuss the psychosocial aspects of how case information is further ingrained in a community through word-of-mouth communication, or how a community may have overly personalized a case through local responses to the crime (e.g., the creation of search parties or involvement in prayer and memorial services). The key is that the expert works to independent conclusions that are then presented to the court in concert with the consultant's work on the venue survey. The utilization of separate experts provides assistance to the judge in interpreting the survey results, places the results in a greater context, and allows for specific recommendations to be made to the court as to whether the trial should be moved to an alternate venue. Ideally, this makes the survey evidence more palatable for judges, who are often quick to dismiss such evidence as invalid, as was the case with Judge Matsch in the McVeigh/ Nichols case discussed earlier in this chapter.

The consultant doing venue work should also limit the role of the defense attorney in writing the survey instrument. Because of the adversarial nature of the trial process, the defense attorney may have difficulty writing or approving survey items that are objective and nonleading. Therefore, to ensure objectivity, it is critical that the consultant clearly communicate to the defense attorney the importance of developing a measure that will objectively assess community attitudes, rather than lead respondents into making statements that produce an overestimation of prejudgment of the defendant. Ideally, attorneys should play only a minimal role in the development of the survey (e.g., reviewing items used to screen for jury eligibility), in part because the courts have looked with suspicion on surveys that were developed with heavy involvement by the attorneys (*American Greetings Corp. v. Dan-Dee Imports, Inc.*, 1985; *Brooks Shoe Manufacturing Co., Inc., v. Suave Shoe Corp.*, 1981; *Frisch's Restaurant Inc. v. Shoney's Inc.*, 1985), as their role as advocates is believed to preclude unbiased participation in the survey research process (Morgan, 1990).

Finally, the consultant must be prepared to honestly interpret the survey data to the defense attorney. If, based on the consultant's experience, the data do not support a change of venue, the consultant should suggest to the defense that a venue motion would likely not be successful, because the data indicate low case recall or little assumption of guilt in the community. In short, rather than acting as an advocate for one side or the other, the consultant who conducts change-of-venue surveys must act as an advocate for the data.

Danger of Tainting the Jury Pool

When conducting the change-of-venue survey, it is necessary to examine not only whether jurors have heard of the case, but the extent of their knowledge regarding those elements of the case that have been reported in the news. One is especially interested in prospective jurors' familiarity with elements that are prejudicial or that would be considered inadmissible in court. This is often assessed using a series of questions that begin with the stem "Have you read, seen, or heard . . . ," followed by a piece of case-relevant information that has been released in the media (e.g., "Have you read, seen, or heard information about a polygraph exam related to this case?") (Moran & Cutler, 1991; Nietzel & Dillehay, 1983; Posey & Dahl, 2002). Inclusion of these items is critical to an understanding of the degree of saturation of media coverage of the case; however, they are not without their complications.

It is often argued, particularly by prosecutors, that these items introduce prospective jurors to information that they did not know about the case prior to participating in the survey (Posey & Dahl, 2002). Accordingly, respondents who are merely familiar with the superficial aspects of the case (e.g., description of the crime and defendant's name) may be hearing these details for the first time. Does their inclusion in the survey cause respondents to remember them as if they had come from another source, such as the newspaper? More important, does their inclusion inadvertently increase bias against the defendant? Research on source misattribution and the sleeper effect suggests that the answer to the first question might be yes (Belli, Lindsay, Gales, & McCarthy, 1994; Kelman & Hovland, 1953; Pratkanis, Greenwald, Leippe, & Baumgardner, 1988; Zaragoza & Lane, 1994). People often confuse the source of their memories, making it likely that they will, over time, give undue weight to information they received from a low-credibility source. Theoretically, in time, survey respondents may recall information from this set of survey questions as if they had learned it through the media. Depending on the degree to which they trust the media, the hypothetical facts that they learned first through the survey may be transformed in their minds into actual events that absolutely occurred.

Consultants can take two measures to protect against the possibility that the survey will produce more biased jurors by introducing them to new case-relevant information. The first measure is that not all survey respondents receive the set of "Have you read, seen, or heard . . . " questions. At an earlier point in the survey, respondents' familiarity with the case is assessed through two case statements (Nietzel & Dillehay, 1983; Posey & Dahl, 2002). The first case statement provides a very general description of the offense, based on only the most widely reported facts in the media (e.g., "On February 21, a 66-year-old waitress failed to show up at work and was reported missing. The next day, authorities found evidence indicating that she had been killed. The defendant in this case is a 26-year-old Caucasian male. Do you recall reading, seeing, or hearing anything about this case or the people involved?"). Respondents who answer yes are then eligible to be asked the "Have you read, seen, or heard . . . " items. Those who answer no are given a second case statement with more specific information (e.g., "Parts of the victim's body were found in several locations outside of her home. The man accused in this case was a neighbor of the victim. Do you recall reading, seeing, or hearing anything about this case?"). If a respondent answers no to the second case statement, one should assume a lack of any familiarity with the case and terminate the interview. Thus, only those who have prior knowledge of the case are asked questions containing more specific information.

The second safeguard the consultant might take to ensure that the survey does not bias respondents is to ask only whether they have read, seen, or heard about information that has in fact been reported in the primary media sources (e.g., the local newspaper) in the community. Because most respondents' familiarity with the case would have originated from that source, the chances that the survey will expose prospective jurors to new information are quite low (Posey & Dahl, 2002).

Challenges in Small Jurisdictions

Many change-of-venue motions are filed in relatively small jurisdictions. Violent crime, especially murder, is rare is such communities; therefore, when it does occur, it receives much media attention and is a frequent topic of conversation among residents (Vidmar, 2002). There is also a likelihood that many prospective jurors will at least be acquainted with some of the people involved in the case, including victims and their families. The increased attention and personal involvement pose a threat to the defendant's right to an impartial jury, and defense attorneys are likely to want to move the trial elsewhere. However, the small jurisdiction presents several unique challenges to the consultant conducting a change-of-venue survey. Among the practical issues that arise is the fact that one must obtain an adequate sample size from which to draw reliable conclusions, while being careful not to contact so many prospective jurors that the court feels that the survey biased the jury pool. Several researchers have offered guidance regarding the sample-size issue in small venues (American Society of Trial Consultants, 2003; Nietzel & Dillehay, 1983; Posey & Dahl, 2002). There is also the possibility that respondents have been made aware that a change-of-venue survey would be conducted. Such information generally comes as a result of media coverage of pretrial hearings on the matter. For instance, in Rush County, Kansas, population 3,678, just after the judge approved a survey during a pretrial hearing in which the instrument's rationale and methodology were explained, the regional newspaper wrote an article proclaiming "Survey to Determine If Prejudice Exists in Murder Case" (Ogle, 1999). There is the danger that such knowledge will predispose respondents to answer in such a way as to try to keep the trial in the community or, at the very least, to try to appear as unbiased as possible for self-presentation purposes. Whatever the motivation, the respondent who is aware of the purpose and sponsor of the survey may not be completely honest in his or her answers to venue survey questions. Even when a change-of-venue survey is conducted in a venue where no presurvey publicity has occurred, people in small communities may view the venue survey with suspicion and question its intent (Posey & Dahl, 2002).

In addition to the legal issues, we are interested in the ethical issues that arise for the consultant conducting change-of-venue surveys in small jurisdictions. The primary dilemma along those lines concerns preserving the confidentiality of all respondents. Perhaps more than in larger venues, there is a good deal of concern about personal anonymity among individuals who participate in a survey in smaller communities. Respondents will often qualify their answers by reminding the interviewer that they do not want to be associated with their answers. For example, Posey and Dahl (2002) report that respondents have told their interviewers: "If anything I say helps the defense of that man, I will not say that I said this, but . . ." (p. 118); "I can't talk about some of the things I know because I teach in a school and this is a small community, but . . ." (p. 118); and "I made a comment about what my job is and I don't want that to be in your report because that will reveal who I am and I don't want anyone to know that I put my opinion on this, but . . ." (pp. 118–119). While some are hypervigilant about confidentiality, other respondents may inadvertently disclose their identities through their open-ended comments. For example, one individual may reveal that he first found out about the case because he lives across the street from the victim, another because her husband is the one who organized the search party to find the victim's body. Without saying their names, individuals reveal themselves in ways that other community members could associate with their responses if they were to read the comments that become part of the court record in the venue motion. In this instance, the consultant is faced with a dilemma. The American Association of Public Opinion Research (AAPOR) Code of Professional Ethics and Practices (1986) states, "unless the respondent waives confidentiality for specific uses, we shall hold as privileged and confidential all information that might identify a respondent with his or her response" (§II.D.2). To fully follow AAPOR's code of conduct in a small venue would entail deleting some of the most telling data, which could illustrate to the court the extent of community involvement with the crime or the case. Therefore, researchers in small venues face a dilemma of either deleting vital data or disclosing potentially identifying information about their respondents.

Effectiveness of Change-of-Venue Surveys

Trial consultants are often challenged to justify their existence by demonstrating that their techniques are effective—that they are really worth the money that is spent on them (Mahoney, 1982; Saks, 1976a). For example, one might question whether scientific jury selection truly results in a more favorable jury for one side or the other than does traditional, attorney-conducted voir dire. However, proving that one's methods result in greater success is nearly impossible, as consulting work is done in the field, where there is limited control over extraneous variables. It is for that reason that the ASTC

Code of Professional Standards prohibits consultants from publishing win-loss records (American Society of Trial Consultants, 2003); they are misleading and not possible to accurately determine (but see Lawson, 1994, in which a trial consultant is quoted claiming a 90% success rate at selecting juries in civil cases and a 70% success rate at selecting juries in criminal cases).

The first problem in assessing the effectiveness of change-of-venue surveys lies in defining "effectiveness." Is a survey effective only if a change of venue is granted? What if, as in a case described by Faber (1973), the judge grants a change of venue, but moves the trial to a location that was also shown to possess a bias against the defendant? Or what of those cases for which the survey results suggest that a change is not warranted? Is it a success when the defense attorney uses that information to withdraw the motion for a venue change? Nietzel and Dillehay (1983) describe two cases for which they conducted venue surveys and the motions for a change were not granted. However, defense attorneys in both cases successfully used the survey data to support arguments in favor of a more extensive voir dire than was originally planned. Were those venue surveys effective?

Nietzel and Dillehay (1983) describe a total of five cases for which they conducted change-of-venue surveys. They provide a brief description of each case, followed by the survey results and the judge's decision regarding the change-of-venue motion. In the first case, they found clear and significant differences between the original and an alternate venue regarding familiarity with the case and the belief that, because his codefendants had already been convicted, the current defendant was also probably guilty. The judge granted a change of venue in this case. In the second case, significantly more respondents from the original venue than from an alternate venue were familiar with details surrounding the case, but there was no difference in their reported beliefs that the defendant was guilty. The judge granted the motion for a change of venue in this case, as well.

In the third case, respondents in the alternate venue possessed significantly less knowledge of the case than did those in the original or an adjacent venue. In addition, those in the original and adjacent venues were more likely than those in the alternate venue to believe that murder charges against the defendant in a separate case (information that was not admissible in the current case) were linked to the current murder charges against the defendant. The change-of-venue motion was denied in this case.

In the fourth case, which involved the retrial of a defendant whose prior conviction had been overturned, respondents in the original venue were more likely to know about the prior conviction, to agree with the original conviction, and to disagree with the court's decision to grant a new trial. The motion for a venue change was denied in this case, as well. Finally, in the fifth case, the defense made the decision not to pursue a change of venue based on the survey results.

A review of the first four cases suggests that it is difficult to predict when a judge will grant a motion for a change of venue and that other factors besides the survey data influence that decision. Carroll et al. (1986) note that changes of venue are expensive, inconvenient for litigants, and may be viewed by judges as an admission of their inability to deal with news coverage in their jurisdictions. It is also possible that some judges, especially those who are elected, are concerned about community sentiment. In many cases, members of the community feel strongly that the trial should not be moved, and there is a very real inconvenience for the victims and their families, who may feel twice victimized by having to travel to witness the trial. The apparent minimal influence of survey data relative to other factors may also be due in part to judges' wariness of relying too heavily on social science data. Hans and Vidmar (1982) examined specifically why motions for change of venue are not granted even when venue survey evidence is presented on behalf of the defense. They suggest that judicial conservatism, or a reluctance to stray from established legal principles, may be operating and note that judges are reluctant to relinquish their discretionary power and intuitive judgment when making a decision. Judges may be concerned that, by relying on survey results, the decision whether to change venue is essentially being made for them.

Indeed, Hans and Vidmar (1982) have identified inherent weaknesses in survey methodology as a primary reason that judges reject survey evidence in change-of-venue hearings. Because respondents are anonymous, not under oath, and answering questions in the privacy of their own homes rather than in a courtroom before the judge and attorneys, some judges question the validity of their responses. That may have been the rationale underlying Judge Matsch's apparent dismissal of the survey data presented in the change-of-venue hearing for Timothy McVeigh, as indicated in his statement, "Such surveys are but crude measures of opinion at the time of the interviews.... There is no laboratory experiment that can come close to duplicating the trial of criminal charges" (*United States v. McVeigh and Nichols*, 1996, p. 15). Although it is likely that surveys will actually result in more honest responses than those obtained in a courtroom, where demand characteristics loom large, one cannot be certain that it is not the other way around. Judges are especially likely to believe that, because jurors are under oath and responding in a setting that emphasizes the discovery of truth, they will provide more honest responses in a courtroom than they do when speaking on the phone to a stranger in the privacy of their own homes.

Finally, the disparity in change-of-venue decisions may be attributable to a lack of clear guidance from the existing case law. In the face of ambiguity, judges fall back on more conservative and less costly methods of coping with pretrial publicity effects. Whellan (1990) focuses on the varying standards that state courts apply to change-of-venue rulings. He notes that the Supreme Court has evaded the task of setting a minimum standard of due process, leaving it to the states to determine how much prejudice is too much. This lack of guidance has resulted in a continuum of standards in state courts, ranging from the most stringent requirement that the defense show that the seated jurors possessed bias against the defendant, to the more lenient standard provided in *Sheppard v. Maxwell* (1966). This standard requires that trial judges grant continuances or motions to change venue when there is a "reasonable likelihood" that prejudicial pretrial publicity will prevent a fair trial. As Whellan (1990) points out, the reasonable likelihood standard has not been well defined, leaving judges to decide for themselves what the standard should be. In some states, such as Missouri ("Rule 32.03," 2003), motions for change of venue are granted automatically if the crime occurred in a relatively small county (in Missouri, in counties with a population of 75,000 or less).

Nietzel and Dillehay (1983) refer to the task of determining how much prejudice is too much as the "criterion problem" (p. 335). For example, if survey results reveal that 50% of respondents in the original venue believe that the defendant is probably guilty, should the judge automatically change the venue? Or should the court require a higher number, such as 70%? The use of absolute standards is not appropriate, as the court must have some discretion to consider the totality of the circumstances (Hans & Vidmar, 1982). However, social scientists can help to provide the sort of guidance that judges often get from case law by pooling the results of their venue surveys. Nietzel and Dillehay (1983) recommend that surveys be conducted even when a change of venue is not being sought. This would allow for the creation of a database from which norms might be established, and judges could then know whether survey results being presented as evidence in a given case exceed those obtained in a majority of cases. Although the judge's decision on the motion remains subjective, at the very least this would make possible guided discretion in these cases.

Conclusions

Clearly, highly publicized cases present a conundrum for the courts. On the one hand, members of the media have the right, even the obligation, to report significant events to the community. This includes reporting that a crime has been committed and also the measures being taken by law enforcement and other public servants to apprehend and prosecute suspects. On the other hand, the rights of the accused must be protected, including the right to a presumption of innocence and a trial before a fair and impartial jury. Although the court has a number of remedies available to assist in ensuring a fair trial in highly publicized cases, research suggests that those remedies are generally ineffective, particularly voir dire and deliberations, which happen to be the remedies most frequently relied upon by judges.

One remedy that has the potential to be highly effective is the change of venue. If an appropriate alternate venue is selected, the defendant will be tried before a jury that has little or no exposure to the publicity surrounding his or her case. However, changes of venue are costly, both monetarily and in the court of public opinion, and judges are often reluctant to grant them. Judicial reluctance is bolstered by case law, which requires that the defendant demonstrate not only that case-relevant publicity has been extreme, but also that the venue has been sufficiently prejudiced by that publicity so as to make it highly unlikely that a fair and impartial jury can be found. This is a difficult standard to meet, allowing considerable discretion on the part of the trial judge in determining when the "highly unlikely" threshold has been surpassed.

Trial consultants are in an optimal position to assist the defense in assessing the degree of prejudice in a venue as a consequence not only of publicity, but also of the less tangible, such as word-of-mouth effects, candlelight vigils, and community fear. Through the use of a change-of-venue survey, the defense can demonstrate the amount and degree of prejudice in the original venue relative to that in an alternate venue not exposed to the publicity. While judicial response to venue survey data has been inconsistent, these data continue to provide the most reliable means of assessing the likelihood that a fair and impartial jury can be found in the original venue. Additional research is certainly needed to determine the role that survey results play in judges' decisions in these cases.

We believe that conducting the change-of-venue survey and presenting the results of that survey to the court are among the most beneficial and least controversial ways in which social scientists can act as consultants in the pretrial process. Consultants bring with them expertise in survey design, data collection, and data analysis, as well as knowledge about the effects of pretrial publicity based on a significant body of empirical research. In addition, the work that they do in this capacity is in the interest of providing judges with the information they need to determine whether the defendant's Sixth Amendment right to a fair and impartial jury is in jeopardy. Thus, more for this than any other role discussed in this text, they are able to act as objective researchers rather than as advocates for one side or the other.

4

Small-Group Research

In chapter 1, we described a brief survey that we distributed to the ASTC membership in the fall of 2003. According to the responses we received, work related to focus groups and mock trials made up, on average, 32% of consultants' practice, making it the most common professional activity engaged in by trial consultants. When you want to know how jurors will respond to your expert witness, high-profile attorney, day-in-the-life video, negligence claim for the plaintiff, or nonnegligence defense, what better way than to try it out on a group of ordinary, jury-eligible people? Attorneys are often surprised by jurors' reactions to them, their witnesses, or the evidence. Conducting pretrial small-group research (SGR) does not necessarily eliminate all surprises, but it can open the attorney's and the client's eyes to unforeseen problems or opportunities.

The trouble with small-group research methods is that they don't have the scientific rigor of other methods of research, such as the survey method discussed in chapter 3. How can one draw conclusions and make recommendations based on the reactions of a small, nonrepresentative sample? In this chapter, we will describe various SGR methods and their uses, as well as the methodological shortcomings and attempts by the profession to deal with those shortcomings through the development of small-group research guidelines.

What Is Small-Group Research? An Exercise in Semantics

In its proposed Code of Professional Standards, the American Society of Trial Consultants (American Society of Trial Consultants, 2003) defines small-group research as "[methods used] to study individuals' beliefs, attitudes and opinions and behavior relevant to issues in litigation. SGR is characterized by participant interaction in a group setting" (p. 29). SGR takes a variety of forms, and the ASTC does not endorse one form over another. However, most SGR can be categorized as either a *focus group* or a *mock trial* (also called a *trial simulation*). The distinction between these two methods is sometimes fuzzy, with the difference being primarily one of format. With a focus group, anywhere from 6 to 12 (Millward, 2000) people are convened for what is essentially a discussion among a moderator and the group participants. Although there is great variation in the specifics, a typical focus-group protocol has the moderator introduce a summary of essential case facts, obtain initial reactions to those facts, and then lead a discussion, focusing on the most important case issues, viability of claims, and so forth. The key defining feature is that the direction of the discussion is determined, or focused, by the moderator, and participants are generally not expected to reach a verdict.

With a mock trial, a streamlined version of the actual trial is presented to mock jurors. There are attorneys presenting both sides of the case, with the firm sponsoring the mock trial providing counsel to present the opponent's case. There are generally opening statements; some manner of presentation of evidence, such as videotaped or actual witness testimony, documents, or photographs; followed by closing arguments. Someone playing the role of judge instructs the mock jurors, who then deliberate to a verdict in the case. There are no attorneys or moderators present during deliberations, so that their focus is determined by the mock jurors themselves and is verdict-driven. Time permitting, the consultant will then question the mock jurors in a fashion similar to that used in focus groups. Deliberations are videotaped, and jurors are usually asked to provide individual written feedback at various critical points throughout the trial.

Although we have described a general distinction between the two methods, there is not consensus, among the ranks of trial consultants or litigators, that the distinction we have made is adequate. For example, the focus-group format most commonly used by consultant Eric Oliver (1998) includes deliberation to a unanimous decision, and attorney Stephen Gorny's (2000) description of a focus group includes attorney presentations of both sides of the case, including witnesses, jury instructions, and deliberation to verdict. In short, his description of focus groups is consistent with the way that most trial consultants would describe a mock trial. Rather than an either-or situation, trial consultant Bernadette Grant (1993) describes a continuum of small-group research methods, ranging from exploratory groups at one end to elaborate, structured trial simulations at the other. In between are a variety of focus-group methods designed to meet the specific needs of the client.

In our survey, we asked respondents to identify the objectives of focus groups versus mock trials, and those responses are described later in this chapter. In their answers to that item, most respondents also provided descriptive distinctions between the two methods. Commonly provided distinctions included the fact that focus groups are conducted prior to mock trials; mock trials are more elaborate and include deliberations; and focus-group discussions are led by a moderator and do not culminate in a verdict. However, several respondents noted an increasingly blurred distinction between the two methods. According to one:

> It used to be that a focus group was reserved for more of a free-flowing discussion with jurors. . . . We were true to the concept of focused discussion—that is, we as moderators would focus the discussion to the topics we wanted to consider. Somehow—and I think it's more the lawyers who got us into this terminology—we started calling almost everything a focus group. All the sudden [*sic*] we could have focus groups with formal plaintiff-defense presentations followed by deliberations and then a focused discussion. . . . I'm OK now with including deliberations after the free-flowing presentation, but at one time I thought that if there were delibs you must be doing a trial simulation. I think the attorneys have driven the change in terminology, and we are being forced to go along with it.

Objectives of Focus Groups Versus Mock Trials

Although there is not complete consensus as to the distinction between focus groups and mock trials, the fact that a distinction is made at all suggests that the two methods serve different purposes. So, when should one use a focus group, and when should one use a mock trial? There is virtually no definitive answer to this question, and, as was true of their descriptive differences, the distinction between their objectives is somewhat blurred.

Some published sources, written by both lawyers and consultants, indicate that focus groups allow one to discover the case theme, the points that will be important to jurors, and the type of questions to ask during voir dire; to critique opening statements, determine witness credibility, and assess juror reactions to exhibit evidence; and to observe the way in which jurors converse about the case (Barnett, 1999; Gorny, 2000; Mullins, 2000; Singer, 1996b; Twiggs, 1994; Wenner, 1998). In addition, focus groups are said to be useful in determining whether one should settle the case versus go to trial, or even whether one should take the case in the first place (Grant, 1993; Singer, 1996b; Twiggs, 1994).

If one is guided only by published sources, it appears that the objectives of mock trials overlap considerably with those of focus groups. Trial consultant Carolyn Koch (2001) notes that mock trials serve the purpose of identifying the important issues, strengths, and weaknesses of a case for the attorneys and their clients. Additionally, observed connections between juror characteristics and their perceptions of the case can be used to construct questions for voir dire. Similarly, consultant Bernadette Grant (1993) states that mock trials are used to evaluate the case and the effectiveness of proposed trial strategy, noting that they can be used for many of the same purposes as focus groups, but explaining that the difference rests primarily in the method of presentation and the fact that mock trials are verdict-driven. The decision whether to use a mock trial or a focus group depends on the amount of time one has to conduct and analyze research (mock trials require more time), the amount of money one is willing or able to spend (mock trials are generally more expensive), and "the kind of data the attorney needs in order to prepare for trial" (Grant, 1993, p. 21). Unfortunately, Grant does not elaborate on this last point, and the difference between the kind of data gleaned from a focus group versus a mock trial remains unclear.

For the individual consultant or litigant, the perceived function of focus groups versus mock trials determines the timing of each method, relative to each other as well as to other pretrial activities. Because mock trials are verdict-driven, Grant (1993) recommends conducting them as close to the trial date as possible. Trial consultant Amy Singer (1996b) recommends the use of focus groups before mock trials. For her, focus groups are used to determine the main trial issues, identify problems with one's case, and develop the best case theme. Therefore, a series of focus groups should be conducted early in the trial preparation process in order to provide clear objectives for discovery, and then a second series of focus groups should be conducted when discovery is complete. Using information gleaned in the focus groups, one then conducts a mock trial to determine which of several trial presentation strategies works the best.

Boyll and Parshall (1998) similarly advocate using focus groups very early in the trial preparation process, at least in some cases. Early research into the effectiveness of various case themes, for example, provides guidance for the construction of deposition questions for expert witnesses. Early focus-group research also allows attorneys to decide which among several witnesses will be the most effective, or whether the retention of an expert witness is actually necessary. Finally, conducting SGR early in the process could lead to an early settlement, ultimately saving the client money in legal fees. On the other hand, Greenbaum (1998) recommends that the mock trial precede the focus group, as the mock trial serves the purpose of identifying key issues, best presentation strategies, confusing points, and the biggest problems with the case for each side in the dispute. A series of focus groups is then used to test the relative effectiveness of various arguments.

Is the semantic and functional fuzziness that exists in published articles on the subject of focus groups and mock trials representative of a general lack of agreement within the trial-consulting profession? In our survey, we asked ASTC members to name the objectives of a focus group versus a mock trial. The most striking characteristic of their responses is the fact that no single objective was named by a majority of respondents for either method. The most frequently named objective for focus groups, named by 35% of respondents, was "to discover case themes." Other commonly identified objectives for focus groups were "to assess general reactions to the case" (named by 30%) and "to test one or two aspects of the case in depth" (named by 26%). The most commonly named objective for mock trials encapsulated the stylistic difference between the two methods. Thirty percent of respondents identified "to assess reactions to a more comprehensive version of the case" as an objective for mock trials, in direct contrast to the more narrow testing of one or two aspects of the case that can be achieved with a focus group.

Many of the objectives named for focus groups were also named for mock trials. In fact, the second most frequently named objective for focus groups, "to assess general reactions to the case," was also named for mock trials by 23% of respondents, and "the in-depth assessment of one or two aspects of the case" was named by 9% as an objective for mock trials. In fact, "assessment of specifically identified aspects of the case" was named in the objectives for both methods, including determining reactions to witnesses and to graphics and exhibits. Other objectives that were named for both methods were "to identify case strengths and weaknesses," "to determine the financial worth of the case," "to identify relevant juror characteristics," and "to explore areas of confusion."

On the other hand, there were also a number of nonoverlapping objectives. Focus groups appear to be distinctively used to discover case themes, guide the process of discovery, develop trial strategy, and provide an inexpensive means of testing reactions to a case. Mock trials, on the other hand, are uniquely designed to assess reactions to a comprehensive version of the case, determine the most compelling points for jurors, minimize weaknesses and bolster strengths, provide attorneys with practice for trial, and test reactions to attorneys, jury instructions, and verdict forms.

Our conclusion regarding the objectives for focus groups and mock trials is that the focus group is a tool that is best used early in the litigation process, uniquely designed to guide discovery and determine the main themes of the case. The more expensive and elaborate mock trial is appropriate for those cases that are likely to go to trial, providing insight into juror responses to the comprehensive case, including demonstrative evidence, the trial attorney, witnesses, and even jury instructions and verdict forms. In addition, mock trials allow the attorneys to practice selling their case to the jury and may even provide the impetus to get attorneys thinking about case presentation, which they might otherwise delay until shortly before the trial. The many overlapping objectives, combined with the lack of consensus for even one objective for each method, may be most problematic from the standpoint of the lawyer-client, who must be aware that the same terms can mean very different things from one consulting firm to another. Therefore, it is prudent to first identify one's own objectives and then to match them against those promoted by the consultant for each technique.

Methodological Issues

The use of focus groups as a research method dates back to the 1940s, when they were used by sociologists at Columbia University to measure the effectiveness of wartime propaganda and the social effects of mass communication (Millward, 2000; Sommer & Sommer, 2002). Since that time, the method has been used in the marketing of everything from products to politicians to movie endings. The method is also gaining in popularity among research psychologists. On PsycLit, an electronic database of research articles and books in psychology, there were 210 papers from 1991 to 1997 that used focus-group methodology, compared with only 10 from 1974 to 1991 (Millward, 2000). However, the use of focus groups as a research method is still criticized on several grounds.

First, some argue that focus groups do not yield genuine participant responses, because comments are not made under anonymous circumstances, such as with a survey, and participants respond to the social demands of the group (Sommer & Sommer, 2002). One cannot know whether expressed opinions represent true feelings or are simply outward conformity (Kidd & Parshall, 2000). Albrecht, Johnson, and Walther (1993) point out four threats to validity: (1) participants may respond in a way that they believe the questioner wants them to, either to please the questioner or to make the session end sooner; (2) participants may simply agree with other group members to win their admiration; (3) the desire for group cohesion might reduce some members' likelihood of voicing opposing views (called *groupthink*, this is most likely to occur in groups that must reach a unanimous decision, such as a verdict [Janis, 1982]); and (4) especially when respondents are asked, one at a time, for their opinions, those responding last are likely to simply echo the views expressed by those ahead of them.

On the other hand, Albrecht et al. (1993) point out that the focus-group method has good ecological validity because we often form our opinions based on discussion with others—attitudes are social constructs. Focus groups are especially useful when the goal is to observe decision making in a group context. According to Kidd and Parshall (2000), "coercion, going along to get along, and the acquiescence of less committed individuals to positions more passionately argued by others" (pp. 294–295) may be relevant to the task, representing the reality of how some decisions are made. Focus groups are preferable to individual interviews, because they allow participants to agree or disagree, negotiate, confront, and criticize one another (Grant, 1993; Kidd & Parshall, 2000; Millward, 2000). Certainly, jury deliberations are often characterized by confrontation, conformity, and negotiation; therefore, methodological concerns regarding the genuineness of responses of focus-group participants may not be applicable in this context.

The focus-group method has also been criticized on the grounds that its results are not generalizable because the sample size is too small to be representative, and members are not randomly selected. However, in its true form, the method is not intended to yield data that are generalizable, but to provide a more complete understanding of the issues of a case (Krueger, 1998; Millward, 2000). When done correctly, the focus-group population is defined on theoretical grounds, targeting those who will provide the most meaningful information to meet research objectives. Focus-group participants should then be randomly selected from the theoretically relevant population, so as to be representative of it (Greenbaum, 1998; Krueger, 1993, 1998). At the very least, therefore, all participants in litigation-related SGR should be jury-eligible. In the end, sample size is not important, as long as enough groups are conducted to "saturate the topic," which occurs when groups begin to yield redundant information (Krueger, 1998).

Both trial consultants and attorneys have addressed the sampling issue as it relates specifically to the use of small groups for pretrial research. Among those who have written on the subject, it seems that researchers are somewhat lax in the representativeness requirement as it pertains to focus groups, but recognize its importance for mock trials. For example, trial consultant Bernadette Grant (1993) notes that some consultants caution against recruiting participants through classified or personal ads in the newspaper, because those who read and respond to such ads are not likely to be representative. However, she does not explicitly rule this out as a legitimate means of recruitment for exploratory focus groups, and attorneys Stephen Gorny (2000) and Stacey Mullins (2000) include newspaper ads as an acceptable means of recruiting, even for groups with more advanced objectives. In contrast, when recruiting for mock trials, Grant states that the sample must be representative of those likely to be seated on a jury in the case being tested. Therefore, beyond screening for jury-eligibility, one must screen for any potential bias or connection to the case for which a prospective mock juror would likely be dismissed for cause in the actual trial.

Attorneys Kathryn Barnett (1999) and Howard Twiggs (1994) rely on old jury pool lists for recruiting focus-group participants. Barnett recommends that attorneys seek out people who are different from themselves in terms of socioeconomic status, attitudes, and reasoning skills in order to get a fresh perspective on the case. Likewise, trial consultant Amy Singer (1996b) recommends recruiting people who are likely to oppose the client's side of the case—people who are highly negative and extremely verbal (she refers to this as "a room full of Hitlers" [p. 322]). To get such a sample, she suggests running a targeted classified ad whose phrasing is likely to attract people who endorse a particular belief.

In our survey of ASTC members, we asked about respondents' primary means of recruiting participants for focus groups and mock trials, and found that recruiting practices are generally consistent with those advocated by Grant (1993). The vast majority of respondents used market research firms or random-digit dialing (which is often conducted by the market research firms) to recruit for both focus groups and mock trials; some reported using focus-group facilities, in-house recruiters, and temp agencies. Only a handful of respondents relied on newspaper ads as their primary means of recruiting. All respondents required that focus-group and mock-trial participants be jury-eligible.

A third criticism of the focus-group method is that the analysis is too subjective (e.g., Kidd & Parshall, 2000). Unlike quantitative methods for which numerical data are statistically analyzed, focus-group analysis requires that the researcher extract themes and draw conclusions from the group dialogue, a process that can easily be influenced by researcher bias. To combat this problem, methodologists (e.g., Kidd & Parshall, 2000; Krueger, 1993; Millward, 2000) recommend the use of software packages, such as The Ethnograph, which are designed to organize textual data. Kidd and Parshall (2000) describe the software application NUD*IST (Nonnumerical Un-structured Data Indexing Searching and Theorizing), used to code and analyze focus-group transcripts. Among other things, this software allows one to determine how many statements in a coding category were made by the same person or people. This is useful because it is easy to falsely conclude that an issue constitutes a theme for the group rather than a strongly held position taken by a vocal minority. Of course, the use of any software package requires that a transcript be constructed of the group interactions, which is very time consuming, especially when multiple groups are conducted.

Noting that there is little in the way of specific direction from the scholarly community when it comes to analyzing focus-group data, some researchers make a distinction between meeting the needs and desires of a client and satisfying the rigors of peer review to demonstrate that one's reported findings are reliable and valid (Kidd & Parshall, 2000; Knodel, 1993; Krueger, 1998). For the former, one may merely trust in the virtues of the method and rely on the experience and expertise of the moderator. The method of analysis depends on the objectives of the research (Knodel, 1993). For most marketing and pretrial research, where the goal is practical recommendations in a relatively short period of time, the analyses can be based on careful listening to tapes, field notes from the sessions, and memory, if reported immediately following the session (Knodel, 1993; Krueger, 1998). If, on the other hand, the objective is publication of research findings in a peer-reviewed journal, there is a much higher standard of proof of the reliability and validity of one's conclusions, and transcript-based analysis is necessary (Kidd & Parshall, 2000; Krueger, 1998).

There are a number of recommended means of improving the validity of focus-group analyses, all of which can be easily applied to pretrial SGR. First, to determine whether issues that have been tentatively identified by the researcher as important accurately represent the views of the group, the moderator should run those issues by group members or have each participant sum up his or her position at the end of the session (Kidd & Parshall, 2000; Krueger, 1993). That way, the researcher can correct misperceptions before group participants walk out the door. Second, one should conduct multiple groups. Validity of the results is demonstrated to the extent that the groups yield the same themes (Kidd & Parshall, 2000; Krueger, 1998). Finally, a technique that allows one to assess the validity of pretrial SGR specifically is to conduct posttrial interviews with actual jurors who serve on those cases that go to trial. If their remarks are consistent with those obtained from focus-group or mock-trial participants, as well as with the consultant's interpretations and conclusions, one can conclude that the SGR was valid (Grant, 1993).

ASTC Professional Standards and Guidelines

Over a period of 3 years or so, members of the SGR subcommittee of the ASTC worked to establish standards and guidelines for consultants conducting pretrial SGR. In the preamble to the ASTC Code of Professional Standards, a distinction is made between professional standards, which are enforceable by the society, and practice guidelines, which are suggested business practices that "should be considered by trial consultants in arriving at an ethical course of action and . . . may be considered by the Board of Directors or other designated Committee in interpreting the Professional Standards specifically and the Code generally" (American Society of Trial Consultants, 2003, p. 2). In 2003, a set of SGR standards and guidelines was approved by the ASTC membership.

The SGR standards govern appropriate applications of SGR, duties to clients and participants, and methodological issues. Perhaps because of the lack of a clear definition of individual methods of SGR, the standards and guidelines have been written to apply to all methods. The first standard consists of a somewhat vague statement regarding the appropriate use of SGR. The remaining standards require that consultants not knowingly overstate the applicability of SGR results and that they draw inferences and make interpretations that are consistent with the research findings. Consultants are to protect the confidentiality of the participants as well as the clients and keep confidential the fact that SGR has been conducted at all with regard to a specific case. Finally, the standards require that consultants inform participants that their participation is voluntary, obtain permission to make videotapes or audiotapes of participants and their remarks, and treat participants with respect.

The practice guidelines for SGR pertain to the same four areas that the standards do (appropriate applications, duties to clients, duties to participants, and methodological issues) but are more numerous. In some cases, the guidelines seem to be a list of recommended practices that will allow the consultant to meet the standards. For example, the guidelines provide a list of steps that might be taken in order to maintain the confidentiality of the client. There are other guidelines that are supplemental to the standards, that is, recommended practices not tied to requisite actions. Among those are several that have led us to wonder why they are not standards. Specifically, under the section Appropriate Application of SGR, one guideline recommends informing clients about the limitations of using SGR to predict litigation outcomes, and another recommends that, when appropriate, consultants inform the client of the purpose, estimated costs, and appropriate uses for the proposed SGR research. Why the hesitation in requiring that the consultant be up-front about the limitations, costs, and appropriate uses for the research? Under what circumstances would it *not* be appropriate to provide such information to the client? We have similar concerns related to the first four guidelines under Duty to Participants, pertaining to confidentiality, freedom to withdraw from the research, use of deception, and provision of a contact person to whom concerns can be addressed.

The guidelines for conducting SGR do not contain the same degree of specificity found in the guidelines for conducting change-of-venue surveys. The survey guidelines are based largely on prior guidelines established by other professional organizations, such as the American Association of Public Opinion Research, as well as on academic survey research sources. Although many books and articles on focus-group research have been published, there does not appear to be a consolidated list of best practices (Greenbaum, 1998). The Qualitative Research Consultants Association (QRCA) provides ethical standards and professional competencies for conducting qualitative research, but these contain the same fairly low level of specificity as the standards and guidelines established by the ASTC. For example, QRCA's Research Competency section recommends that the consultant be someone who "[u]nderstands and applies the social science research process, including the differences and appropriate conditions for application of qualitative and quantitative research and common specific research applications" (Qualitative Research Consultants Association, 2003, p. 2).

Establishment of standards and guidelines represents an opportunity to educate consultants regarding the proper use of the focus-group method. Although professional organizations have yet to compile a list of best practices, there is a significant body of literature providing specific guidance regarding methodological issues, such as sampling, designing interview guides, and moderating groups (e.g., Carey, 1995; Greenbaum, 1998; Knodel, 1993; Krueger, 1993, 1998; Millward, 2000), as well as a growing list of sources on analysis of focus-group data (e.g., Bertrand, Brown, & Ward, 1992; Kidd & Parshall, 2000; Krueger, 1998). It is unfortunate that more of the specifics did not make their way into the ASTC's standards and guidelines, where specifics are mostly limited to matters of confidentiality and ethical considerations associated with conducting research with human participants.

Regarding methodology and appropriate application of SGR, the specifics have been left to the better judgment of the consultant. For example, the first standard reads, "Trial consultants shall recommend and employ small group research in those instances when, in their professional judgment, such research is well suited to the research problem at hand" (American Society of Trial Consultants, 2003, p. 30). The way the standard is worded, if a member uses SGR for purposes that are not typical, or that strike many members as inappropriate, the member cannot be disciplined as long as his or her own professional judgment suggests that its use was appropriate. Although it is true that with SGR there is rarely just one correct way to do things, that does not mean that there are no *incorrect* ways to do things, and leaving so much to the discretion of the consultant opens the door for sloppy methodology. This is especially true because ASTC does not have minimal education standards for membership, so that many consultants have no formal training in research methodology.

Threats to the Profession, or Signs of Progress?

In recent years, two changes have occurred in the use of pretrial SGR: attorneys have begun conducting their own focus groups, and online providers have begun conducting focus groups on the Internet. Do these developments represent a threat to trial consultants, shifting one of their most common practices into the hands of other professionals, or are they merely a sign that trial-consulting practices have become an expected component of all pretrial preparation?

Attorney-Conducted Small-Group Research

In the last 10 years or so, several attorneys have published how-to articles to guide members of the legal profession through the process of conducting their own pretrial SGR (e.g., Barnett, 1999; Mullins, 2000; Twiggs, 1994). Is this advisable? Do attorneys have the necessary educational background and skills to conduct their own SGR? Apparently, the answer to that question depends on the profession of the person you ask, and the magnitude of the case. Stacey Mullins (2000) warns her fellow attorneys, "Trial consultants will vigorously discourage attorneys from conducting their own focus groups on the grounds that the attorney doesn't possess the requisite skill, training, or knowledge to fully appreciate, understand, and decipher the information obtained" (p. 433). Although she acknowledges that in many cases that may be true, she argues that, for smaller cases, attorneys can conduct their own focus groups, and she provides instructions in doing so. Attorney Kathryn Barnett (1999) similarly argues that lawyers are capable of conducting focus groups without the expertise of "expensive consultants" (p. 74), and she also provides instructions in doing so. However, both authors stop short of dismissing the usefulness of trial consultants' services altogether. Mullins (2000) includes the caveat that attorney-conducted focus groups should not be considered a substitute for *any* use of trial consultants, whose analyses are "scientifically based and of exceptional assistance" (p. 435), and Barnett acknowledges that small-budget groups cannot provide a valid list of juror characteristics that will ultimately lead to a court victory, implying that the (large-budget?) groups conducted by consultants can produce such a product. Twiggs (1994) also recommends the do-it-yourself groups for small cases only.

We are curious about the deference to the services of trial consultants for "large" cases only. Yes, there is more at stake in a high-dollar case, so the investment in consultants can be justified financially, but is the financial investment the only difference they see? Do attorneys reason that they (or their clients) should spend a lot of money to prepare for cases that might result in high damage awards, and make only a small expenditure for cases where the stakes are lower? Or do they really see a tradeoff in the quality of groups they conduct themselves and those conducted by consultants, but are willing to sacrifice quality in the smaller cases? In other words, if they truly believe that they get quality feedback from the small-budget groups, why not stick with the small-budget groups for all cases? On the other hand, if the feedback gained through small-budget groups is questionable, why conduct the groups at all?

Although we have not encountered, in writing, the unequivocal dismissal by trial consultants of attorneys' abilities to conduct their own SGR, there certainly seem to be doubts about the appropriateness of their doing so. Consultants observe that, on their own, attorneys often present a very weak opponent's case (Koch, 2001), and they do not appreciate the importance of having a representative sample, often inviting fellow attorneys or family members to serve in the role of jurors (Grant, 1993; Koch, 2001). Also, because attorneys are trained to evaluate cases based on the rule of law, they generally do not do a good job of anticipating lay responses to the case (Koch, 2001). Finally, consultant Amy Singer (1996b) argues that the focus-group moderator should be an expert interviewer who is capable of identifying case themes, problem areas, and jurors' value beliefs. The moderator should then hand that information over to a litigation psychologist, who can analyze, interpret, and make recommendations to the attorneys regarding trial strategy. Singer argues that the opinions expressed by the focus-group participants "must be scientifically evaluated and interpreted to achieve meaning" (p. 325), suggesting that attorneys are not the appropriate people to be doing this.

Of course, many professional trial consultants are not psychologists, and many do not have training in scientific methodology. The bottom line is that a lack of understanding of the scientific method, or lack of familiarity with relevant research findings, might lead *anyone* to use small-group research methods that are not reliable or to draw conclusions that are unfounded. For example, in his how-to article on focus groups, attorney Stephen Gorny (2000) recommends gathering profiles of mock jurors prior to the start of the research. This is, of course, a common practice in small-group research. However, Gorny advocates using this information to "determine how particular categories of jurors (such as men, women, senior citizens, minorities, and so on) will view your case" (p. 113), which can then be applied during voir dire. Gorny makes the common mistake of assuming that demographic characteristics will emerge as predictive of reactions to the case, when the empirical research evidence suggests otherwise (Bornstein, 1999; Feild, 1978; Fulero & Penrod, 1990a). (Incidentally, several trial consultants who responded to our survey also named the identification of relevant juror characteristics as an objective for focus-group research.) A lack of familiarity with that and similar other bodies of research can lead to poorly constructed research objectives and, ultimately, to greater expense to the client, regardless of who is conducting the research.

Small-Group Research Online

Another recent trend is the use of online focus groups (Greenbaum, 1998; Hsieh, 2001). These work in a number of ways. In some cases, the litigant posts a case summary, depositions, photos of evidence, and so forth on an online bulletin board (Hoeschen, 2001; Hsieh, 2001). This method is not technically a focus group and should really be called something else, as participants log-on at their convenience and provide reactions to the case, but never interact with each other. In other instances, online providers coordinate real-time focus groups, recruiting participants who meet specified criteria and instructing all of them to log-on at a designated time, in order to respond immediately to trial materials and to each other's remarks (Greenbaum, 1998; Hoeschen, 2001; Hsieh, 2001; Sweet, 2000).

At least one site, eJury, conducts "summary trials," for which opposing attorneys present their respective sides of the case to a group of e-jurors, and the attorneys agree ahead of time whether the jurors' decision will be binding. Electronic jurors on the eJury site review the evidence and render verdicts individually, never interacting with each other. Even nonattorneys, such as neighbors with a dispute, can post their case on iCourthouse and have the dispute settled by "jurors," which consist of essentially anyone who wishes to review the case materials. Jurors never interact with each other, but they are allowed to submit questions to the interested parties and can read the questions posted by other jurors and the answers to those questions.

For sites that do not allow just any interested person to act as a juror, participants might be recruited electronically from established panels or targeted Web sites or selected randomly by telephone. The better sites use electronic screeners to include only qualified participants, such as those who are jury-eligible and not likely to be removed for cause from the particular case. Participants are provided with passwords and instructions and may be rescreened when they log-on in an effort to ensure that the person attending the group is the one who was originally screened. For example, the screener might ask for the answer to a specific question that was asked during the initial screening (Sweet, 2000).

The better sites also offer technical support for the moderator and participants, sometimes welcoming and engaging the participants as they log-on for the session. Sweet (2000) warns that the moderator, who might be the attorney or someone hired by the attorney, must have excellent keyboard skills. Participants type their responses in real time to questions posed by the moderator, who must then be capable of monitoring participants' responses to the question and to each other, presenting follow-up questions, and keeping the group on-task, all through typed correspondence.

Possibly the greatest selling point for online focus groups is that they have the potential to reduce SGR costs dramatically, as there are no costs for renting a space and video equipment or for feeding participants, and the pay for online participants is generally lower than that for those participating in person (Greenbaum, 1998; Hsieh, 2001). According to trial consultant La-Donna Carlton, for example, the pay to a participant in an in-person mock trial runs about $275 per day, while it only costs about $10–25 to pay for a participant to take part in an online group (Hsieh, 2001). Reduced costs make online groups especially useful for small law firms or those handling small cases (Hsieh, 2001).

Additionally, the use of online focus groups allows one to sidestep the transcription problem associated with conducting in-person groups, as some sites make transcripts available for analysis soon after the completion of the group (Hsieh, 2001; Millward, 2000; Sweet, 2000). Because transcription represents the greatest hurdle to analyzing focus-group data using computer software, online groups could result in more objective data analysis.

Most of the criticisms of online SGR are aimed at ecological validity, or the extent to which the group interactions are representative of true juror decision making. Although some argue that people will make more honest comments online than they would in a face-to-face setting (Hsieh, 2001), recall that one of the methodological strengths of focus groups is that they are ecologically valid with respect to jury decision making, which is characterized by conforming, arguing, compromising, and so forth. The group dynamic in online groups is artificial, absent the same peer pressures and nonverbal interactions that occur with in-person groups (Greenbaum, 1998; Hoeschen, 2001; Hsieh, 2001). Removal of the face-to-face interaction reduces validity, which is further threatened when the online verdict is submitted individually by jurors who never interact with each other.

Others argue that focus groups should not be conducted on the Internet because the leadership role of the moderator is greatly diminished (Greenbaum, 1998). With an electronic group, the moderator cannot maintain eye contact with participants or ensure that they are engrossed in the task. There is also no way to ensure the security of the information (e.g., someone may be looking over the shoulder of the participant at trial materials or reading remarks made by other participants), raising concerns from an attorney work-product perspective (Greenbaum, 1998). Although some real-time online groups require that mock jurors agree to stay at the computer throughout the session, there is no way of ensuring that they do nor that someone else is not responding in their place (Hsieh, 2001).

Another methodological concern is that online groups are not representative of jurors because they only include those with a computer, those who are Internet savvy, and those who have an interest in the law (Hoeschen, 2001; Hsieh, 2001). Attorney Vic Anderson responds to that criticism by stating, "The people without computers are the people who don't show up for jury duty, and when they do they are the followers. I want to find out what the leaders are thinking, and those people have computers" (Hoeschen, 2001, p. 26). Of course, this observation has virtually no empirical support and demonstrates the common reliance by attorneys on stereotypes about jurors. If Anderson's comments are representative of the level of critical evaluation applied by attorneys regarding online groups, there may be some truth to the concern expressed by Philip Monte, former trial consultant and current prosecuting attorney, that "lawyers who are unsophisticated in social science run the risk of being hoodwinked by the bells and whistles of the Internet" (Hsieh, 2001, ¶6).

We agree that the greatest shortcoming of online groups is the lack of face-to-face interaction among participants because, from a methodological standpoint, that interaction is the focus group's best feature. However, we do not necessarily feel that online groups, especially those that are well run, are any worse than some of the low-budget groups described in the literature. Every method has its strengths and weaknesses, and the attorney-as-client does well to be capable of such an evaluation. However, we do feel that the so-called online focus groups that, in fact, do not involve any interaction among participants represent too great a sacrifice of ecological validity to yield trustworthy data.

Conclusions

For one of the authors, the power of the mock jury became apparent a number of years ago. In 1979, the shah of Iran was deposed by Islamic nationalists headed by Khomeini. The United States was desperately in need of foreign oil, but the majority of American oil companies terminated their ongoing contracts to purchase oil from Iran. One company, Ashland Oil, agreed with the new Iranian government to purchase $283 million worth of oil, and a contract was signed in April 1979. The oil was shipped to Ashland Oil, but the American oil company refused to pay for it, claiming that it had signed the contract under duress. Hence, the Iranians—formally, the National Iranian Oil Company—filed suit in 1985 to recover the unpaid amount. The case dragged on, but finally a trial was scheduled to be held in Jackson, Mississippi, in late 1989.

At this time, the Islamic Republic of Iran was held in very low esteem by citizens of the United States. This was the country where Islamic nationalists had kidnapped a group of American diplomats and held them hostage for more than a year. The U.S. law firm representing the Iranians questioned whether they could get a fair trial in this country. Nevertheless, the law firm agreed to carry out a day-long mock trial in Jackson, Mississippi, in August 1989, and arranged for the trial-consulting firm of Lititech to supervise it.

Jury-eligible mock jurors were recruited by a local marketing firm, and enough jurors for three mock juries watched a slimmed-down presentation of the trial, with local lawyers and staff members role-playing witnesses as well as attorneys for the other side. (The mock jurors were not told which side had hired them.) After watching the mock trial, which took most of a Saturday, the three mock juries deliberated. Each jury found for the Iranians and made awards of hundreds of millions of dollars to them. Most jurors, in their deliberations, voiced their hostility toward the Iranian government but also their overwhelming feeling, sometimes expressed with reluctance, that the Iranians were justified in their claims.

When used correctly, focus groups, and their SGR siblings, can be an invaluable tool for attorneys and their clients as they prepare for trial, as they decide whether to go to trial, or even as they decide whether to pursue a case. Small-group research is methodologically well suited for the task, allowing for the kind of give and take that is characteristic of actual jury deliberations. When participants are jury-eligible and otherwise representative of the kind of people likely to serve as jurors for the case in question, and when enough groups are conducted to allow for saturation of the issues, SGR allows trial consultants and their clients to make reasonably confident decisions as to how to proceed with a case.

On the other hand, when SGR is not properly conducted, it can amount to little more than wasted time and money. It is critical that trial consultants get clear in their own minds, and make clear to their clients, the circumstances under which one SGR method is preferred over others. It is equally important that consultants comply with the established ASTC standards and guidelines for conducting SGR, although we would like the guidelines to be more specific with regard to appropriate methodology and more explicit with regard to what constitutes minimally expected practices by converting some of the current guidelines into standards.

Finally, we see it as a testament to the accepted utility of SGR that it is now being conducted in cyberspace and by attorneys without the aid of consultants, at least for small cases. We do not believe that either trend represents a threat to the trial-consulting profession (some online groups are conducted by trial consultants), but both require that lawyers and their clients be knowledgeable about methodological issues. We especially rec-ommend that trial consultants play an active role in educating attorneys and their clients about the limitations of online focus groups. The temptation of saving money by rejecting face-to-face groups in favor of cyberspace groups is likely to be hard to resist, and validity issues may not be readily apparent to those with no training in research methodology.

5

Trial Strategies and Procedures

When the decision is made to proceed to trial, the attorney's strategy becomes relevant, beginning with construction of the opening statement, followed by presentation of evidence, questioning of witnesses, and closing arguments. Attorneys might look to various professional sources, such as *Trial* magazine, for advice on such things as timing and style of delivery of the opening statement, or appropriateness of an aggressive cross-examination. However, attorneys are also increasingly turning to trial consultants to assist them with trial strategies. In this chapter, we will briefly describe the elements of a trial and evaluate the overall state of the research on jurors' responses to various trial strategies. Next, we will examine specific techniques used by attorneys at each stage of the trial and evaluate the recommendations of trial consultants and legal professionals alike in light of empirical research findings. Finally, we discuss the utility of attorneys' turning to trial consultants for assistance with their trial strategies.

As we embark on a discussion and evaluation of consultants' recommendations,[1] it becomes necessary to explain the distinction between the empirical research, as an entity, and the writings of trial consultants, who may or may not be conducting such research. As discussed in chapter 1, trial

---

1. We do not claim to have accessed the entire universe of published recommendations by trial consultants but feel that we provide a representative sample of that which is published. Recall, however, that consultants are often reluctant to share "trade secrets," so we cannot know the extent to which our sources represent the recommendations of all members of the profession.

consultants come from many backgrounds with varying degrees of education and training. Those with advanced degrees in the social sciences, including psychology, sociology, political science, and communications, have generally received extensive training in empirical research methodology. Some of them are publishing empirical research at the same time that they are working as trial consultants. However, not all social scientists/consultants conduct research, and advanced degrees in the social sciences are not guarantees that all of their recommendations as consultants are supported by research findings. In fact, we have been struck by the dearth of empirical research citations in the writings of many trial consultants. Jo-Ellan Dimitrius and Mark Mazzarella's (1998) *Reading People* does not contain a single citation and there is no bibliography. Likewise, Weiser and Latiolais-Hargrave (2000) do not include citations in their book on how to read people. There is a bibliography, but it does not include any research published in peer-reviewed journals. Curiously, these authors do make occasional reference to empirical research (e.g., they briefly describe social psychologist Bella DePaulo's research on deception), but they do not include a citation, and DePaulo is not included in their bibliography. Dick Crawford's (1989) book on courtroom persuasion also includes neither citations nor a bibliography.

There are several possible explanations for the absence of empirical citations in consultants' work. First, the consultant may not come from a background that regularly cites empirical research. Those with an advanced social science degree (i.e., M.A. or Ph.D.) will have been trained to support nearly every factual statement with a citation. However, those with a background in theater and those with no advanced degree generally do not have such training and apparently are comfortable making claims without providing the reader the means of checking the support for those claims.

Second, the consultant may not feel that empirical citations are appropriate for the audience, which might explain why even social scientists/consultants sometimes write without citations. Dick Crawford and Jo-Ellan Dimitrius both have doctoral degrees, but their books are written for attorney and lay audiences, respectively. The assumption might exist that attorneys and nonacademic readers would be put off or distracted by writing that is interrupted by frequent citations or that alludes to empirical research. If that assumption is being made with regard to attorneys, however, it is contradicted by the many footnotes and references to research that can be found in most legal periodicals.

The third reason for the minimal use of empirical citations is that there is very little empirical research relevant to many of the issues to which trial consultants speak. Ronald Matlon, a trial consultant and communications professor, presented a research review regarding opening statements and closing arguments at the 1991 meeting of the American Society of Trial Consultants (Matlon, 1991). In it, Matlon identified 11 major areas for which little or no research has been conducted, and he appealed for greater collaboration between social scientists and legal scholars to fill in those research gaps.

Elements of a Trial

The trial begins with the opening statement of the side responsible for bringing the case to trial. Hence, in criminal cases, the prosecution delivers the first opening statement, and in civil trials, the plaintiff is heard first. In both criminal and civil trials, the defense then has the option of delivering its opening statement or waiting until after the prosecution or plaintiff has presented all of its evidence. Strategy issues relevant to opening statements include statement length, amount of detail, organization, whether to make concessions to the opposing side, and, for the defense, the timing of the statement.

Presentation of evidence occurs through the testimony of witnesses. Again, the prosecution or plaintiff always presents its evidence first. Following the direct examination of each witness, the opposing side has the opportunity to question, or cross-examine, the witness. Strategy issues relevant to the presentation of evidence include questioning style, degree of aggressiveness, especially during cross-examination, and proxemics, or interpersonal distance between the attorney and the witness during questioning.

The last phase of the trial is the closing argument. Like the opening statement, closing arguments are not evidence. However, they differ from the opening statements in that they are argumentative, characterized by attempts to persuade the jury to reach a specific verdict. While attorneys are not free to introduce new facts or evidence during closings, they can, within limits, appeal to the emotions of jurors as they summarize key components of their case and retell the stories first constructed during openings. Trial strategies relevant to closing arguments focus on organization, content, and use of ingratiation strategies.

Finally, throughout the trial, the presentation style, mannerisms, and even appearance of the attorneys may be scrutinized by and affect the responses of the jurors. Therefore, it is important to include in a discussion of trial strategies an evaluation of attorney characteristics. For each of these trial elements, we will compare and contrast the recommendations made by attorneys, by trial consultants, and by the research findings.

Overall State of the Research

Research on jurors' responses to trial strategies has been criticized by members of the legal community, as well as by some social scientists, on the grounds that it lacks ecological validity (Bray & Kerr, 1982; Davis, Bray, & Holt, 1977; Diamond, 1979; Ellsworth, 1988; Gerbasi, Zuckerman, & Reis,

1977). Much of the research relies on college students as participants rather than on a more representative sample of jury-eligible citizens; mock jurors rarely deliberate; and trial simulations generally range from written descriptions of trials to videotapes of actors reconstructing a trial. The only research method that exposes its respondents to an entire, actual trial is the use of shadow jurors who observe a trial and then render an individual verdict. However, even in this most ecologically valid research design, jurors don't deliberate, and they are aware that their decision will not actually affect the parties involved in the case. Furthermore, this method lacks experimental control, rendering it difficult to draw cause-effect conclusions from the research results. So, is the social science research useful? Should attorneys make strategic decisions based on recommendations that stem directly from this body of research?

In his evaluation of the usefulness of mock-jury research, Bornstein (1999) conducted a review of the research examining the effects of the characteristics of the research sample and of research comparing various types of trial presentation on mock-juror verdicts. In his review of studies comparing the use of college student versus nonstudent samples of mock jurors, he found that the sample made a significant difference in only 5 of 26 studies. In 3 of the studies where a significant effect was present (Berman & Cutler, 1996; Schuller & Hastings, 1996; Simon & Mahan, 1971), the college student sample reached verdicts that were somewhat more favorable to defendants in criminal cases and to plaintiffs in civil cases. In one case, however, the college students were less likely than the older adult sample to accept a self-defense argument (Finkel, Meister, & Lightfoot, 1991). Bornstein also found little effect for any demographic variables (including age and level of education) in most jury decision-making research.

Furthermore, in his examination of the effects of trial presentation medium (e.g., live trials, videotaped trials, written transcripts, brief written descriptions of the trial), Bornstein (1999) found that medium does not have an effect on verdicts in most cases. This was true for research involving direct experimental comparisons of medium, as well as for research attempting to replicate findings across medium type. Taken together, Bornstein's findings support the use of mock-jury research findings by attorneys and trial consultants in the development of trial strategies. However, one would feel greater confidence in relying on this research if one also knew whether the absence of deliberations, the brevity of simulated trials, and the knowledge that they are reaching a "fictional" verdict also do not significantly affect the validity of mock jurors' research responses.

Opening Statements

Although attorneys will often begin their persuasive attempts during voir dire, the opening statement represents the first formal opportunity for them to make an uninterrupted presentation of their case. What weight is given to preparation of the opening statement by attorneys? Is it of a similar degree of importance to consultants? What does the research suggest regarding the impact of opening statements on jurors' decisions?

Impact of Opening Statements

A review of the social science, trial advocacy, and trial-consulting literature reveals a prevailing belief that, in spite of the fact that it is not technically considered to be evidence, the opening statement is highly influential in jurors' decisions. In their advice to each other, attorneys have suggested that the art of converting the opening statement into a persuasive plea can "condition the jury favorably" to one's side (Nizer, 1961, p. 42) and "greatly enhance [the attorney's] position in the trial" (Marshall, 1973, p. 32). More recently, attorneys have advised that it is during opening statements that "most jurors actually take sides and start pulling for one party" (McElhaney, 2000, p. 51) and that attorneys must "establish a rapport with jurors, earn their trust, and, hopefully, plant the seeds that will later yield a victory for the client" ("Opening Statements," 1998, p. 66). Finally, Perlman (1994) argues that "the opening statement may be a trial lawyer's most important weapon" (p. 68), and Allison (1998) cautions that "it's easier to win at the beginning of the case than at the end" (p. 5).

Trial consultants also generally take the position that the opening statement carries great persuasive weight in the trial process (Ball, 2002; Crawford, 1989; Matlon, 1988; Vinson, 1986; Vinson & Davis, 1996). For example, in his chapter on opening statements, Matlon (1988) describes their importance this way:

> We at least know [that opening statements] are of such importance that every attorney should attempt to prepare and present an opening statement that virtually cripples the opposition. Just as in a football game, an attorney should try to get the game out of reach through the opening statement and have the other side play catch-up the rest of the trial. As one witty writer succinctly put it, "the opening statement is not the time for foreplay; it is the time to score!" (p. 179)

Finally, social scientists writing on the application of psychology to law have noted the significance of the opening statement in jurors' decisions (Kassin & Wrightsman, 1988; Linz & Penrod, 1984; Linz, Penrod, & McDonald, 1986; Matlon, 1988).

In spite of the dominant perception that the opening statement is a critically important component of the trial process, there has been surprisingly little research examining whether jurors' leanings immediately following opening statements predict post- or even predeliberation verdicts, and much of the research that does exist is dated. Weld and

Danzig (1940) had mock jurors observe a simulated trial in the Moot Court room at Cornell Law School. Jurors were asked to record judgments for the plaintiff or defense at 18 different points throughout the trial, including immediately following opening statements. Results revealed that, for 9 (or 22%) of the 41 mock jurors participating, verdict preference following opening statements predicted verdict preference throughout the remainder of the trial. In a separate study conducted as a component of the University of Chicago Jury Project, Broeder (1958) found that 80% of jurors formed judgments immediately following opening statements. In both studies, the post-opening opinions of some jurors were the same as those taken into deliberations; presentation of the evidence in the trial did not change judgments made after listening to opening statements.

Several more recent studies have yielded conflicting results on this issue. In a posttrial interview study with civil jurors (Hans & Sweigart, 1993), the majority of jurors reported that they remained neutral following opening statements, in part because they had not yet heard any evidence. Similarly, Hannaford, Hans, Mott, and Munsterman (2000) reported that less than 10% of their juror-respondents indicated in posttrial interviews that they began leaning toward one side or the other during opening statements, with even fewer reporting that they had made up their minds at that point. In fact, more than 95% of their participants stated that they changed their minds at least once during the course of the trial. However, the results of both of these studies are somewhat suspect because the researchers relied on jurors' self-reports of their behavior. Jurors are generally aware that they are supposed to suspend judgment until the end of the trial and may therefore respond in the posttrial interview by describing what they *should have done*, rather than what they *actually did*.

Results obtained by Diamond and her colleagues (Diamond, Casper, Heiert, & Marshall, 1996) are more consistent with those of the early research. They presented jury-eligible citizens with a videotaped simulation of a death penalty case, stopping to take attitude measures at various points throughout the trial. They found that 70% of jurors reached a verdict following opening statements that remained constant until the end of the trial (the jury in this study did not deliberate). Because of the conflicting findings, we can draw no conclusions at this point regarding the oft-stated assumption that trials are won or lost during the opening statement. However, the research with the greatest experimental control, which does not rely on jurors' own descriptions of their behavior, points to the opening statement as quite influential.

Most of what has been written about opening statements has focused on specific elements, including length, content, organization, and, for the defense, the timing of the statement. Are the recommendations made by legal practitioners consistent with those made by trial consultants? What does the empirical research suggest?

Recommendations

Many specific suggestions regarding the length, organization, and content of opening statements can be found in trial advocacy literature. French (1992) argues that the opening statement should be concise and direct, as jurors' attention spans just 15 to 20 minutes. He further recommends techniques to assist jurors in paying attention, including providing a case theme, internal summaries, and use of repetition. Perlman (1994) advises that the first and last 2 minutes of the opening statement are crucial and should include language that is easily understood and will have a strong emotional impact on jurors. For example, he recommends replacing the word *accident* with phrases such as "violent crash," "severe crash," or "catastrophic event." He also suggests that attorneys end opening statements by citing universal principles, by suggesting to jurors that they have the opportunity to right a fundamental wrong.

Trial consultants have also made a number of specific recommendations regarding the structure and content of opening statements. David Ball (2002) advocates that plaintiff's attorneys begin with the rules, that is, identify the rules we are supposed to follow in life that are relevant to the case (e.g., doctors are supposed to do no harm to their patients). Second, attorneys should tell the story of what happened. The story should be simple, and it should be told in the present tense, as a series of events (the use of the present tense is also advocated by consultants Matheo and DeCaro, 2001). It should begin with and focus on the actions of the opposition, as it was their actions that caused the harm. Attorneys should then describe the harm, point the finger of blame, counter the opposition's arguments, describe the short- and long-term effects of the harm for their clients, and explain to jurors how they can fix things by awarding money.

In contrast to Ball's methodical approach to the opening statement, according to which jurors do not learn of the harm done to the plaintiff or the blameworthiness of the defendant until a foundation has been laid, Crawford (1989) recommends that attorneys "go for the jugular" (p. 111) during the first 2 minutes of the opening statement. This is done with a series of definitive statements right off the bat that identify the person who was harmed, the nature of the harm, and those responsible. The opening paragraph should be clear, vivid, and sum up for jurors what the case is about. All of this should happen in the first 2 minutes in order to make use of the primacy effect, and Crawford recommends that the same critical statements should be made in the last 2 minutes to take advantage of the recency effect. Crawford also advises that attorneys reveal case weaknesses during the opening statement, in order to increase credibility and steal the thunder of opposing counsel.

Licensed psychologist and trial consultant Jeffery Boyll (1989) advocates that attorneys be mindful of the memory capabilities of jurors. He makes reference to (but does not cite) memory research demonstrating that people can retain a limited number of facts in memory, that we typically forget about 70% of information presented in auditory form, and that forgetting occurs rapidly at first and then more gradually. In light of the memory research, Boyll recommends that attorneys focus on no more than four key issues or facts, repeat those key issues throughout the trial, present information visually as much as possible, and take advantage of the primacy and recency effects. Finally, trial consultants Matheo and DeCaro (2001) emphasize the creation of a theme that jurors will latch on to and repeat during deliberations. The attorney must convey a sense that she is passionate about the case (although they do not state specifically how this should be done), use imagery to engage the jurors, and be dramatic without being melodramatic (although the distinction is not made clear).

Primacy, Recency, and the Story Model

For most trial consultants (e.g., Ball, 2002; Crawford, 1989; Matheo & DeCaro, 2001; Matlon, 1988), the story is of critical importance to the opening statement. In their writing, consultants often advocate an opening strategy consistent with Pennington and Hastie's (1992, 1994) Story Model, according to which jurors actively construct stories based on the trial evidence and fill in any gaps in those stories based on their own past experiences and knowledge about the way the world works. Stories are likely to be altered throughout the course of the trial as jurors are exposed to new pieces of evidence and attorney arguments.

Although surprisingly little empirical applied research has examined the effects of the specific content of opening statements, there is a significant body of basic research that supports recommendations regarding primacy effects and the importance of providing jurors with a cognitive framework through which they might organize and interpret the actual evidence presented during the trial (Asch, 1946; Bower, 1978; Brewer & Nakamura, 1984; Langer & Abelson, 1974; Linz & Penrod, 1984; Taylor & Crocker, 1981). In a classic experiment demonstrating the primacy effect, Solomon Asch (1946) presented participants with a description of a person and then measured their perceptions of that person. For one group of participants, the person was described as "intelligent, industrious, impulsive, critical, stubborn, and envious." A second group of participants received exactly the same descriptors, except that they were presented in reverse order. Those who heard the list in reverse, so that the negative descriptors came first, formed more negative impressions of the person than did those who received the positive descriptors first. The first information we receive about a person carries more weight and may even influence the way we interpret additional relevant information.

In a later study, Langer and Abelson (1974) had research participants listen to a conversation between two men. Half of the participants were first told that the conversation was a job interview, while the others were led to believe that it was a psychiatric intake interview. Those who believed that the conversation was a psychiatric intake interview perceived greater pathology in the interviewee's behavior and interpreted additional background data in a way that was consistent with a perception of mental illness. The simple descriptor preceding the interview colored the way participants interpreted the dialogue and influenced their use of additional information. Lingle and Ostrom (1981) labeled such organizing schemata "thematic frameworks," or foundations of existing knowledge that guide the encoding, organization, and retrieval of newly obtained, relevant information. Findings from basic research suggest that attorneys should construct their opening statements so that they provide jurors with a thematic framework that will lead jurors to interpret the evidence in a way that is favorable to the attorney's side in the trial.

However, the basic research does not directly apply to the trial situation, in which jurors are exposed to two sides of an argument. How would Asch's participants have responded, for example, if they had heard from one source that the target was intelligent and from another that the target was envious? Applied research findings specific to the trial situation suggest that understanding jurors' decisions is complicated by the fact that they are exposed to contradictory arguments and must decide which version of the facts to believe.

One empirical study examined the contention that the relative structure of the opening statements delivered by the opposing lawyers might affect verdicts. Pyszczynski and Wrightsman (1981) manipulated the amount of preview information provided by the prosecution and defense in opening statements in a criminal trial. In an attempt to determine at what point in the trial opening statements had their effect, they assessed individual mock-juror verdicts at 13 separate points in the trial. They found that, regardless of the amount of preview presented in the defense opening, participants who had been exposed to an extensive prosecution opening gave fairly strong guilty verdicts early in the trial and maintained their position throughout. On the other hand, those exposed to a brief prosecution opening followed by an extensive defense opening were in favor of acquittal throughout the trial. Taken together, these results suggest that jurors were most influenced by the first strong opening statement to which they were exposed. The authors suggest that an extensive opening statement provides a thematic framework through which jurors then interpret the evidence; however, there is an alternative explanation for their findings. In this study, the highly detailed opening statements were significantly longer than those with less detail. Rather than attending to the content of the opening statements, and using that content to organize the witness testimony, participants in this study may have simply relied on a heuristic, or rule of thumb, that the side presenting the longer argument had the stronger case.

Additional research suggests, however, that there is validity to the notion that jurors utilize a thematic framework as they respond to evidence throughout the trial. Consistent with Pennington and Hastie's (1988, 1992) Story Model, jurors utilize stories when reaching a verdict; story elements are similar for those reaching similar verdicts; and verdicts tend to favor the side whose evidence presentation most resembles a story sequence (Hannaford, Hans, Mott, & Munsterman, 2000; Hans & Sweigart, 1993; Huntley & Costanzo, 2002). Pennington and Hastie (1994) have advised, therefore, that attorneys "remedy the unstory-like form of evidence presentation...during the presentation of opening and/or closing arguments" (p. 195). Recent research suggests that, in civil cases, it is especially important for the plaintiff's opening statement to be constructed according to the Story Model, but that the closing argument should not be a story (Spiecker & Worthington, 2003). We discuss this further later in this chapter.

Causal Focus

What of David Ball's (2002) recommendation that the opening statement should begin with and focus on the actions of the opposition? Social science research supports the contention that focusing attention on a specific individual increases the tendency of others to believe that such an individual caused a particular outcome (Fiske & Taylor, 1991; McArthur, 1981; Storms, 1973). Applying that assumption to a trial situation, Branscombe, Owen, Garstka, and Coleman (1996) manipulated the focus of mock jurors' attention through attorneys' statements that mentally undid the actions of one of the drivers involved in an auto accident. For example, the attorney might state, "This accident could have been avoided if only Driver A had been paying more attention to her driving and had not been driving too fast for the weather conditions." Statements such as this are referred to as "counterfactuals," because they allow for a mental undoing of what actually occurred. Results revealed that the amount of responsibility assigned to Driver A was significantly greater when the focus was on her behavior and when the attorney's statements implied a way in which she could have avoided the accident had she behaved differently. These researchers replicated their findings in a study in which jurors were led to focus on the behavior of either the victim or the assailant in a rape case (Branscombe et al., 1996).

In another series of studies, Creyer and Gürhan (1997) shifted mock jurors' attention away from a freak element of a car accident (a piece of concrete falling from an overpass) and onto the car's driver, who was not wearing a seat belt, by introducing statistical evidence regarding seat belt use. The researchers found that participants constructed more counterfactuals focused on the driver's behavior when the seat belt use information was presented than when it was not presented, demonstrating that it is possible for attorneys to shift jurors' causal focus even when it is naturally drawn to another target.

Making Promises and Stealing Thunder

In the trial advocacy literature, Allison (1998) specifically warns against overstating one's case during the opening statement. However, empirical research suggests that unkept promises might lead jurors to believe that they received evidence that was never presented. The key is the extent to which opposing counsel is paying attention and reminds the jurors of the omission. Pyszczynski, Greenberg, Mack, and Wrightsman (1981) presented to mock jurors an auto theft case with varying defense opening statements. In two conditions, the defense attorney claimed that there would be evidence showing that his client was not at the scene of the crime; however, no such evidence was ever presented during the trial. Some mock jurors then read a reminder from the prosecuting attorney during his closing argument, pointing out that the defense attorney promised, but did not deliver, the exonerating evidence. Participants in a third, control condition received no promise and no reminder. Mock jurors who received the promise, but were not reminded by the prosecution that it was not fulfilled, perceived a lesser degree of defendant guilt than did those who received the reminder statement. Although these results suggest that jurors do attend to the content, and not simply the length, of opening statements, they also suggest that attorneys should not rely on jurors to critically evaluate opening statements or test them against the evidence that is actually presented during the trial. If opposing counsel promises more than he or she delivers, it should be brought explicitly to jurors' attention during closing arguments.

So, it is risky to overstate one's case during opening statements, but should attorneys disclose case weaknesses, as recommended by Crawford (1989)? This recommendation is supported by research conducted by Williams, Bourgeois, and Croyle (1993). Weaknesses in the defense case were presented first by the defense attorney or presented first by the prosecutor. When the defense attorney presented the information first, jurors were less likely to believe that the defendant was guilty. In addition, when the defense attorney admitted to the weaknesses, he was rated as more trustworthy than when he did not. These results were replicated in a second study in which there was information damaging to the plaintiff's side in a civil trial (Williams et al., 1993). By admitting to weaknesses in one's own case, the attorney inoculates the jury against opposing counsel's most harmful weapons. In other words, this strategy allows one to steal the thunder from one's opponent.

Timing of the Defense Opening Statement

In criminal as well as civil trials, the defense has the option of making its opening statement immediately following that of the prosecutor or plaintiff's attorney, or waiting until after the prosecution or plaintiff has presented all of its evidence. Most legal experts advocate that defense attorneys not delay presentation of the opening statement (Linz & Penrod, 1984).

Trial consultants also generally advise against delaying the opening. For example, Crawford (1989) suggests that by delaying, the attorney forfeits her ability to impeach opposing witnesses before they have taken the stand, to challenge opponents' arguments immediately after they are made, and to permanently persuade jurors at the outset of the trial, as the defense opening constitutes the "last words jurors will hear in a formal speech-making sense until the closing argument" (p. 107).

The importance of immediately challenging the statements of the prosecutor or plaintiff is debated among legal experts. Allison (1998) argues against delaying the defense opening statement on the grounds that delaying provides the prosecution the benefit of a "steamroller effect," holding jurors' attention from the start of the opening statement and clear through to the completion of its case in chief, with no challenge from the opposition. Jeans (1975) takes the contrary position that the defense *should* delay its opening, but uses the same rationale; by delaying, the defense benefits from the effect of presenting its opening statement followed immediately by witnesses testifying on its behalf. Simply put, Allison argues that the defense should not delay, so as to prevent a steamroller effect for the prosecution, while Jeans argues that the defense should delay, so as to secure the steamroller effect for itself.

Only one empirical study has directly investigated whether the defense should delay its opening statement. Gary Wells and his colleagues (Wells, Miene, & Wrightsman, 1985) presented undergraduate mock jurors with a trial transcript from an auto theft case. The primary experimental manipulation was the timing of the defense opening statement, which was placed either immediately following the prosecution's opening, immediately prior to the prosecution's opening, or immediately after the testimony of prosecution witnesses. Although not allowed by law, researchers included the second condition for theoretical purposes. First, it allowed them to test whether the early creation of a defense schema would adversely affect the impact of the prosecution's opening. Second, it allowed them to test competing theoretical positions, one stating that preserving the continuity of one's own case is the most critical (and therefore the defense should delay its opening) and the other stating that the creation of cognitive schemata for the jurors is most critical (and therefore the defense should not delay its opening, but should provide jurors with a conceptual model to compete with the prosecution model prior to the presentation of prosecution evidence). Two additional experimental manipulations involved the quality of the opening statement made by the defense (poor quality versus high quality) and strength of the defense case (strong versus weak).

Results revealed that mock jurors judged the defendant to be significantly less guilty in the second condition (defense opening immediately prior to prosecution opening) than in the other two conditions. Furthermore, delaying the opening statement adversely affected the defense in terms of judgments of witness testimony, defendant testimony, and perceptions of prosecution and defense opening statements and closing arguments. Under no circumstances was delaying the defense opening statement advantageous to the defense case. It is interesting to note that in this study, there were no effects for quality of the defense statement and that the strong and weak statements were roughly the same length. Taken together with the Pyszczynski and Wrightsman (1981) findings that the more extensive opening had the greatest influence, one might conclude that the content of opening statements matters less than their length. Maybe jurors really do rely on a "longer is better" heuristic.

Evidence Presentation

Evidence is presented through the testimony of witnesses and demonstrative materials, such as courtroom reenactments, photographs, and videotapes. Although some have argued that a case is won or lost during opening statements, without the evidence to back it up, a good opening becomes little more than an empty promise. At the same time, it might be argued that this is the phase of the trial over which attorneys have the least control. The evidence is what it is. Ideally for the prosecution, there are fingerprints at the crime scene matching those of the defendant; often there are not. Ideally for the plaintiff, one has copies of documents ordering employees not to disclose the harmful effects of a manufacturer's waste products. In reality, one may only have a disgruntled former employee who states that he was ordered to shred such a document. Attorneys must make the most of what is given to them. In chapter 2, we discussed methods used by attorneys to prepare their witnesses to testify. In the end, however, as noted at the beginning of chapter 2, the attorney has little control over how the witness performs on the stand or responds to questions posed by opposing counsel.

During the evidence presentation phase of the trial, attorneys only really control a few things: the medium through and order in which the evidence is presented, the questions they ask, and the manner in which they ask them. In this section, we will review the advice of attorneys and trial consultants, as well as the empirical research findings relevant to the direct and cross-examination of witnesses.

Direct Examination

Most of the evidence presented during a trial is delivered through witness testimony. Direct examination of a witness is conducted by the attorney who calls that witness to testify. Under most circumstances, this exchange will be friendly, characterized by the use of open-ended questions that allow the witness to simply tell his or her story. "The purpose of direct examination, therefore, is to allow the jury an opportunity to relive the events of the case from your client's point of view so that the jury understands, accepts, and remembers the case from your client's perspective" (Klein & Kochman, 1998, p. 24). The direct examination often does not have the drama that is associated with cross-examination, but some legal scholars argue that it can, and should, be just as interesting (Gray, 1997; Klein & Kochman, 1998). They liken direct examination to a script from a movie or a play, noting that, although the facts outlined in the script cannot be changed, the attorney as director should inject his or her perspective, and lines should be delivered "in a persuasive, interesting, compelling, and clear manner" (Gray, 1997, p. 46).

Many of the specific recommendations regarding direct examination are similar to those for the delivery of a good opening statement: be clear and concise, use simple language that does not confuse the witness and paints a picture for jurors, elicit information in an organized (often chronological) fashion, and elicit the most dramatic or critical information at the beginning or the end of the witness's testimony (Klein & Kochman, 1998). It is further suggested that attorneys consider revealing case weaknesses through direct testimony, so as to steal the thunder of opposing counsel on cross-examination (Gray, 1997; Klein & Kochman, 1998). As discussed above, there is a significant body of evidence from social psychological research supporting the creation of a cognitive framework through which jurors can organize a witness's testimony in a story-like manner, as well as the importance of primacy and recency effects. We have also discussed research supporting a strategy which reveals one's own case weaknesses before the opposition has the chance to do so (Williams et al., 1993). The importance of using simple language, specifically avoiding the use of confusing questions, was highlighted by the research findings of Kebbell and Johnson (2000), which revealed that witnesses who had been asked confusing questions (i.e., those containing negatives or double negatives, those including multiple questions, those using complex syntax and vocabulary) were less accurate than those asked simpler questions.

A number of additional recommendations specific to direct examination can be found in the legal literature. For example, it is suggested that attorneys allow their witness to bond with the jury by allowing the witness to share information about occupation, family, and the like and by instructing the witness to speak directly to the jury. It is also recommended that the attorney slow things down during critical pieces of the testimony, encouraging the witness to relate important details "in an almost agonizingly slow manner" (Klein & Kochman, 1998, p. 25) in order to help the jury visualize and retain crucial information. Finally, attorneys advise each other to ask primarily open-ended questions (leading questions are generally not allowed during direct examination), to have the witness explain confusing or complicated answers, and to listen carefully to one's own witness, both to diminish the appearance that the testimony is rehearsed and to be sure to catch any errors in testimony (Klein & Kochman, 1998).

The recommendations of trial consultants regarding direct examination are largely consistent with those of attorneys, as well as with the research findings. In his chapter on conducting the direct examination, Crawford (1989) focuses on the perceived credibility of the witness and strategies available to attorneys that will enhance their witnesses' credibility in the eyes of jurors. Attorneys are specifically advised to make frequent eye contact with the witness, to convey a sense that even the most unsavory witness is liked by the attorney, and to shield the witnesses from a difficult cross-examination by discussing their weaknesses with them on direct. Crawford returns to his commitment to the primacy and recency effects in his recommendations regarding the ordering of the questions for each witness, as well as the order in which witnesses are called to testify. Attorneys are instructed that under most circumstances they should call their strongest witnesses first in order to affect juror attitudes and commitments as soon as possible. For witness questioning, he suggests that attorneys use an anticlimactic order, whereby the witness's pivotal and essential point is revealed during the first 2 minutes of questioning and is then revisited during the final 30 seconds.

An alternative approach, both for questioning the individual witness and for determining the order in which witnesses are called, is to do so in chronological order. Although we applied Pennington and Hastie's (1988) Story Model to our discussion of opening statements, and in spite of the fact that they recommend its application to both opening statements and closing arguments, their empirical research has focused on their model's application to the order of presentation of evidence (Pennington & Hastie, 1988, 1992). Their findings suggest that evidence should be presented in chronological order to correspond with the story one is telling to the jury. Unfortunately, social science research findings do not always transfer neatly to the realm of the real world, including the courtroom. To present testimony in strict chronological order, a witness might be called to testify about one part of the story, leave the stand for a while as subsequent events are described for jurors by other witnesses, and then recalled to provide the rest of her testimony so that it all makes for a coherent story.

Legal scholar Richard Lempert (1991) explains that, in fact, the Federal Rules of Evidence allow this to happen. An attorney can ask for and receive the court's permission to call a witness for a segment of testimony, allow him to step down, and then recall him later. However, this does not happen very often because of the reality of the trial situation. First, it would be an inconvenience to witnesses, who might have to spend several days at the courthouse waiting to be recalled, as an actor waiting to return to the stage the next time his character appears in the play. Second, delivering testimony in this way is inefficient, and the Federal Rules of Evidence require that the judge see to it that witness testimony does not consume more time than it should (Lempert, 1991). The shuffling of witnesses to and from the stand may try the patience of the judge. Finally, calling and recalling a witness might lead jurors to perceive that the witness had not been entirely forthcoming the first time on the stand and would certainly allow opposing counsel to better prepare for cross-examination (Lempert, 1991).

Cross-Examination

Cross-examination involves an entirely different questioning strategy. While the direct examination of a witness is characterized by open-ended questions that allow the witness to fully develop and make clear for the jury his or her position, questions delivered during cross-examination tend to be closed-ended, often limiting the witness to a one- or two-word response. Goals of cross-examination occasionally do include clarification of direct testimony and acquisition of additional information that is helpful to one's case (Matlon, 1988). Neither of these is especially adversarial in nature; in fact, the witness might be questioned in a way that is more similar to a direct examination. However, cross-examination is more often conducted with the goal of reducing the credibility of the witness and his or her testimony. It is this goal that has led to the greatest disagreement among legal experts regarding appropriate attorney behavior.

Robert Lawry (1996) argues that legal practice is steeped in the tradition of the "lawyer-statesman, a person of practical wisdom, sound judgment, and resolute public-spiritedness" (p. 563). He points to cross-examination as an example of how that tradition has been lost, giving way to an emphasis on win-at-all-costs, extreme client loyalty. To support this contention, Lawry points to the changes in wording across revisions of the American Bar Association's *Standards for Criminal Justice: Prosecution Function and Defense Function.* In the first edition, adopted in 1971, the ABA admonished defense attorneys regarding cross-examination: "[a lawyer] should not misuse the power of cross-examination or impeachment by employing it to discredit or undermine a witness if he knows the witness is testifying truthfully" (Standard 7.6(b), as cited in Lawry, 1996, p. 577). In the commentary to that standard, the authors, acknowledging that circumstances surrounding cross-examination are likely to be subjective and that the standard is largely unenforceable, leave it to the lawyer's conscience and honor to comply with the standard.

In the second edition (ABA, 1980), the revised standard (now 4–7.6[b]) included somewhat softer language, so that, in cases where the defense consists solely of a challenge to the prosecution's known truthful witnesses, attempts to discredit those witnesses is allowable. The commentary recommends that attorneys avoid such attempts at discrediting truthful witnesses, but only when such avoidance can be done in the context of an effective defense. The third edition of the *Standards* was adopted in 1993. In that edition, the revised defense standard states very succinctly, "Defense counsel's belief or knowledge that the witness is telling the truth does not preclude cross-examination" (as cited in Lawry, 1996, p. 579). Lawry notes that, while the commentary to the standard touches on ethics, it is largely dedicated to a discussion of tactics with an emphasis on zealous representation and does not include a discussion of morality or the truth-seeking function of the adversarial system. Rather than admonishing against attempts at discrediting witnesses, the authors state, "Witnesses should not be subjected to degrading, demeaning, or otherwise invasive or insulting questioning *unless counsel honestly believes that such questioning may prove beneficial to his or her client's case*" (Lawry, 1996, p. 580; italics added). Others in the legal literature have debated the truth-seeking function of cross-examination, as well (e.g., Brown, 1991; Metos, 1990).

Not all legal scholars agree that the focus on zealous representation is a bad thing (e.g., Freedman, 1966). While acknowledging that there is no place for the bullying of innocent witnesses, Philip Corboy (1986) argues that the only worthwhile goal of cross-examination is to prejudice the case of one's opponent. However, in making his point, he appears to struggle with the legal-moral distinction as it pertains to certain cross-examination strategies. He notes, for example, that questioning that has "no purpose other than degradation and humiliation of the witness...is surely not condoned as embodying those principles of decency and fairness espoused either by the legal profession or society as a whole" (p. 2). However, in the next sentence, Corboy argues that, while such questioning "may be a boorish violation of legal etiquette, it is not unethical if it at all bears upon the veracity of the witness" (p. 2). Furthermore, he states that the distinction between the truthful witness (whom Lawry seeks to protect) and the un-truthful witness is not one that the attorney is ever in a position to make. Therefore, a zealous cross-examination of every witness is in order.

Gibbs, Sigal, Adams, and Grossman (1989) examined the effects of attorneys' attempts to discredit a witness during cross-examination. In their research, a videotaped reenactment of a personal injury case was presented to mock jurors. The trial included the cross-examination of an expert witness, and the attorney's questioning style was either hostile (including angry voice inflection and pronounced hand gestures) or nonhostile and either included or did not include leading questions. Participants rated the attorney on the extent to which they found him convincing and effective and reached a verdict in the case. Attorneys in the hostile/leading question condition and the nonhostile/nonleading question condition were rated as less effective than those in the hostile/nonleading question and nonhostile/leading question conditions. Therefore, it appears that attorneys who are either too aggressive or too soft in their attempts to discredit the witness are perceived least positively by jurors, suggesting that jurors will hold attorneys to the lawyer-statesman ideal endorsed by Lawry (1996). However, although perceptions of attorneys were affected by cross-examination style, verdicts in this particular case were not. More research is needed to determine whether, and under what circumstances, jurors might actually punish overly aggressive attorneys with their verdicts.

A second concern expressed by Corboy (1986) regarding the ethics of cross-examination strategies lies with the use of another dirty trick: the introduction of inadmissible evidence. Corboy sees this as a greater evil than attacking the truthful witness. When attorneys make reference, through leading questions, to information that has been ruled inadmissible or that is clearly not legally relevant, this has the potential to cause irreparable damage. According to Corboy, objections to information that has reached the eyes and ears of the jury come too late; the damage is already done.

Social psychologist Saul Kassin and his colleagues (Kassin, Williams, & Saunders, 1990) examined this contention. They presented mock jurors with the transcript from a trial involving the rape of a woman in the dimly lit corridor of her apartment building. Participants read her testimony, the testimony of the accused, and the testimony of an expert witness regarding the effects of high stress levels on eyewitness performance. For some participants, the cross-examination of the victim included two presumptuous questions that invited the introduction of inadmissible evidence regarding past claims of having been raped. For other participants, two presumptuous questions were asked of the expert, which suggested that his work was poorly regarded by his colleagues. In each condition, the presumptuous questions were met with either an affirmative response from the witness, a denial from the witness, or an objection by opposing counsel. There was also a control group whose transcript did not include presumptuous questions asked of either witness. Research participants were asked to rate the credibility of the witnesses and the effectiveness of the attorneys and to reach a verdict in the case.

The results of the study were somewhat complex and varied by participants' gender. Of those who read the presumptuous questions asked of the victim, females were more likely to favor conviction, but only when the questions were met with denial from the victim. Inclusion of the presumptuous questions did not diminish the credibility ratings of the victim. Of those who read the presumptuous questions asked of the expert witness, females were more likely than males to view the defendant as guilty, regardless of whether the questions were met with denial, admission, or objection. Inclusion of the presumptuous questions did decrease the credibility of the expert regardless of the response to the questions; those who received the questions rated the expert as less credible than did those in the control group. Therefore, Corboy's (1986) contention that alluding to inadmissible information in the course of cross-examination creates irreversible damage is somewhat supported. It seems to depend on the response to the question, the nature of the information, and the nature of the case, as rape cases generally lead to discrepant responses based on juror sex.

As some legal scholars debate the ethics of certain cross-examination techniques, others give more specific advice to their fellow attorneys. For example, defense attorneys are told: ask only questions that are consistent with defense theory; be natural; focus on leading questions and "boxing in" the witness, but don't be afraid to ask a nonleading question if it can't hurt you; ask the toughest question first; move around in the courtroom; and have fun (Brown, 1991). Others advise that one should not interrupt the witness, as such behavior is perceived by jurors as unintelligent and unfair (Bernstein, 1994), and that the attorney should call attention to the witness's nonverbal expressions in order to increase witness anxiety (Klein, 1993). Finally, Lempert (1991) recommends that attorneys use cross-examination as a means of disrupting the opponent's story. Even if there are no substantive points to be made on cross, simply breaking up the story being told by one's opponent makes the cross worthwhile. However, he cautions against simply taking the witness through the testimony he or she has already provided, as the story told twice is more likely to be recalled.

Trial consultants' recommendations regarding cross-examination overlap somewhat with those made by attorneys. Ronald Matlon (1988) suggests that cross-examination should be brief, hitting only the most crucial points of a witness's testimony. In addition, he suggests that the first question should address the issue for which the witness has the least confidence or that which is most directly relevant to the attorney's case theory. For example, if a defendant is pleading that he acted in self-defense, all cross-examination should focus on diminishing the self-defense argument. Third, Matlon recommends that cross-examination "end on a high note" (p. 235), one that damages the credibility of the witness or the strength of the opponent's case. The following is an example of how a defense lawyer cross-examining an eyewitness might end on a high note or, alternatively, how he might blow it:

> Q. Where were the defendant and the victim when the fight broke out?
> A. In the middle of the field.
> Q. Where were you?
> A. On the edge of the field.
> Q. What were you doing?
> A. Bird watching.
> Q. Where were the birds?
> A. In the trees.
> Q. Where were the trees?
> A. On the edge of the field.
> Q. Were you looking at the birds?
> A. Yes.
> Q. So your back was to the people fighting?
> A. Yes.

Now what do you do? You stop and sit down. And what will you argue in summation? He could not have seen it. His back was to them. You have challenged perception. Instead, you ask the one question too many:

> Q. Well, if your back was to them, how can you say that the defendant bit off the victim's nose?
> A. Well, I saw him spit it out. (Younger, 1976, pp. 30–31)

Trial consultant Dick Crawford (1989) makes a number of recommendations to attorneys regarding cross-examination strategy. Among them is the suggestion that attorneys think of the cross-examination as a speech made in the form of a series of leading questions. The witness essentially becomes irrelevant, relegated to yes-or-no responses to questions which are designed to convey information to jurors. Attorneys are advised to always use leading questions, even with a gentle witness; interrupt witnesses only when it makes sense to do so (e.g., when the witness is argumentative or when the witness is clearly lying); and to never relinquish power or control over the witness.

Many of the recommendations of attorneys and trial consultants alike include the use of aggressive tactics to control the witness or, at the very least, to make him or her uneasy. However, research suggests that attorneys must be careful about the degree of aggression they display during cross-examination. Astrid Schütz (1998) asked research participants to view videotaped interviews with two German politicians during an election campaign. When the candidates engaged in such behaviors as interrupting journalists and personally attacking their opponent, they were judged to be aggressive and arrogant. On the other hand, when the candidate engaged in a calm, focused attack on his opponent, he was characterized as confident and self-assured.

Proxemics

The influence of testimony evidence is not limited to the questions and answers themselves; jurors attend to the nonverbal as well as the verbal when judging the credibility of witnesses. We discussed in chapter 2 steps that attorneys take to prepare the witness, including attending to nonverbal behaviors such as eye contact and posture. However, the behavior of the questioning attorney is also observed by the jurors and may have some bearing on the perceived credibility of the witness, as well as on the perceived effectiveness and credibility of the attorney. One nonverbal behavior that has received considerable attention in trial advocacy literature is proxemics, or social distance. Proxemics refers to the spatial relationships between people or between a person and an object (J. D. Smith, 1991). Legal scholars have suggested that an attorney can manipulate that space in a way that will make the witness feel more or less anxiety while testifying (see Brodsky, Hooper, Tipper, & Yates, 1999, for a review). For example, it is recommended that, during cross-examination, the attorney should invade the witness's personal space in order to convey dominance, to increase witness anxiety, and to serve as an obstacle between the witness and the jury (Klein, 1993; Klein & Kochman, 1998; Peskin, 1980; J. D. Smith, 1991, but only when counsel believes that a witness is not testifying truthfully). On the other hand, attorneys are advised to give the witness space during direct examination, except when it may be appropriate to touch the witness in order to convey sympathy and support (Givens, 1981; Klein, 1993; Klein & Kochman, 1998; J. D. Smith, 1991). As is the case with most of the recommendations in the legal literature, however, these authors do not cite empirical support for their contentions.

Brodsky et al. (1999) conducted some preliminary research on proxemics in a courtroom setting. They observed 12 attorneys engaged in direct and cross-examination, and recorded the interpersonal distance between the attorneys and the witnesses. They found that attorneys conducted cross-examination from a closer proximity than they did direct examination, suggesting that attorneys are behaving in ways consistent with professional recommendations. However, social scientists and attorneys alike have yet to address the critical question as to the effects of attorney-witness proximity on jurors' judgments of witness credibility. One study conducted outside the legal domain gives some indication that jurors' perceptions will depend upon the gender and relative power status of the witness and the attorney (Burgoon, 1991). In that study, participants were asked to make judgments about photographs depicting same- or mixed-sex dyads interacting at varying distances and engaged in various touching behaviors (e.g., a handshake, hand holding, touch on forearm, touch to the face). Photos depicting people in close proximity generally were interpreted as conveying dominance of one over the other, and interpretations of the interaction varied with target sex and style of touch. Clearly, additional research specific to the courtroom domain is needed in this area.

Closing Arguments

The closing argument represents the attorney's final shot at persuading the jury. Like the opening statement, it is not evidence. However, unlike the opening, during closing arguments, attorneys are allowed some latitude to draw on emotion as they seek two primary goals: to clarify the evidence and to persuade jurors to their side (Matlon, 1988). It seems that all phases of the trial are believed by some to be the critical phase; the closing argument is no exception, described by some as the point at which the trial is won or lost (e.g., Bergman, 1989; Cotchett & Rothman, 1988). In one study, Rieke (1971) found that, although the presence or absence of a closing argument did not affect assignments of liability, mock jurors who heard only a plaintiff's closing argument awarded the highest damages, and those who heard only a closing argument by the defense awarded the lowest damages.

Attorneys have plenty of advice for each other as to the proper design and delivery of a closing argument that will lead to a win. McElhaney (2000), for example, warns that it is a waste of time to go over with jurors all of the testimony they have already heard, as is common practice with some lawyers. Instead, he recommends that the lawyer act as a teacher, listing on a display board the most important points from the trial. In this way, the attorney gains credibility (because teachers are "a fundamental symbol of credibility" [p. 56]), and the jurors become actively involved as they reach a conclusion on their own, rather than having it handed to them by the attorney. Other legal scholars (e.g., Schuetz & Snedaker, 1988; L. Smith, 1981) and some trial consultants (e.g., Ball, 2002) also advocate this strategy.

The contention that it is best to allow jurors to draw a conclusion on their own is ultimately not supported empirically. Linz and Penrod (1984) acknowledge that research has demonstrated that, when the audience is motivated to draw a conclusion and is capable of doing so based on the content of the message and other situational factors, allowing them to reach a conclusion on their own does produce longer-lasting attitude change. However, attorneys can never assume that jurors are drawing any conclusions, much less the conclusion they want them to draw. Therefore, the strategy is a risky one. Social scientists argue that the best approach is for the attorney to draw rather explicit conclusions for jurors (Hovland & Mandell, 1952; Linz & Penrod, 1984; McGuire, 1969; Weiss & Steenbock, 1965; Zimbardo & Lieppe, 1991).

Crawford's (1989) recommendations regarding closing arguments include to begin with the most compelling information, stated definitively, confidently, and conclusively; to avoid a simple summary of the evidence that was presented during the trial; to provide a rationale for the expected verdict; to inoculate the jury against opposing counsel's upcoming closing argument; to include an appropriate degree of narrative, pathos, and vivid word pictures; and to conclude with a few sentences of great significance. The persuasion research suggests that attorneys should ingratiate themselves to jurors to increase liking, and some legal experts advise that this be done at the beginning of the closing argument in the form of a thank you to jurors for fulfilling their duty (e.g., Schuetz & Snedaker, 1988). Crawford recommends against it on the grounds that jurors are most attentive at the beginning of the closing argument, and the primacy effect will be wasted if used for a simple appreciation. Starr (1983) laments the absence of empirical research examining when ingratiation is likely to be effective and when it will backfire.

There is some debate among social scientists as to the most appropriate structure of the closing argument. On the one hand, Rieke and Stutman (1990) recommend that the closing argument provide a narrative such as that used during the opening statement. The attorney should leave jurors with a vivid and compelling story and should point out ambiguities in the story told by opposing counsel. On the other hand, research conducted by Spiecker and Worthington (2003) and McCullough (1994) suggests that attorneys should use an expository approach, which delineates each legal element that must be proven, followed by an argument that the prosecution or plaintiff either did or did not meet its burden, depending on which side is making the closing argument. The expository approach is more closely aligned with the jury's task at this phase of the trial: having heard narratives and evidence for both sides, the jurors must apply the law as it is given to them in the judge's instructions. The expository approach has the additional benefit of providing deliberation ammunition to jurors who are allied with the attorney's side going into deliberations (Wrightsman, 2001).

Other closing-argument recommendations that can be drawn from social science research include the suggestion that attorneys repeat their strongest points in order to increase acceptance and understanding (but no more than three times, as additional repetitions may become tedious for jurors) and that they limit the number of major points to around seven, as additional persuasive points will be difficult for jurors to track and will have minimal persuasive effect (Calder, Insko, & Yandell, 1974; Linz & Penrod, 1984; Petty & Cacioppo, 1979). Research conducted by Lupfer and his colleagues (Lupfer, Cohen, Bernard, & Brown, 1987) suggests that attorneys should employ closing arguments that encourage jurors to base their decisions on the facts of the case rather than on some moral principle (i.e., attorneys should appeal to jurors according to a conventional, rather than postconventional level of moral reasoning, according to Kohlberg's 1976 model).

Social science research also suggests strategies appropriate to specific trial circumstances. For example, Stallard and Worthington (1998) tested the effectiveness of a closing-argument strategy designed to reduce the effects of the hindsight bias among civil jurors. The *hindsight bias* is a tendency for individuals to exaggerate the foreseeability of a particular outcome when they know that the outcome has occurred (Fischhoff, 1975). Hindsight bias is especially likely to produce liability judgments in favor of the plaintiff, as jurors conclude that the defendant should have known that the negative effect would occur.

To combat the hindsight bias, Stallard and Worthington (1998) examined the effectiveness of a defense closing argument that informed jurors of plaintiff's attempts to make them "Monday-morning quarterbacks" and that ended with an appeal to jurors to not use hindsight when judging the defendant by reminding them not to second-guess the defendant's decisions. Results suggest that the inoculation strategy was effective; participants exposed to the debiasing strategy were less likely to find for the plaintiff than those who were not exposed to that strategy.

Attorney's Style

In their writings, especially regarding opening statements and closing arguments, trial consultants have focused on the stylistic, as well as content, characteristics of attorney presentation. It seems that most consultants who write on the subject of attorneys' style have their backgrounds in communications and theater. In a series of articles published in *Court Call*, the quarterly newsletter of the ASTC, trial consultant Gary Genard applies what is known about effective dramatic performance to the trial scenario. Arguing that a trial is "like a drama played on a 'real' stage" (Genard, 2000, p. 8), Genard compares trial participants and evidence to the actors, audience, and props used in a dramatic play. He advises that attorneys attend to three areas of persuasion: competence, rapport, and delivery (Genard, 2001a). Without providing specific detail as to how to accomplish it, he states that attorneys should "[a]dvertise your competence in everything you say and do in the courtroom. When you trust yourself and what you are saying, your audience will trust you" (p. 14). He recommends that attorneys use plain English rather than legalese; tell an interesting, engaging story; speak with conviction and enthusiasm; and maintain eye contact with members of the jury.

In his column, Genard also gives advice regarding voice quality, stating, "All listeners react instinctively to the *quality* of our individual voices. This means that you can use your voice to build trust, to elicit sympathy, to validate honor, . . . the list is virtually endless" (Genard, 2001b, p. 10). Finally, Genard argues that jurors enjoy a fight between equals, so attorneys must take steps to make themselves worthy advocates (Genard, 2002). They must convey a sense that they are up to the task, that they are pleased to be representing their client in that particular case. They must be themselves, and they must show respect to all trial participants, including their adversaries. The message is that jurors do not want to watch a highly experienced attorney beat up on a young associate; that is not a fair fight. Therefore, the experienced attorney must be humble and respectful, avoiding any form of rude or condescending behavior toward the opposing attorney, especially when the opposing attorney is not doing a good job. Genard applies his recommendations not only to opening statements, but to all aspects of the trial, from voir dire to closing arguments. Although the use of citations would be appropriate for *Court Call*'s audience, Genard does not provide empirical citations for any of his recommendations.

Other trial consultants also have built their practices around the assumption that the lawyer in the midst of a trial is much like the actor on stage—this is a performance, and the jury-as-audience must be persuaded, convinced, and emotionally moved. Consultants Katherine James and Alan Blumenfeld, both professional actors, produced a series of four instructional videos entitled *What Can Lawyers Learn From Actors?* In the videos, they advise attorneys how to act "like a human being" (James, 2002, p. 9) through their demeanor in the courtroom and the way they tell their stories during opening and closing statements. They provide instruction as to how to control the jurors' focus, how to question witnesses, and the appropriate development and use of the voice. On their Web site, James and Blumenfeld indicate that they have "endeavored to become expert consultants through the careful study of learning theory and education theory, as well as the study of human behavior, how people learn, how jurors learn and how they deliberate" (James & Blumenfeld, n.d., "Who We Are," ¶1).

Lisa DeCaro and Leonard Matheo are also professional actors who have become trial consultants. A short biography provided in the ASTC 2002 conference materials describes their work, indicating that they "teach litigators how to compose a compelling opening statement and closing argument, how to use non-verbal communication and eye contact to emphasize their message, how to build a relationship with each juror, how to call the jurors to action, and how to advance their story through each element of the trial" (American Society of Trial Consultants, 2002, "Production Design," ¶5). Although they state that "courtroom performance has little to do with 'acting' and much to do with communicating" (Matheo & DeCaro, 2001, p. 59), much of their advice encourages attorneys to do the same things that actors do "day in and day out" (p. 59). For example, they encourage attorneys to make use of vocal inflection, conveying different meaning depending on whether voice pitch rises, falls, or remains constant. They state that jurors are unconsciously influenced by voice inflection, which elicits a visceral response. Use of falling inflection, for example, might convey to jurors that the attorney already knows or does not care about the answer to the question he has asked of a witness. On the other hand, use of rising inflection indicates a question for which one desires an answer, and the questioner "seems warm, friendly, and genuinely interested" in the response (p. 60).

Finally, Matheo and DeCaro note that the use of a sustained inflection gives the impression that one is not finished speaking, so that even if one stops speaking, the listener will mentally finish the statement. They advise that attorneys use sustained inflection with incomplete sentences during closing arguments so that jurors will draw their own conclusions. Here again, however, the consultants are assuming that jurors will finish the statement in favor of the speaker's position and that allowing the jurors to draw their own conclusion is more persuasive than drawing it for them. Recall that these assumptions are not necessarily supported by the research (Hovland & Mandell, 1952; Linz & Penrod, 1984; McGuire, 1969; Thistlethwaite, De Haan, & Kamenetzky, 1955; Weiss & Steenbock, 1965; Zimbardo & Lieppe, 1991).

Matheo and DeCaro (2001) also advise attorneys to memorize their opening statements, as a thorough memorization will then free up the attorney to improvise if needed. In making this point, the authors state the following:

> The key is that you can't "sort of" memorize the material. You have to know it so well that you *never* have to think about what you are going to say next. The best way to do this is to memorize out loud. Just as your muscles remember to put the clutch in even when your brain is thinking about the fight you just had with your kids, your muscles will also remember words they have spoken many times, even when your brain can't. (p. 61; italics in original)

There is no research to support the contention that the *muscles* are capable of memorizing anything. What the authors are describing is divided consciousness, which allows us to automatically perform a well-learned task while focusing our attention elsewhere (Hilgard, 1975). There is research to support the existence of divided consciousness, but Matheo and DeCaro oversimplify when they state that, after thorough memorization, attorneys will have little difficulty cutting, adding to, or editing the sections they have memorized. Research on memory shows a clear interference effect, whereby previously learned information interferes with our ability to recall new information, especially when it is similar (Underwood, 1957). Therefore, the attorney who has edited a thoroughly memorized opening statement will need to exert great concentration during its delivery in order to give the newly edited, rather than the original version.

Finally, Matheo and DeCaro (2001) give attorneys advice about body language:

> Crossing your arms means that you are cutting yourself off from listeners. Hands in your pockets means you're hiding something. Rubbing hands together says you're greedy. . . . Whether the theories are accurate or not, most potential jurors are aware of them. To win, you must be aware of how your body language is perceived. (p. 65)

They do not cite, and we are not aware of, any research to suggest that the body-language assumptions are correct nor that most jurors are aware of them (or, more important, that jurors endorse them).

In his book on courtroom persuasion, Dick Crawford (1989) indicates that there are three key "credibility factors" that determine whether jurors will be persuaded by an attorney: trust, competence, and likability. He elaborates extensively on each, educating his reader as to strategies for achieving the desired persona. For example, the competent attorney is prepared, does not rely extensively on notes, moves comfortably about the courtroom, and conveys a sense of purpose throughout the trial. The trustworthy attorney admits mistakes, informs the jury of weaknesses in his case, and uses objections to point out to jurors that, while he is following the rules of the court, his opponent is not (e.g., "Your Honor, Johnnie and I are required to object to that leading question and we would like for you to urge the prosecutor to follow the well-established court rules just as we are doing" [p. 27]). Finally, the likable attorney engages in an appropriate level of self-disclosure to allow jurors to get to know her as a person, portrays her humanity by conveying natural emotional responses to statements made during the trial, and achieves a delicate balance between being combative and being courteous toward opposing counsel.

Crawford (1989) also places the burden on the attorney to hold jurors' attention throughout the trial, indicating that attention relates to perceived credibility. To keep jurors' attention, Crawford states that attorneys must communicate, nonverbally as well as verbally, a deep commitment to the virtue of their case. He cautions that research has demonstrated that when the nonverbal message conveyed through facial expression, eye contact, posture, or gestures contradicts the verbal message, listeners will dismiss the words and believe the message being conveyed by the body. Attorneys can also keep jurors' attention through the use of vocal inflection, varied pace of speech, and moving about the courtroom during opening and closing statements and while questioning witnesses.

Contrary to Matheo and DeCaro (2001), Crawford (1989) recommends against memorization of the opening statement and closing argument. He notes that memorizing long speeches such as those consumes precious trial preparation time and sets the attorney up for embarrassment due to forgetting or losing one's place in front of the jury. Crawford advises that an alternative to memorization is the use of a mnemonic system that assists the attorney as he moves from one point to the next; by linking key points to previously learned anchor words (or "pegs"), the attorney moves forward through the speech without losing his place or leaving out important arguments.

Although he does not cite empirical research findings in his book, many of Crawford's recommendations are supported by research on persuasion. Speakers are most persuasive when they are perceived as likable, credible, and trustworthy (Chaiken & Maheswaran, 1994; Patton & Kaericher, 1980). Speakers who present both sides of the argument, revealing weaknesses in their own side while refuting the other side's arguments, are perceived as trustworthy (Crowley & Hoyer, 1994; Schlenker, 1980; Williams et al., 1993). We do like those whom we perceive to be similar to ourselves, so when the attorney reveals personal information to jurors and conveys natural emotional responses, jurors are likely to become aware of commonalities, which may enhance their liking of the attorney (Mackie, Worth, & Asuncion, 1990). In addition, likable sources tend to be more persuasive than unlikable sources; however, this tendency is dependent on argument quality and listener involvement in the message. When listeners are highly involved (i.e., motivated and able to attend to the message content), likability is not important; their persuasion is based on argument quality. It is the low-involved listeners who are most likely to be affected by the likability of the speaker, as they are less likely to scrutinize the arguments and more likely to rely on the mental shortcut that a likable speaker is more credible (Chaiken, 1980). Therefore, attorneys must be advised that they cannot get by on charm alone, as long as the jurors are paying attention and caring about the outcome of the case.

Crawford's recommendation that attorneys allow jurors to get to know them personally through some degree of self-disclosure is consistent with the suggestion discussed in this chapter's section on direct examination: allow your witness to reveal personal information about him- or herself to create an emotional bond with jurors (Klein & Kochman, 1998). People do have greater liking for those who are demographically and behaviorally similar to themselves (Glaman, Jones, & Rozelle, 1996). However, research suggests that attorneys need to be careful when using self-disclosure as an ingratiation tool (Chaiken & Derlega, 1974a, 1974b; Chelune, 1976). In one study, Chaiken and Derlega (1974a) found that unreciprocated self-disclosure was considered less appropriate than the same disclosure when it was reciprocated. In another study, Chelune (1976) manipulated the amount of self-disclosure to a stranger by either a male or a female speaker. Results suggested that observers tend to like male speakers more when they disclose less, but like female speakers more when they disclose more. Although both male and female observers made this distinction, it was more pronounced for female observers, who had strong feelings against high-disclosing men and in favor of high-disclosing women.

All of this attention paid to the attorney's style may be much ado about nothing (or about very little). Shari Seidman Diamond and her colleagues (1996) showed more than 1,900 jury-eligible citizens a videotaped simulation of either a death penalty trial or an antitrust price-fixing trial. Following the trial, jurors completed a questionnaire assessing their reactions to the trial, the witnesses, and the attorneys, and they then deliberated in groups of 6 to 12 jurors. The deliberations were videotaped. Researchers found that specific references to the attorneys were made at a rate of just four per deliberation, and only 7% of those comments referred to jurors' personal reactions to the attorneys. The majority of comments related to substantive points brought out by the attorneys during arguments or through questioning of a witness.

Conclusions

We have reviewed a sampling of recommendations made by attorneys and by trial consultants regarding trial strategies and have found considerable overlap between recommendations that attorneys make to each other and those made by trial consultants. We have also shown that some of those recommendations are supported by empirical research findings; some are refuted by those findings; and for a number of recommendations, there is not sufficient research to either support or refute them. Trial consultants and lawyers recommend that opening statements tell a story and that they take advantage of primacy and recency effects, all of which are supported by the research. Trial consultants additionally suggest that attorneys, in making their opening statements, focus on the behavior of the opposing party, reveal their own case weaknesses, and deliver the defense opening immediately following the prosecution's opening. Again, all of these recommendations are supported empirically. Similar suggestions are made by attorneys and trial consultants regarding direct examination and, while most have not been tested in that context, it seems likely that the research would generally support the existence of primacy, recency, and thunder-stealing effects there, as well.

Less is known about support for recommendations regarding cross-examination. Specifically, research is needed to examine the effects of the use of aggressive strategies during cross-examination, as those strategies are recommended in some type and degree by attorneys and trial consultants alike. How do jurors respond when an attorney interrupts the witness, questions the witness's credibility, or points out witness behaviors in an attempt to make him or her anxious? Do the age and sex of the attorney and the witness make a difference? And what of the recommendations made by attorneys regarding proxemics during direct and cross-examination? How do jurors respond when an attorney invades a witness's space during cross, or touches a witness during direct? The proxemics issue was not addressed in the sample of trial-consulting literature we reviewed and has not been adequately addressed in the empirical research.

Recommendations made by attorneys and trial consultants regarding closing arguments receive mixed support from the research. Reliance on primacy and recency effects is again consistent with research findings. However, research suggests that lawyers should not leave it to jurors to draw their own conclusions—this is a risky strategy, as there is no guarantee that the conclusions reached by jurors will be the same as those desired by the lawyers. More research is needed to determine whether, and to what extent, lawyers should rely on emotional appeals or ingratiate themselves to the jury during their closing statements.

Finally, a number of stylistic recommendations can be found in the trial-consulting literature. Some of the recommendations are so vaguely stated in the literature that they are virtually untestable. For example, what does it mean to act like a human being, or to advertise your competence in everything you say or do? In some cases, the authors offer no more specific recommendations. For some suggestions, such as memorizing the opening statement, research findings are directly contradictory. For others, there has been little or no research conducted to examine their validity. These include the use of vocal inflection changes, various forms of body language, or moving around in the courtroom while addressing the jury. Finally, some of the recommendations regarding attorney style are directly consistent with empirical research findings relevant to persuasion.

Our evaluation of the trial strategy recommendations made by trial consultants leads us to conclude that, for the most part, they are supported by research findings. This is especially true for opening statements and direct examination and less so for stylistic suggestions. Where there is not empirical support for the recommendations, it is more often due to an absence of any research on the recommended strategy than it is to a direct contradiction with research findings. Although the absence of research might be viewed as a failure within the academic or social scientific communities, we also question the ethics of making recommendations that have not been empirically validated.

As to the question of the extent to which attorneys can really benefit from the aid of trial consultants in their trial strategies, it appears that attorneys have a good sense of what they should and should not do during the course of a trial. They recognize the importance of primacy and recency effects and of making clear opening statements that provide jurors with thematic frameworks, and most recommend against delaying the defense opening statement. Furthermore, they caution against promising too much in the opening, as an alert opposing attorney will likely make the jury aware of any unfulfilled promises. When it comes to trial strategy, then, attorneys may not have much need for trial consultants once the trial begins. Before settling on this conclusion, however, it is prudent to ask, how likely is it that attorneys, on their own, will follow their own advice?

Linz et al. (1986) had trained undergraduate students observe and code the trial behaviors of prosecuting and defense attorneys during their opening statements in 50 criminal trials. Behaviors were coded according to level of articulateness, friendliness, enthusiasm, formality, humorousness, nervousness, and arrogance. The statements were coded for degree of complexity, organization, emotionality, repetitiveness, education on relevant law, emphasis on victim or defendant background, use of exhibits, informativeness, and the tendency to relate opinions rather than facts. In addition to the student evaluations, the attorneys were questioned after the trial regarding their perceptions of their own performance, and jurors were asked to evaluate the attorneys posttrial.

The trained in-court observers rated the prosecuting attorneys as more legally and factually informative and better organized than they did the defense attorneys; defense attorneys were perceived to be more enthusiastic than were prosecutors. At the same time, defense attorneys' evaluations of their own opening statements systematically differed from the observers' ratings on the variables of emphasis on facts, educating on the law, and building one's argument. Furthermore, when compared to ratings made by actual jurors, defense attorneys consistently rated their overall performance more favorably than did the jurors. Self-perceptions of defense attorneys with the most trial experience were the most discrepant from jurors' assessments, especially regarding the stylistic qualities of articulateness, enthusiasm, friendliness, likableness, and arrogance. Defense attorneys overrated their own performances on all variables except arrogance, which they underestimated. Prosecutors' self-ratings, on the other hand, did not differ from those made by jurors. Therefore, defense attorneys, at least, might benefit from frank feedback from a trial consultant regarding both the content of their opening statements and their demeanor in the courtroom.

6

What Do We Know About Jury Deliberations and the Determinants of Jury Decisions?

The ultimate goal of all trial consultants is an outcome that achieves success for their clients, whether it is a favorable settlement or the desired trial verdict. Since many of the cases lead to a trial by a jury, it is important to describe just what we know about how juries operate and what determines their verdicts. For example, what motivates jurors? How much do juries pay attention to the evidence? Do those who possess prior experience as jurors play a dominant role? Knowledge gleaned from empirical research on jury deliberations dates almost entirely from the last 4 decades, but it is increasing at a rapid rate, especially with regard to juries in civil cases. Trial consultants need to make these research results available to their clients. Thus the goal of this chapter is to move beyond the empirical knowledge about courtroom procedures described in chapter 5, to substantive matters relevant to the jury's decisions.

Jurors Differ; Juries Differ

The fact-finding task is a difficult one; two jurors can view the same set of facts differently, and each may emphasize a different set of facts in forming his or her individual verdict. The sheer variety of backgrounds of jurors— even those few participating in the same trial—virtually assures that in some respects, they will think differently. Terms like "reasonable doubt" in a criminal trial and "pain and suffering" in a civil trial have different meanings for different jurors. Consider the task of deciding the value of a lost human life. The special master whose job is to allocate the U.S. government's compensation fund for the deaths in the September 11, 2001, attacks on the World Trade Center and the Pentagon had to decide the compensation for the families of each of the 3,200 victims. While it is true that lawyers and actuaries determined a payment structure for catastrophic death years ago, the emotion associated with the terrorists' attacks has made the task of the mediator, Kenneth Feinberg, exceedingly subjective and difficult. How does the loss of a 25-year-old janitor compare with the loss of a 65-year-old stockbroker? Doubtless if the decision were to be made by a set of individuals—rather than left solely in Feinberg's hands—they would produce different decisions in the awards made to any specific victim.

Likewise, juries differ. Samples of only 6 to 12 persons, drawn from a diverse population of potential jurors, can lead to different biases from one jury to another; it is not uncommon, when several mock juries hear the same set of facts, that they lead to wide variations in verdicts or awards. By the luck of the sample, one holdout in a criminal trial can lead to a hung jury—and perhaps to no retrial—even when the vast majority of jurors stand in agreement. Similarly, in a civil trial, one juror's individual judgment of the appropriate award to the plaintiff may be quite out of line with those of the remaining jurors and yet still influence the jury's eventual award.

But diversity of responses to the same set of facts is human, and judges—supposedly more experienced and informed than jurors—can also reflect such diversity. For example, a number of years ago, 47 district court judges at a workshop were asked to read the facts of a hypothetical case and to render a verdict and sentence. Of these, 29 found the defendant guilty and 18 found her not guilty, and a similar lack of consensus was found in the sentences assigned by the 18 judges who gave a punishment (Austin & Utne, 1977; Austin & Williams, 1977).

Jury verdicts have a reputation of being unreliable, in the sense that many experienced trial attorneys believe that you can't predict what a given jury's verdict will be. But are the decisions of several juries for the same set of facts any more inconsistent than those of several judges? Even Supreme Court justices can differ; in the 2001–2002 term of the U.S. Supreme Court, 28% of the cases were decided by the closest vote possible, a 5–4 vote, and only in a little more than one third of the cases (36%) were the justices in unanimous agreement. Granted, the task of Supreme Court justices is different from that of a trial jury—the Court determines the applicability of laws or constitutional principles—but the justices, like jurors, have their own subjective evaluations of terms, and sometimes their decisions rest on their idiosyncratic selection of facts or definition of terms. For example, in a 1992 case (*Jacobson v. United States*), a defendant convicted of obtaining child pornography claimed he had been entrapped, and the majority of the justices agreed that the government's attempts to tempt him to break the law were too heavy-handed. A minority opinion by Justice Sandra Day O'Connor, however, disagreed with the majority over just what constituted a "predisposition" by the defendant. In a case decided in 2002 (*Carey v. Saffold*), again by a 5–4 vote, a crucial aspect was that the justices disagreed about the meaning of the term "pending."

So individuality and subjectivity are pervasive human phenomena. Certainly individual jurors and the group verdicts of juries differ, but can we draw some general conclusions about the determinants of their behavior? We believe we can.

The rest of this chapter presents a summary of the knowledge of jury behavior provided by 4 decades of social science research. First, we confront the stereotypes about juries, especially that they are lenient. Then we evaluate whether they differ from judges and other experts in their decisions; the results here are more complex than the stereotype. Then we consider the causes of individual jurors' decisions, and finally we examine what is known about the procedures that juries use in making their group decisions. Thus the chapter considers the determinants of individual jurors, prior to deliberation, before turning to the final issue of the effects of deliberations on eventual outcomes.

Do Juries Differ From Judges and Other Experts?

Juries are often faulted for their "erroneous" verdicts; generally the public believes that juries reach outcomes that are too lenient. That is, they believe criminal juries let guilty defendants "off" and that civil trial juries make excessive awards to plaintiffs. It is impossible, in most cases, to determine whether the verdict was an incorrect one; there is no correct answer in the back of the book. But we can compare the verdicts of juries with those of judges and other experts. When we do so, we find that juries are not as deviant as the public presupposes.

Kalven and Zeisel's Study of Juries and Judges

In comparing juries and experts, we first ask: how similar are their verdicts? Given the same information, would judges presiding at a trial render the same decision that juries, given this responsibility, make? An empirical answer exists for this question, and it is reassuring, although it is flawed.

Starting 50 years ago, a law professor and a statistician/sociology professor at the University of Chicago, Harry Kalven, Jr., and Hans Zeisel, began a series of studies of the jury system in the United States that was eventually published in 1966. In one of their studies, each trial judge in the United States (whether a state or federal judge) was sent a questionnaire by mail. The judge was asked to select a recent jury trial over which he or she had presided and to respond to a number of questions, including the judge's hypothetical verdict as well as the jury's actual verdict. The first wave of questionnaires was distributed in 1954 and 1955; somewhat more structured questionnaires were sent to judges in 1958. A total of 555 judges responded; some judges described only one trial, but others provided a large number. The result was a database of thousands of trials, clearly an impressive number but, unfortunately, by no means a random sample of jury trials.

In the 3,576 trials that were criminal trials, the judge's hypothetical verdict agreed with the jury's actual verdict in approximately 75% of the cases; the specific percentage depends on whether one includes the 5–6% of the trials in which the jury did not reach a verdict. These findings are sometimes interpreted as supporting a conclusion that the jury system in the United States "works," that juries agree with judges' verdicts to a significant and hence satisfactory degree. Perhaps implicit in such a conclusion is the treatment of the judge's verdict as a criterion, as the correct decision. But such an assumption is too simplistic; first of all, judges possess certain information about the case that jurors may not have. For example, in the United States, if a criminal defendant does not testify, the jury will not know whether he or she has a criminal record. Judges have defendants' past records in their files, and Kalven and Zeisel's study was not able to control how many individual judges actually used such information in determining their hypothetical verdicts. If many did, this means that the "75% agreement" is actually an *underestimate* of the true level of agreement.

What do these results say about leniency? It is true that the jury convicted the defendant less often than the judge would have (64% versus 83% of the time). But juries still found the defendant guilty in most of the cases; the results fail to substantiate a rampant fear that citizen-juries are giving defendants unlimited freedom. When we place this outcome with the fact that the vast majority of those charged with a crime plea bargain (85–95% do), the system is generally achieving its goals of convicting those suspected of law breaking.

Another source of uncontrolled variation was the reason or reasons for selecting particular trials by the judge. Did the judge select a particular trial to be the one included in the survey because in that one, the jury's verdict was consistent with what the judge would have done? Or because it was inconsistent? Or simply because it was the most recent jury trial? We do not know, but we can be sure that different judges had different reasons, and this uncontrolled aspect of the procedure makes interpretation of the results more problematic. But the overall results have been substantiated by a recent survey of 300 jury trials in four different jurisdictions (Eisenberg, Hannaford-Agar, Hans, Mott, & Munsterman, 2004). In this study, the judges were asked what their verdicts would be while the jury was deliberating. Juries agreed with the judge 75% of the time—amazingly, the same percentage as in the study published 40 years before. The conviction rate for juries was 63% (compared to 64% earlier) and for judges, it was 81% (compared to the earlier 83%).

Kalven and Zeisel chose to focus on some of the possible reasons that jury verdicts sometimes differed from the judges' hypothetical verdicts.

Under a category that they called "jury sentiments" (which accounted for at least half of the disagreements), they included acquittals by juries based on their feeling that the case was too trivial for formal review, plus acquittals based on a belief that the defendant had already suffered enough, as well as other nonevidentiary reactions to the defendant, the prosecution, and the legal system. In contrast, these authors saw judges' verdicts as sticking closer to the law and the weight of the evidence. However, they noted that such jury sentiments were more likely to occur when, according to the judge, the evidence in the case was close and capable of supporting either verdict. Thus they proposed a "liberation hypothesis," arguing that the closeness of the evidence freed the jurors to give weight to their own feelings of justice (Kalven & Zeisel, 1966).

Surveys of jury "accuracy" have also been done in Great Britain, with the result being a general endorsement of jury effectiveness. As Baldwin and McConville (1979) noted, sometimes it is difficult to evaluate the methodology because details are not provided, but McCabe and Purves (1972) concluded that only one out of every eight acquittals by the jury could be described as "perverse" (i.e., contrary to the law and the evidence). Similarly, Zander (1974), studying 200 acquittals in England's two busiest courts, found the proportion of perverse acquittals to be "exceptionally low." Baldwin and McConville (1979), in analyzing jury trial results in both Birmingham and London, reported that "in almost six cases out of seven, there was no serious complaint about the jury's verdict from most of the respondents we contacted" (p. 130). But they also reported, "Looking at the findings of our research, it is clear that we have classified considerably more jury verdicts as questionable than any other researcher has done" (p. 130).

Awards in Medical Malpractice Cases and Other Civil Cases

Part of the leniency stereotype refers to the decisions of civil-trial juries, especially their purported tendency to sympathize with victims (i.e., plaintiffs) and to give them outrageously high awards. Again, Kalven and Zeisel's survey provides relevant data. The jury found for the plaintiff in 59% of the cases, not surprising since plaintiffs brought the suits; the presiding judge would have found for the plaintiff in 57% of the cases, certainly not a dramatic difference. Agreement between jury and judges occurred in 78% of the cases. These results are consistent with more general findings; in cases tried before juries, plaintiffs win about 55–60% of the time (Moller, 1996), although the success rate varies by type of case—over 60% in auto accident cases, 40% for product liability, but only 30% for medical malpractice (Daniels & Martin, 1995; Merritt & Barry, 1999). This last percentage certainly conflicts with the public's stereotype that jurors are easily duped by patients who falsely claim their doctor was at fault.

Another indication that jury decisions are often consistent with those of experts comes from an impressive set of studies in which Neil Vidmar

(1995) compared juries' decisions in medical malpractice cases with those given by experts. In one study, mock jurors' awards were compared with the awards by panels of arbitrators composed of three experienced lawyers. In a case involving a medical accident during elective surgery that led to burns and pain for the patient, the median award to the plaintiff by 21 lawyers acting as arbitrators was $57,000, a figure actually higher than the median award by 89 jurors of $47,850. (The difference was not statistically significant.) However, the awards made by different jurors were much more variable than those by the arbitrators. Among the 89 jurors, awards ranged from $11,000 to $197,000, while the arbitrators' awards ranged from $22,000 to $82,000; thus the *range* of awards by the lawyers was only one third that of the jurors.

A second study, once again considering a claim of medical negligence, used an entirely different group of attorneys, who had been certified by the state as mediators. When the defendant was an individual (a doctor), awards by jurors were slightly less than those by lawyers, $108,450 versus $111,687. When the defendant was a corporation (a hospital), the jurors' awards were slightly higher than those of the lawyers, $115,890 versus $108,146. Differences were not statistically significant.

A recent study by Jennifer Robbennolt (2002), looking at punitive damage awards, confirmed the findings of Vidmar regarding malpractice awards. Laypersons' decisions were compared with the decisions of trial judges; the average punitive damage award by mock jurors was only 5% higher than the average award by judges, a nonsignificant difference. This research, as well as other studies comparing judges and jurors (cf. Wissler, Hart, & Saks, 1999), finds that both groups give similar weight to the severity of the injury in making compensatory damage awards.

The Expert-Novice Distinction

The supposed difference in the determination of verdicts by professionals and by juries reflects the expert-novice distinction that achieved some visibility in experimental psychology in the 1980s (Chi, Glaser, & Farr, 1988). Experts are seen as better able to discern "the big picture" and meaningful patterns in their areas of expertise; they can process information faster than can novices; and they see the deeper implications of the material in their domain. But a faster processing of information does not necessarily mean a more valid one, and the advantage of the expertise of the judge must be balanced against the exceedingly high motivation to do a good job present in most juries. This is especially true when one considers that judgments of credibility of witnesses are central to the fact finding in many criminal trials, and judicial expertise is probably not a contributor to accuracy in this regard.

Like Kalven and Zeisel, like Vidmar, and like Robbennolt, we believe that most jurors are conscientious and try to do a good job. They take their task seriously and, on occasion, show excellent foresight by doing things that increase the likelihood of a well-reasoned and fair verdict. For example, in the trial of Juan Corona, charged with a series of murders, the jury did not take its first vote until the second day of deliberation. This vote was five for guilty and seven for not guilty. But two of the seven who voted not guilty did so in order to prevent the jury from reaching a premature decision. To quote one: "I voted innocent, too. But not because I have any doubts that Corona isn't guilty. I was just afraid we might've convicted him on the first ballot and I don't think that's right. I think we should do all kinds of talking and explaining before we convict a man of murder" (Villasenor, 1977, p. 58).

Conclusions

Some juries find criminal defendants not guilty when the evidence appears to lead to an opposite conclusion. And some juries in personal injury cases make excessive awards to injured parties. These decisions, by the sheer nature of their outrageousness, get attention in the media, and the public remembers them. But we believe the major source of the problem is in the *variability* in jury awards. As we have seen, and as will be illustrated in subsequent sections of this chapter, the group process in jury deliberations exacerbates this effect, and certain activities by trial lawyers do also.

However, in general, jurors "tend to reach decisions that largely agree with those of legal experts" (Feigenson, 2000, p. 4). Law professor Alan W. Scheflin (1995), commenting on the diary of a juror in the Menendez brothers' trial, wrote:

> By reading juror books, such as those written by Villasenor (1977)
> on the Juan Corona mass murder trial, by Kennebeck (1973) on
> a trial of thirteen Black Panther party members, and by Timothy
> (1974; see Scheflin, 1977) on the Angela Davis trial, one's faith is
> restored. We see how neighbors and strangers from all walks of life
> and from diverse backgrounds conscientiously work together to
> reach a common verdict with which they can all be satisfied. (p. 140)

Thus, trial consultants can provide a useful function when they remind defense attorneys of the role of sentiments in jury decisions and the findings relevant to a decision whether to ask for a jury trial or a bench trial.

The Study of Jurors and the Study of Juries

The goal of this chapter is to specify what we know about jury deliberations: specifically, we want to identify the processes that are used and the substantive qualities that influence outcomes. Those eventual outcomes are *jury* verdicts, that is, one outcome that (often) reflects agreement by every individual juror. (A few jurisdictions do not require unanimity.) Research findings suggest that this eventual group outcome is mostly accounted for by the individual jurors' predeliberation positions. That is, the eventual verdict is quite predictable from the first-ballot votes of the individual jurors (Kalven & Zeisel, 1966). However, the act of deliberating, the group discussion, can have an influence. First, new information can be presented that changes votes, and second, the sheer process of discussion seems to have predictable effects. We discuss these, but first we consider individual jurors' leanings, prior to deliberations.

Given the above, in this chapter one of our emphases is on the processes used by jurors in decision making; we reserve an examination of their content-based beliefs for the next two chapters. As human beings, jurors claim they use "common sense" and that they attempt to be "logical"; they often apply seemingly reasonable standards for evaluating evidence, called *heuristics*; and they have conceptions of what are fairness and justice.

Conceptions of Fairness and Justice

Several recent books that explain jury behavior emphasize a proposition that the prime motive of jurors is to achieve *justice*. Neil Feigenson (2000), in explaining jurors' decisions in accident cases, proposed that jurors seek "total justice." He wrote: "By 'total justice' I mean that jurors are more concerned with making things come out right than with strictly following the relevant legal rules.... jurors *try* to follow the relevant law but are guided by the total justice imperative as they do so" (2000, p. 16; italics in original). "Total justice" is reflected in several different ways:

Jurors "want to balance accounts between the parties" (Feigenson, 2000, p. 16), i.e., they see a contest between the good guys and the bad guys, and they want the good guys to win.

Jurors want to make a just decision in the sense that "it incorporates all the information they think is relevant" (p. 17). Even inadmissible evidence is used if they consider it to be relevant.

Jurors reach their decision through a holistic process; they may "blur distinctions between judgments of responsibility and judgments of compensation, so that the former is improperly influenced by perceptions of the severity of the injury and the latter is improperly influenced by perceptions of blameworthiness" (p. 17).

Jurors want procedural justice among their colleagues; they want to appear to be respectful of other viewpoints, open to persuasion, and generally justice-oriented in an interpersonal sense.

Commonsense Justice

In an influential set of publications, Norman Finkel (1995, 1997, 2001) has coined the term *commonsense justice* to refer to what citizens (and jurors) consider to be just and fair. His empirical work and that of others (Haney,

1997; Horowitz, 1997; Olsen-Fulero & Fulero, 1997) leads to a conclusion that, as Kalven and Zeisel argued 40 years ago, jurors' sentiments may differ from the "black letter" law; that is, they may modify or even reject legal standards if these do not coincide with their sense of justice.

One typical contrast between commonsense approaches and black-letter law is that the latter is more analytic; that is, the law asks jurors to focus on specific factors and determinants. But jurors may believe that it is just to take a wider number of factors into account. Consider, for example, a personal injury case: "the law asks jurors to make compensatory damages assessments . . . by focusing primarily on the severity of the plaintiff's injuries [but] [m]any jurors might prefer to focus on the bigger picture, including the actions of the defendant in causing those injuries. For these jurors, considering only the consequences does little to reveal the entire drama or to deliver justice" (Greene & Bornstein, 2003, p. 39).

Decision Criteria in Criminal and Civil Trials

If a juror serves on a jury in a criminal trial, it is difficult for him or her to avoid entering the courtroom free of predispositions. As we will illustrate in detail in chapters 7 and 8, decision making is not done by jurors who are "blank slates."

Probability of Commission and Reasonable Doubt

With regard to jurors' decisions in criminal trials, virtually all the legal and psychological conceptions of how a juror makes decisions propose that verdicts reflect the implicit operation of two judgments on the part of jurors. One is an estimate of the *probability of commission*; that is, how likely is it that the defendant committed the crime? Individual jurors will base their estimates of the probability of commission on the relative weight of the evidence on either side. (But it is likely that their beliefs and previous experiences will also have an impact.)

A second judgment by the juror concerns the standard of *reasonable doubt*; jurors in criminal cases are instructed that they should bring back a verdict of not guilty if there is any reasonable doubt of the defendant's guilt. But conceptions of justice can affect the application of this standard. For example, Horowitz (1997) considered the level of certainty necessary to convict in a criminal trial. The standard for conviction in a criminal trial is, of course, that the defendant be proved guilty "beyond a reasonable doubt." But the definition of this standard varies from jurisdiction to jurisdiction, and sometimes these definitions are not very helpful.

In fact, judges are loath to quantify "reasonable doubt" (they are uncomfortable with statistics and percentages) but Dane (1985) applied statistical reasoning to Justice Byron White's descriptions of the term in his opinion in *Johnson v. Louisiana* (1972) and estimated that it reflected an 88%

certainty of guilt. But research by Irwin Horowitz and his colleagues (Horowitz, 1997; Horowitz & Kirkpatrick, 1996) concluded that jurors "set the bar for conviction at a level significantly lower than anticipated by jurists" (Horowitz, 1997, p. 298). Horowitz (1997) suggested:

> One potential explanation is that jurors in recent years may have altered the balance between due process and crime-control values. An emphasis on crime control may have resulted in a decrease in the jurors' subjective threshold of certainty of guilt: thus juries may be willing to convict on a lower standard than generally envisioned by the courts. Given the inherent imprecision that characterizes definitions of *beyond reasonable doubt*, jurors have ample room to construe the level of certainty required for conviction. (pp. 298–299; italics in original)

Individual Jurors' Decisions in Civil Trials

In a civil trial, the decision-making process by jurors is somewhat different from that in a criminal trial. Jurors must determine fault, and if the defendant is at fault, must judge the extent and severity of the plaintiff's losses. They must convert these judged losses into a dollar value. They may award punitive damages as well as amounts for actual damages or losses.

It has been proposed (Kalven, 1958; Greene, 1989; Greene & Bornstein, 2003) that jurors may use one of two processes in converting their assessments of injuries into dollar values; they may use a process called *anchoring and adjustment*, in which they calculate individual components of the loss and then add them together, or they may use a more *holistic reasoning process*, in which analysis and computation are not used.

Anchoring and Adjustment

In some jurisdictions, plaintiffs' lawyers may suggest what they consider to be an acceptable damage award, and they may employ economists or other experts to testify about earning potential that would have accumulated had not the plaintiff been injured or killed. Similarly, defense attorneys may counter with their own recommended figures. These may serve as anchors, or numerical reference points, for jurors; as Greene and Bornstein (2003) observe, "anchors are likely to carry weight in decisions about damages because people may lack confidence in their own ability to assign dollar values to various injuries" (2003, p. 150). When they do so, they are using what Tversky and Kahneman (1974) called the *anchoring and adjustment heuristic.*

But when an anchor is suggested, one of two types of responses can occur. If the anchor falls within the range of response alternatives considered acceptable by the juror—called originally by Sherif and Hovland (1961) the *latitude of acceptance*—then *assimilation* occurs, and the juror's ballpark value moves toward the anchor value. But if the suggested anchor amount falls outside the juror's range of acceptable amounts—the juror's *latitude of rejection*—then a *contrast effect* occurs, with the juror shifting away from the anchor. The research on this phenomenon certainly leads to a conclusion that assimilation occurs more often than does contrast. Summarizing their review, Greene and Bornstein (2003) supported a conclusion that "the more you ask for, the more you get" (p. 152):

> In a particularly compelling demonstration of this effect, Hinsz and Indahl (1995) showed mock jurors a re-enactment of a civil trial in which the defendant was being sued for wrongful death by the parents of two children killed in an automobile accident. In one condition, the plaintiff's lawyer requested $2 million, and in a second condition requested $20 million. Jurors were asked to fairly and reasonably compensate the plaintiffs for the losses they had sustained. The mean award for the "$2 Million" condition was $1,052, 917, and the mean for the "$20 Million" condition was a whopping $9,061,538! (p. 152)

What are the limits of assimilation? Chapman and Bornstein (1996) included an inordinately high request, for $1 billion, by a plaintiff who testified that her birth control pills had led to ovarian cancer. In contrast, in the other condition, the same plaintiff asked for relatively much less, $5 million. Even though the jurors rated the plaintiff who asked for more as being more selfish and less honorable, they still awarded her significantly more money than those exposed to the $5 million request. This is an example in which the trial advocacy manuals—those that advise the plaintiff's attorney to exaggerate the amount requested for damages—are supported by the results of empirical research. Although some studies find a boomerang effect for requesting a high award—or possibly a contrast effect (Malouff & Schutte, 1989; Marti & Wissler, 2000)—they are in the minority.

What happens when the jurors are confronted with two proposals for compensation, one from the plaintiff's attorney and one from the defendant's? Logic would expect that—assuming the parties are credible—some intermediate figure, between these two anchors, would become the award. Studies find that the defense is effective in reducing the award, but little support was found for an expectation that jurors would "split the difference" (Ellis, 2002; Marti & Wissler, 2000; Raitz, Greene, Goodman, & Loftus, 1990).

Reports of jury deliberations in some actual trials reflect jurors' use of a component-by-component assessment of damage awards (summarized by Greene & Bornstein, 2003, pp. 157–158). Many states use special verdict forms that instruct jurors to break down awards into elements or components. One study concluded that this requirement to focus on individual elements of damages causes the awards to be higher than a condition in which the jury is allowed to select a figure that "just seems right" (Wiggins & Breckler, 1990).

The Holistic Approach

Economic damages are susceptible to a component-by-component determination of awards, but other types of damages are less so—for example, awards for pain and suffering. The few studies relevant to this approach "support the notion that jurors may have an overall impression of what an injury or loss is worth, and rather than concerning themselves with the damage components, as an accountant might, instead search for a sum that they feel is appropriate" (Greene & Bornstein, 2003, p. 160).

Determining Punitive Damages

In civil trials, if the jury finds that the defendant is at fault, it may also have the opportunity to award punitive damages against the defendant in addition to compensatory damages.

Instructions to the Jury

Although the judge's instructions about punitive damages vary from jurisdiction to jurisdiction, the following is typical:

> Defendant's mental state—General instruction:
> If you find from the evidence that [the defendant] is guilty of wanton, willful, malicious, or reckless conduct that shows an indifference to the rights of others, then you may make an award of punitive damages in this case.
> Defendant's mental state—"Willful" and "wanton" defined:
> In order for the conduct of the defendant to constitute willfulness or wantonness, his/her acts must be done under circumstances which show that he/she was aware from his/her knowledge of existing conditions that it is probable that injury would result from his/her acts and omissions, and nevertheless proceeded with reckless indifference and without care for the rights of others. . . . It is not necessary to find that the defendant deliberately intended to injure the plaintiff. It is sufficient if the plaintiff proves by the greater weight of the evidence that the defendant intentionally acted in such a way that the natural and probable consequence of his/her act was injury to the plaintiff. (Sunstein, Hastie, Payne, Schkade, & Viscusi, 2002, p. 12)

Also the jury may be told that it must conclude that harm to the plaintiff was the "foreseeable and probable effect" of the defendant's behavior.

Once the jury concludes that the defendant's behavior has reflected the above descriptions, its task is to set the dollar amount of the punitive damages. Again, specific instructions vary; here is California's:

In arriving at any award of punitive damages, you are to consider the following:

1. The reprehensibility of the conduct of the defendant.
2. The amount of punitive damages which will have a deterrent effect on the defendant in light of the defendant's financial condition. (Sunstein et al., 2002, p. 13)

Typically, jurors are told that "the law provides no fixed standards as to the amount of such punitive damages, but leaves the amount to the jury's sound discretion, exercised without passion or prejudice" (Sunstein et al., 2002, p. 13).

Problems With Punitive Damage Awards

Although theoretically the opportunity to award punitive damages occurs in only a few cases, the incidence of punitive damage verdicts and the magnitude of awards have increased dramatically in the United States in the last 2 decades, such that legislation has been introduced to limit them. Furthermore, the U.S. Supreme Court has tried to restrict punitive damages; in 1996 it found that a jury award of punitive damages was excessive (*BMW of North America, Inc. v. Gore*), and in 2003 (in the case of *State Farm Mutual v. Campbell*), it ruled that such damages should not excessively exceed the award of compensatory damages. Here are some of the awards that have fueled the movement to put caps on punitive damage awards:

In May 1999, an Alabama jury made a punitive damage award of $580 million, although the economic damages to the plaintiff were claimed to be no more than a mere $600.

In July 1999, a California jury awarded punitive damages of $4.8 *billion* in a class-action suit against General Motors.

In December 1999, a federal judge upheld a jury's punitive damages award of $250 million against Chrysler Corporation. (Sunstein et al., 2002, p. 1)

Social scientists and law professors have recently sought to understand the decision-making process of jurors in their awards of punitive damages. For example, one of the goals of the tort-reform movement is to put caps on damage awards in civil cases. Robbennolt and Studebaker (1999) found that when the court placed a cap on compensatory and punitive damage awards, this action affected the actual size of the awards made by jurors. For example, when the punitive damage cap was $100,000, the average award was

$83,100, but when it was $50 million, the average award skyrocketed to $9 million.

A recent interdisciplinary contribution is the book *Punitive Damages: How Juries Decide*, by a team of law professors and social scientists affiliated with the University of Chicago (Sunstein et al., 2002). One of the features of the studies reported in this book is that, thanks to foundation support, the researchers were able to recruit respondents from the jury pool and pay them for their time. A total of more than 8,000 respondents participated, forming more than 600 juries. Each study reported in this book used large numbers of respondents and took the time to question them in detail about their decision making. The cases given to the respondents were based on real cases.

Sunstein, Hastie, and their colleagues, in developing a psychology of punitive awards, established what they called the *outrage model*:

> The essential claim is that the moral transgressions of others evoke an attitude of outrage, which combines an emotional evaluation and a response tendency.... Under the outrage model, punitive damages are considered to be an expression of an angry or indignant attitude toward a transgressor. The evaluative aspect of the attitude is labeled *outrage*; the response tendency is labeled *punitive intent*. Outrage is basic, and punitive intent is measured by outrage and additional factors, such as the degree of harm suffered by the plaintiff. Although punitive intent is affected by some factors that do not affect outrage, our original hypothesis is that most of the determinants of the two states are shared—and we therefore expect them to be highly correlated. (Sunstein et al., 2002, pp. 32–33; italics in original)

Outrage and punitive intent are internal psychological states; they must be converted into a behavior of assigning a value, in this case a dollar amount.

Specific Factors That Affect Punitive Awards

Stereotypes—often plausible ones—abound about the specific aspects of a situation that affect the award of punitive damages. To assess whether demographic factors affected awards, Sunstein et al. (2002) gave 899 jury-eligible respondents from Travis County, Texas, summaries of 10 realistic personal injury cases. In each case, compensatory damages in the amount of $200,000 had already been awarded; the juror's job was to consider whether to award punitive damages. Different sets of jurors answered one of the following three questions for each of the 10 cases:

1. How outrageous was the defendant's behavior (on a scale of 0 = *not at all outrageous* to 6 = *absolutely outrageous*)?
2. How much should the defendant be punished? (The scale was from 0 = *no punishment* to 6 = *extremely severe punishment*.)

3. How much should the defendant be required to pay in punitive damages?

To determine if members of different demographic groups responded similarly, rankings of the different trial summaries were computed. For different groups, the correlations were "essentially perfect.... Men and women, Hispanics, African Americans, and Whites, and respondents at very different levels of income and education produced almost identical orderings of scenarios used in the study" (Sunstein et al., 2002, p. 35). This finding reaffirms the earlier conclusion that jurors share a common view of what is fair, what is right and what is wrong; this shared moral sense is similar regardless of the jurors' age, gender, or race.

The size of the defendant's company—whether a large corporation or a family business—has also been postulated to affect punitive-damage awards. Sunstein and his fellow researchers hypothesized that the size of the firm would not affect levels of outrage or punitive intent, but would affect the size of punitive damage awards. Respondents in the previous study were presented scenarios in which the size of the defendant's company varied, with "large" companies having profits of $100 million to $200 million a year, and "medium-sized" companies having profits of $10 million to $20 million per year. As expected, only with regard to punitive damage awards did this make a difference; large firms were punished with much larger dollar awards (an average of $1,009, 994) than were medium-sized firms (an average of $526,398).

Is there a "home-town" bias, that is, do jurors make larger awards if the plaintiff is local and the defendant is distant? A total of 375 jury-eligible respondents in Reno, Nevada, saw a videotaped narration and read a summary of a case in which a train derailed and dumped toxic herbicide into a river. The amount of $24 million in compensatory damages had already been paid. The identities of the plaintiff were varied so that half of the jurors were told that the plaintiff was either a local fish hatchery or a division of a food company with headquarters in Toronto, Canada. Also, half were told the defendant was either a local railroad company there in Nevada, or a railroad company with headquarters in Chicago.

A little more than one fourth of the jurors indicated no punitive damage award should be made. Among those who did make awards, larger awards were made against remote defendants and larger awards were given to local plaintiffs, but neither effect was statistically significant. Yet local plaintiffs received 36% higher awards than did remote plaintiffs on average, a difference in median awards of $4.2 million. Thus a second study was done in an attempt to clarify these inconsistencies.

Again, respondents were from Reno, Nevada; these 293 respondents gave significantly greater awards to the local plaintiffs, a difference of $25 million. But remote defendants were assessed only a slightly higher penalty than local defendants; this effect was not significant. The authors concluded: "This finding is not inconsistent with wealth redistribution, but it may be better described as a bias to favor local recipients" (Sunstein et al., 2002, p. 73).

The Effect of Plaintiff's Strategies: Is It Better to Ask for More?

Previously we discussed the anchoring and adjustment process, in which jurors consider a tentative value and work from there. Sunstein and his collaborators sought to determine if this process is applicable to the award of punitive damages. In the study described above that involved a train derailment, two award-anchor conditions were created by changing the plaintiff's request in the closing argument from a relatively low level of punitive damages ($15–50 million) to a relatively high level ($50–150 million). The mock jurors made awards that were about two-and-one-half times larger when the request was high. The researchers commented:

> Thus, there is some order to the highly variable dollar awards. In particular, the results underscore the central role of salient anchor values in mock jurors' reasoning about awards. The numbers highlighted in the plaintiff's closing argument and the amount of the compensatory award dominated the process of transforming punishment intent into a dollar value. The power of the plaintiff's request is especially impressive given the large collection of numbers that were presented to the mock jurors as evidence to describe the defendant's financial status (two tables containing approximately forty numbers plus accompanying exposition). (Sunstein et al., 2002, p. 69)

Thus, trial consultants can advise lawyers regarding the size of the request. Furthermore, most attorneys will be surprised to learn that the research cited here indicates that demographic characteristics offer little predictability.

Jury Deliberations

We now switch from the individual juror to the jury's group verdict as the topic of study. First, we consider the legal system's ideals about deliberations. These are worthy of scrutiny because they establish the ground rules for how deliberations are supposed to proceed. Then we consider what social science research has uncovered about the typical procedures in jury deliberations. Finally, we seek to answer the question: what is the effect of the deliberation process on outcomes?

The Legal System's Conception of Jury Functioning

All of us have a conception of how a jury deliberates, even if we have never been on a jury. And the legal system has its own conception of how a jury should deliberate. Although expressions of this conception are only sporadically found in court decisions and statutes, three aspects seem salient.

Independence and Equality

The legal system focuses on decisions by *juries*, not *jurors*. The newspaper and television accounts of a spectacular trial announce that "the *jury* found a verdict of..." One of the supposed benefits of the jury is its functioning as a *group*. In such representations, the legal system seems to make several assumptions about the nature of individual jurors. First, it is assumed that the jury is composed of 12—or 6, or 8, or however many required—*independent* and *equal* individuals who each contribute to the final verdict. As Kassin and Wrightsman (1988) noted:

> The courts attempt to foster this ideal in a number of ways. For example, judges instruct jurors to refrain from discussing the trial with each other until they retire for their deliberations. In this way, each juror develops his or her unique perspective on the case, uncontaminated by others' views. This ensures not only the independence of individual members but also the diversity of the group as a whole. (p. 172)

When the legal system sets an ideal of each juror being *independent* and *equal*, it establishes a high standard, because in most real-life groups such qualities do not exist. It is true that in the jury room, each juror is equal to every other in the sense that everyone has been exposed to the same evidence and also everyone has only one vote. But juries, like all other groups, are composed of people who differ in their degree of participation and influence on others, and a few people do almost all the talking (Stephan & Mishler, 1952). Some jurors talk more than others; some choose not to try to influence others; and jury forepersons differ in their ability to facilitate group decision making. Some jurors bring in their personal experiences when they believe these are relevant to the decision, and evidence is a stronger determinant of the verdict for some jurors than for others. Some trial attorneys go so far as to propose that the 12-person jury is composed of only 2, 3, or 4 members who make any difference. Robert Duncan, who was a highly successful Kansas City trial attorney, asserted that "most juries consist of one or two strong personalities with the rest more or less being followers. Thus, often the jury actually consists of a one- or two-person jury" (Kassin & Wrightsman, 1988, p. 177).

Perhaps the above is an exaggeration, but empirical research has shown the unequal pattern of comments that typically occur during jury deliberations (Hastie, Penrod, & Pennington, 1983). More than 800 persons watched the reenactment of a murder trial and then were assigned to one of 69 juries. The deliberations of each jury were videotaped, to permit a later tabulation of the number of statements made by each juror. In each mock jury, a few participants dominated the discussion, while others spoke much less frequently. In fact, most of these 12-person juries had as many as 3 jurors who remained silent, except to cast their votes.

Similarly, we can ask: what does it mean that jurors are assumed to be independent of each other? They are admonished not to discuss the case with each other prior to the beginning of deliberations (except in Arizona, which is experimenting with giving jurors in civil trials this opportunity). Do they in truth refrain from discussing the case? It is, of course, difficult to say: the few accounts by jurors of their participation in trials reflect the temptations to confirm one's impressions with one's colleagues (cf. Roth, 1986). We imagine that jurors convey to their fellow jurors their reactions to the testimony of some witnesses by frowns or other nonverbal indicators, even if they try not to.

Openness to Informational Influence

It is infrequent for a jury of 6 or 12 persons, at the beginning of the deliberations, to agree on a verdict. Hence, the process of deliberation is, by and large, an example of persuasion and social influence. The legal system has its ideals for how juries should (and should not) manage the tensions that inevitably result from the clash of opinions. The task is formidable: how to maintain the goals of independent expression and yet reach a consensus.

The courts assume that the discussion during deliberations emphasizes the weight of the evidence and the instructions regarding the application of the law. Its idealized jurors use logic and facts as they try to express their verdicts and influence those of the other jurors. Psychologists refer to this as *informational social influence* (Deutsch & Gerard, 1955).

Avoidance of Heavy-Handed Pressure

The third ideal reflects the opposite of the second: consensus should *not* be achieved through intimidation or heavy-handed pressure, or what psychologists have labeled *normative social influence* (Deutsch & Gerard, 1955). Jurors who differ from the majority view should not be bullied, browbeaten, or harangued into submission. The Supreme Court, in *Allen v. United States* (1896), expressed this ideal: "the verdict must be the verdict of each individual juror, and not a mere acquiescence in the conclusion of his [*sic*] fellows" (p. 501).

Innovations to Achieve the Ideal

To achieve its goal of reaching its ideal in jury deliberations, the legal system on occasion has instituted well-meaning innovations in its procedures. Unfortunately, these innovations may have the opposite effect from those intended. For example, in some trials of alleged Mafia bosses in New York City, precautions were instituted never to identify potential jurors by name in the courtroom. The goal was to prevent jury tampering, especially threats to jurors to coerce them into rendering acquittals. But prospective jurors soon became aware of the intent of the actions, and these instilled in their minds a presumption of guilt rather than innocence.

Two innovations which, we believe, have had unfortunate consequences are described here: the sequestration of jurors and the use of what is called the "*Allen* charge" when the jury is deadlocked.

JUROR SEQUESTRATION   The general purpose of sequestration is to free the jury from pressures from the community and to isolate each juror from access to nonevidentiary, potentially biasing information about the case, including that coming from friends and family, as well as from the print and electronic media. Its goal to further the due process of law is a worthwhile one, but are the costs to jurors greater than the benefits?

The decision to sequester the jury received national attention during O. J. Simpson's criminal trial; the jury in that case was sequestered for almost 9 months, and two jurors wrote books about their unpleasant experiences (Kennedy, Kennedy, & Abrahamson, 1995; Knox & Walker, 1995). While the length was unusual, the judicial decision to sequester is not. *All* criminal juries in New York state were required to be sequestered while they deliberated until the state law was changed in 1995; if the case involves a serious felony, sequestration is still the rule there (Levine, 1996).

To our knowledge, no evidence exists that sequestration facilitates its goal of achieving unbiased jury decision making. We question whether sequestration effectively curtails unwanted information; what may occur is a *reactance effect*, in which the juror—when denied freedom—increases his or her effort to obtain the forbidden information. Beyond that, what is clear is that, for jurors, sequestration is highly unpleasant. Chopra, Dahl, and Wrightsman (1996) summarized their interviews with most of the jurors who had been sequestered during a very emotional Missouri death-penalty trial. The jurors' reactions were similar to those of the Simpson jury; they felt like prisoners themselves, locked in their dreary hotel rooms, under scrutiny by the marshals. Jurors who are sequestered lose control of their own lives. They have little or no solitude or privacy; deputies escort them wherever they go (even to the bathroom), and the deputies can enter their rooms at any time. They have little choice in their leisure activities, and they are bound by the schedule provided by the court.

Negative reactions to sequestration will differ from juror to juror and of course will be exacerbated as the confinement is extended. But the review by Chopra et al. (1996) found such a consistency of responses that they proposed the existence of a *sequestered-juror syndrome*, which includes the following symptoms:

Depression, restlessness, anxiety, and insomnia (partially due to removal from their usual surroundings)

Obsessive-compulsive disorder, including a shift toward a narrow, inward-looking obsession

Feelings of hopelessness, helplessness, and despair, especially when confronted with a dispute during deliberations

Cognitive impairment, including difficulty in concentration and memory

Reduction in self-confidence and self-esteem, leading to possible capitulation of the minority to the majority's preferences in a verdict

Loneliness

A sense of disempowerment, including an inability to escape from the day's aggravations

Kaplan's (1985) interviews with 40 jurors in death-penalty cases support these conclusions; 27 of the 40 had one or more discomforting physical or psychological symptoms, including everything from general nervousness to heart palpitations.

Some of the symptoms in this syndrome, such as the cognitive disorders, impinge directly upon the jurors' ability to judge and, therefore, upon the defendant's right to due process. Does jurors' bitterness about their confinement create a bias? Perhaps they blame the defendant ("He's the one who got us in this mess"); perhaps they blame the state ("They're the ones who locked us up"). Little systematic research exists on the effect of sequestration on verdicts; our position is that sequestered jurors are likely to blame *someone* for their plight, but it could be either side. Attribution of blame for a distressing situation is typically used as a coping mechanism.

Regardless, much indirect evidence indicates that the deleterious effects of sequestration can undermine the system's goal of a fair trial. Trial consultants can assist attorneys who wish to lobby against the procedure.

THE USE OF THE *ALLEN* CHARGE   Kalven and Zeisel's (1966) survey of jury trials in criminal cases found that between 5 and 6% of juries could not reach a unanimous verdict, and hence were "hung." As jury composition has become more heterogeneous in the United States over the last 4 decades, the hung jury rate has probably increased beyond this percentage. It is a problem for the courts.

Judges do not like hung juries; they result in mistrials that mean wasted time and money and often lead to a second, repetitive trial. In such a case, the judge will frequently read to the jury what has come to be called the *Allen* charge, a special instruction, first used in Massachusetts and later approved by the Supreme Court. The purpose of the *Allen* charge is to undo the logjam of a hung jury. It usually works so well that lawyers have given it colloquial names, including the "nitroglycerin charge," the "hammer instruction," and, most frequently, the "dynamite charge" (Levenson, 2003; Marcus, 1978). While the specific language may vary, the following is the original 1896 formulation:

> That in a large proportion of cases absolute certainty would not be expected; that although the verdict must be the verdict of each individual juror, and not a mere acquiescence in the conclusion of his fellows, yet they should examine the question submitted with candor and with a proper regard and deference to the opinions of each other; that it was their duty to decide the case if they could conscientiously do so; that they should listen with a disposition to be convinced, to each other's arguments; that, if much the larger number were for conviction, a dissenting juror should consider whether his doubt was a reasonable one which made no impression upon the minds of so many men, equally honest, equally intelligent with himself. If, upon the other hand, the majority was for acquittal, the minority ought to ask themselves whether they might not reasonably doubt the correctness of a judgment which was not concurred in by the majority. (*Allen v. United States*, 1896, p. 501)

Kassin and Wrightsman (1988) ask us to think about a jury that hears this instruction:

> Having already discussed the case at great lengths, the jurors are called into the courtroom and read this supplemental instruction. Their state of information and their arguments over the evidence remain unchanged. What then transpires back in the jury room, in light of this latest directive? (pp. 193–194)

And what kind of influence takes over? It can be a coercive influence (Levenson, 2003). We believe that the *Allen* charge, unless the judge revises its wording, unfairly points a finger at those jurors who are in the minority. As one court described it:

> The dissenters, struggling to maintain their position in a protracted debate in the jury room, are led into the courtroom and, before their peers, specifically requested by the judge to reconsider their position. . . . The charge places the sanction of the court behind the views of the majority, whatever they may be, and tempts the minority juror to relinquish his position simply because he has been the subject of a particular instruction. (*People v. Gainer*, 1977, p. 850)

Yet other judges maintain that it is acceptable to pressure the dissenters. One judge argued, "They may properly be warned against stubbornness and self-assertion" (*People v. Randall*, 1961, p. 425). More important, the U.S. Supreme Court (in *Lowenfield v. Phelps*, 1988) ruled that the *Allen* charge is not necessarily coercive and reaffirmed its use on a routine basis, and in

2002 (in *Early v. Packer*), the Court overturned a circuit court decision that had concluded that the use of the *Allen* charge *was* coercive (Levenson, 2003).

Research by social psychologists Saul Kassin and Vicki Smith (Kassin, Smith, & Tulloch, 1990; Smith & Kassin, 1993) confirmed the fears of the critics; they found that those mock jurors who were in the minority in a deadlocked jury changed their verdicts more often than those in the majority; furthermore, those in the minority felt heightened pressure to shift. In contrast, the effects of the instruction on jurors in the majority was to exert increasing amounts of social pressure.

One of the problems with the use of the *Allen* charge is that jurors, upon hearing it, assume that they have no choice but to return a unanimous verdict. The case of *Lowenfield v. Phelps* (1988), in which the Supreme Court upheld its use, is an example. In that case, a hung jury in Louisiana was told by the judge, "I order you to go back to the jury room and to deliberate and to arrive at a verdict" (Kassin, Smith, & Tulloch, 1990, p. 549). Shortly thereafter, the jury voted unanimously to convict the defendant of first-degree murder. Surely such an instruction encourages the worst kind of normative influence.

In encouraging the use of the *Allen* charge, the legal system apparently has a one-sided view of the image of holdout jurors, that they are "obstinate, uncooperative, and closed-minded . . . the chronic nonconformist" (Kassin & Wrightsman, 1988, p. 194). Examples exist of a single holdout juror who "sang, looked out the window, made jokes, and refused to talk about the case or to go along with the majority view" (Hawkins, 1960, pp. 136–137). But sometimes juries deadlock because the weight of the evidence is about even from one side to the other, and there exists well-reasoned disagreement. Kalven and Zeisel (1966) found that most hung juries occur in close cases. We conclude that there are properly hung juries, marked by legitimate disagreement over the evidence, and improperly hung juries, suffused with irrationality and normative influence. Given that, the law's goal should be to blast improperly hung juries into a verdict, while leaving the others unaffected (Notes and Comments, 1968).

Our conclusion, then, is that the *Allen* charge is an overreaction if it is indiscriminately applied to all hung juries. Fortunately, there is an alternative. A number of years ago, the American Bar Association proposed an instruction to be included in the judge's instructions before deliberations begin, but it could be reread to the jury as needed. It states:

> It is your duty, as jurors, to consult with one another and to deliberate with a view to reaching an agreement, if you can do so without violence to individual judgment. Each of you must decide the case for yourself, but do so only after an impartial consideration of the evidence with your fellow jurors. In the course of your deliberations, do not hesitate to reexamine your own views and change

your opinion if convinced it is erroneous. But do not surrender your honest conviction as to the weight or effect of evidence solely because of the opinion of your fellow jurors, or for the mere purpose of returning a verdict. (American Bar Association, Project on Minimum Standards for Criminal Justice, 1968, p. 5)

Thus the ABA charge does not single out minority jurors, and it has received some support in the courts. In *United States v. Smith* (1988), the 10th Circuit recommended an instruction that calls upon all jurors, not just those in the minority, to reflect on their positions. In *United States v. Dorsey* (1989), the District of Columbia Circuit required the use of a similar charge. Judges have some discretion about what instruction to give. Trial consultants need to be sensitive to the alternatives.

The Social Psychology of Social Influence

Let us say that the initial vote of a 12-person jury is 8 for conviction and 4 for acquittal. What are the processes and dynamics that take place, as jurors try to convince their colleagues to shift their votes? The vote shift, if it occurs, is not necessarily a straightforward one in which one juror at a time moves from the minority to the majority. This section describes what research has found about some of the factors influencing the process.

What Happens During Deliberations?

At some point, either initially or after some discussion, an initial vote is taken. If every juror's vote agrees with the others, the deliberation is effectively over. But typically, the group is divided, and the faction in the majority strives for unanimity. Most of the communications are directed to those jurors in the minority; they may reflect informational influence; they may reflect normative influence. Clearly informational influence is more desirable, not just because the legal system idealizes it, but because people want to be correct in their judgments and expect that when others agree with each other, they must be right. But when the influence attempts are normative, the reason people conform is more likely their fear of the negative consequences of appearing deviant. They do not want to be rejected, ridiculed, and punished by the majority (Schachter, 1951).

Compliance in Voting

Normative social influence more often produces *public compliance*; the minority jurors will change in the sense that they may publicly vote with the majority, even though privately they continue to disagree. More desirable is a genuine, private change, which more likely comes from informational influence.

But each type of influence rarely appears in a pure form. As Kalven and Zeisel (1966) noted, the deliberation process "is an interesting combination of rational persuasion, sheer social pressure, and the psychological mechanism by which individual perceptions undergo change when exposed to group discussion" (p. 489). Hazel Thornton (1995), in her diary of the Menendez brothers' trial, reports the following during deliberations, reflecting our view that they combine normative and informational influence attempts:

December 17: Thornton recounts how the group moves from "venting" feelings to "expressing our concerns in a somewhat more civilized manner."
December 20 and 22: She describes what is logical and persuasive for one juror is given a conflicting interpretation by another.
January 3: She refers to jurors yelling and calling each other names, blatant examples of normative social influence.
January 4: She writes, "I lost my temper today and yelled at [another juror], who had interrupted me (among others) one time too many."
January 6: She states, "These guys (I hate to lump them all together after my tirade on Tuesday, but they're all driving me crazy) can't even let us get to our point without jumping in and interrupting for one reason or another." (quoted by Wrightsman & Posey, 1995, p. 124)

These influence attempts were not successful in the first Menendez brothers' trial. But we do know that at least occasionally, jurors publicly conform when their private attitudes have not changed. One example is the following:

In 1981 a Miami jury deliberated for more than six hours on whether four defendants had paid undercover agents $220,000 for 15 pounds of cocaine. At one point the jurors reported that they were deadlocked, so the judge asked that they try further to reach agreement. Three hours later they returned with verdicts: three convictions and an acquittal. When the judge began polling them in open court as to whether they agreed in conscience with their decisions, the very first juror said, "No." The judge sent them back to the jury room. A few minutes later they returned with the same verdicts. Polled again, the first juror agreed, but juror #5 said, "No, it's not my verdict." Again, the judge sent them back. This time, they returned and confirmed the verdicts. But one of the defense lawyers said, "We noticed juror #11 kick the back of juror #5's chair when it was her turn." Polled separately, jurors 1 and 5 both repudiated their verdicts. Sent back a fourth time, the jurors deliberated half an hour more, returned with the same verdicts, and stood by them. Then when the trial ended, jurors 1 and 5 approached two of the defendants and apologized for their convictions. According to their report, two jurors insisted on concluding that night because they had vacation plans. One of them swung at another juror, and four who initially had voted for acquittal were "browbeaten into submission." (Kassin & Wrightsman, 1988, p. 176)

To complicate matters more, public compliance can result even when the majority uses only informational influence. The *Frontline* PBS television program titled "Inside the Jury" presented excerpts from the trial and jury deliberations in a case in which Leroy Reed, a convicted felon then out on parole, purchased a gun in order to apply for a detective-training course. He had, in effect, incriminated himself because—while hanging around the Milwaukee police station—he was asked for identification and showed the police his gun receipt. He was told to go home and bring in the gun (on the bus), and he was then arrested. While the elements of a law violation are present—he was an ex-felon; he possessed a gun; and he knew he possessed a gun—the majority of the jurors wanted to find him not guilty because he was of limited mental ability and his purchase of a gun was only motivated by a well-meaning if unlikely goal of getting employment as a private detective. The holdout juror, after efforts at influence which (from what we are shown of the deliberations) concentrated on logical analysis and absolutely avoided intimidation, agreed to vote with the majority to make the verdict unanimous, but he told them, "I'll never in my heart think this is right."

What Does Research Reveal About the Nature of Jury Deliberations?

In most states, jury deliberations cannot be observed or taped; the above example of Leroy Reed's trial jury deliberations was a special case. But in a few jurisdictions, especially in Arizona, actual jury deliberations are being videotaped. And other information, including court records and retrospective accounts by jurors, provides us with knowledge about the process of deliberations. Diaries kept by jurors on a day-to-day basis are even more illuminating, but only a few have made it to print. For example, one of the jurors in the trial of Bernhard Goetz, the "subway vigilante," prepared a daily memoir of the trial's developments that was especially helpful in showing how the jury logically reached what was, for many observers, an unpopular verdict (Lesly & Shuttleworth, 1988). The diary of Hazel Thornton (1995), one of the jurors in the trial of the Menendez brothers for the murder of their parents, reflects a juror actively and conscientiously trying to make sense of conflicting testimony and impenetrable jury instructions. It also clarifies a misconception held by the public, which remembers that in their first trial the Menendez brothers "got off"; in actuality, in their first trial, each jury (there was a separate jury for each brother) was hung, but not over the question of guilt versus innocence. *Every* juror voted to convict; the division was over whether it was for murder or for voluntary manslaughter. No evidence for sympathy from any juror emerges in this diary. Yet the diary reflects the very heated and acrimonious deliberations over just which crime was applicable. (In a later trial, both brothers were convicted of murder.)

Participation Rates

In any group, some members are assertive and some are shy. Some talk more than others, often much more. Some may not speak unless they are directly addressed. And men talk more than women. It is the same with juries.

Gender Differences

Often, male and female jurors play different roles during deliberations; men assume task-oriented roles more often, expressing opinions and offering observations. Women reflect more socioemotional roles, offering support, showing more concern for bruised feelings, and generally helping to reduce interpersonal tensions (Nemeth, Endicott, & Wachtler, 1976; Strodtbeck & Mann, 1956). Males were rated by their fellow jurors as more persuasive (Hastie, Penrod, & Pennington, 1983).

Prior Experience as a Juror

Prior experience as a juror affects participation, both in amount and content. When Broeder (1965) interviewed jurors after their trials were completed, he encountered several experienced jurors who had assumed the mantle of "experts" and tried to control the rest of the group. For example, he described a woman who, upon entering the room for deliberations, immediately cut paper ballots, explained that it was standard procedure to open with a secret vote, and "did everything but suggest that she be elected foreman" (Broeder, 1965). Empirical research findings support the above observations. Those mock jurors who had previously served on a real jury talked more than those who had not (Hastie, Penrod, & Pennington, 1983). Another study (Kassin & Juhnke, 1983) found that novice jurors participated less and made less persuasive comments than did their experienced peers; novices also conformed more with the majority when the other jurors had prior jury service.

Does prior experience as a juror "harden" one's view and lead to the likelihood of a conviction of the defendant? The limited studies lead to inconsistent conclusions, and it may be that the nature of the previous trials (especially the strength of the evidence) affects whether prior experience leads to a conviction-proneness (Dillehay & Nietzel, 1985, 1999; Kerr, 1981; Kerr, Harmon, & Graves, 1982; Reed, 1965; Werner, Strube, Cole, & Kagehiro, 1985).

We may summarize these findings as follows:

In principle, all jurors are supposed to be created equal. In practice, however, this equalitarian ethic is seldom if ever realized. The fact of the matter is that dominance hierarchies develop, that mirror the differences in status in the real world. Thus, despite the forces designed to place all jurors on an equal footing and neutralize individual differences, juries still consist in predictable ways of leaders, participants, and followers. (Kassin & Wrightsman, 1988, p. 180)

The Group Polarization Effect

A staple of late-night television is the film *Twelve Angry Men*, in which juror Henry Fonda is initially the sole minority juror, in favor of an acquittal, but comes to persuade each of the remaining 11 jurors to vote as he does. It is wonderful drama but quite unrealistic (Bothwell & Abbott, 1999). In reality, the verdict preferred by the majority of the jurors in the initial ballot becomes the unanimous group verdict more than 90% of the time (Devine, Clayton, Dunford, Seying, & Pryce, 2001). Thus, as we have emphasized before, "to predict the outcome of deliberations with a fair degree of certainty, one need only to know where the twelve individuals stand before they enter the jury room" (Kassin & Wrightsman, 1988, p. 182). Kalven and Zeisel (1966) interviewed jurors after the completion of 225 criminal trials and determined how each of these juries split on its initial vote. In only 6 of the 225, the final unanimous verdict was not predictable from the initial breakdown. These researchers concluded: "The deliberation process might well be likened to what the developer does from an exposed film: It brings out the picture, but the outcome is predetermined.... The deliberation process, though rich in human interest and color appears not to be at the heart of jury decision making" (p. 496).

The discussion and vote taking during deliberations lead to a reliable effect that is a corollary of the "majority [usually] wins" rule described above. Called the *group polarization effect*, it has been defined as follows: "The average post-discussion response will tend to be more extreme in the same direction as the average of the pregroup responses" (Moscovici & Zavalloni, 1969, p. 133).

To test whether group polarization applies to jury decisions, social psychologists David Myers and Martin Kaplan (1976) had mock jurors read summaries of felony traffic cases and, for each, rate how guilty they thought the defendant to be. For some of the cases, the evidence against the defendant was strong; for others, it was weak. Afterward, respondents deliberated in six-person groups and then once more indicated their individual verdicts. The results reflected the group-polarization concept; in cases where the evidence was strong, respondents became more likely to find the defendant guilty after talking to others about it. But when the evidence was weak, they became less likely to do so.

The group-polarization effect emerges in deliberations in civil trials as well as in criminal trials. Awards made by the jury as a group may even exceed those by any individual juror. In Sunstein et al.'s (2002) study of punitive damages, in 27% of the cases the jury's award was as high or higher than that of the highest individual judgment prior to deliberation. A few examples of this shift are the following:

> A jury whose predeliberation judgments were $200,000, $300,000, $2 million, $10 million, and $10 million reached a verdict of $15 million.
>
> A jury whose predeliberation judgments were $200,000, $500,000, $2 million, $5 million, and $10 million reached a verdict of $50 million.
>
> A jury whose predeliberation judgments were $2 million, $2 million, $2.5 million, $50 million, and $100 million reached a verdict of $100 million. (Sunstein et al., 2002, p. 52)

The researchers called this effect "the severity shift." In the sense that it favors the plaintiff in a civil trial, it resembles the deliberation-induced shift toward leniency in a criminal trial. It is here where the conception of a commonsense-based decision breaks down.

How does the minority ever "win"? Minorities sometimes persuade the majority to their point of view. In chapter 1, we described one example, the trial of John Mitchell and Maurice Stans for campaign financing irregularities. Juror Andrew Choa almost single-handedly turned the verdict around. But this happens very rarely.

When it does, two strategies seem to contribute. One is for the minority juror or jurors to adopt right from the start a staunch, consistent, and unwavering position; when confronted with a self-confident alternative viewpoint, jurors in the majority may take notice and rethink their own positions (Moscovici, 1985). A second strategy is quite different; it advocates that individual dissenters should first conform to the majority and thus establish their credibility. Thus having accumulated "idiosyncrasy credits," they can start advancing an alternative verdict—and more likely shift the majority (Hollander, 1985). Interestingly, Henry Fonda, in *Twelve Angry Men*, used the first approach, emphasizing consistency, whereas Andrew Choa succeeded by accumulating idiosyncrasy credits. Research has found that, under the right circumstances, either strategy can be effective (Maass & Clark, 1984).

A Leniency Effect, Too

An interesting wrinkle in the above pattern exists; in addition to polarizing opinions, the deliberation process consistently generates a shift toward leniency for criminal defendants. All other things being equal, individual jurors at the beginning of deliberations are less likely to acquit and more likely to convict than they are at the end of deliberations (MacCoun & Kerr, 1988). A jury that is evenly split at the beginning of deliberations is more likely to eventually acquit than eventually convict, especially when the first ballot is delayed (Kaplan, 1999). Apparently, with jurors appreciating the gravity of their task and taking seriously the concept of "beyond a reasonable doubt," it is easier to justify an acquittal than a conviction (Stasser, Kerr, & Bray, 1982).

Conclusions

The above review suggests a number of conclusions and applications when a trial consultant advises an attorney on jury selection and other aspects of a trial.

Implications for Jury Selection

Assuming that the trial attorneys are provided liberal questioning time, it would be helpful to assess the prior jury experience of each prospective juror. This is often overlooked in the questioning, but may reveal the juror's biases as well as his or her potential for influencing others during the deliberations as well as any emotional reactions to trial service.

Reducing the Effects of Hindsight Bias

Chapter 5 discussed jurors' use of hindsight bias and how, in closing arguments, the posing of alternatives may weaken its effect.

The Timing of the Judge's Instructions About Reasonable Doubt

The problem of the instructions being incomprehensible to many jurors is a general one, which we consider in chapter 10 when we discuss reforms of the jury system. We focus here on a specific aspect: the timing of the instructions on reasonable doubt. Ordinarily, these are not given to the jurors until they begin their deliberations. This makes no sense; jurors are not told the rules of the game until after the game has been played. Trial consultants, if they are working with criminal defense attorneys, need them to urge the judge to give these instructions at the beginning of the trial. When mock jurors were given the "requirement of proof" instruction at the beginning of the trial rather than at the end, it reduced the conviction rate from 59% to 37% (Kassin & Wrightsman, 1979). Hearing these instructions at the beginning of the trial also increased the amount of information from the evidence presentation remembered by the jurors. This innovation fits common sense; even Supreme Court justice Sandra Day O'Connor has endorsed it. She wrote, in her recent book:

> Jurors should be given general instructions on the applicable law *before* the case begins. How are they to make sense of the evidence and the mass of information that the parties will put before them, unless they know in advance what they are looking for? Jurors are not mere receptacles in which information can be stored, to be retrieved intact when the jurors are finally told what to do with it. Jurors are people, and people organize information as they receive it, according to their existing frames of reference. Unless they are given proper frames of reference at the *beginning* of the case, jurors are likely either to be overwhelmed by a mass of information they are incapable of organizing, or to devise their own frames of reference, which may well be inconsistent with those that the law requires. (O'Connor, 2003, p. 221; italics in original, footnotes omitted)

7

Jury Selection
Measures of General Bias

Perhaps Clarence Darrow's claim that "[a]lmost every case has been won or lost when the jury is sworn" (Strier, 1999, p. 93) is an exaggeration, but the identification of potential biases in prospective jurors is one of the most important tasks in the trial. Some trial attorneys are increasingly relying on consultants and empirical methods to advise them in making these decisions. These procedures are the main focus of this chapter, as well as chapters 8 and 9. But most attorneys have their own ingrained assumptions about who makes a good or bad juror (Fulero & Penrod, 1990b). If they cannot hire the expertise of a trial consultant, these attorneys will employ their assumptions and stereotypes in their choices. Thus it can be argued that the goals of trial consultants, despite their negative reputation in the eyes of the public, aren't any different from those of trial attorneys—they both seek a jury composed of persons who will be open-minded about (if not sympathetic to) their side's set of facts and arguments. The difference is that litigation consultants use what is called *systematic jury selection*, or scientific procedures, rather than the "seat of the pants" orientation of many lawyers.

Examples of trial attorneys' stereotyped beliefs about jurors are the stuff of legend. Jeffrey Toobin recounted, "Early in my career as a prosecutor, when I first began selecting juries, a senior colleague warned me about men with beards. 'Guys with beards are independent and iconoclastic,' my mentor said. 'They resist authority. Get rid of them'" (Toobin, 1994, p. 42). The master attorney Clarence Darrow believed that, as a defense attorney, he was better off with jurors of an Irish background; he avoided Scandinavians, who—he presumed—had too much respect for the law. The celebrated contemporary attorney Gerry Spence has said: "Women are more punitive than men by a score of about five to one" (quoted by Franklin, 1994, p. A25). And attorney Keith Mossman (1973) has reported that "a nationally-known trial lawyer once told me he would not accept any left-handed jurors" (p. 78).

Such stereotypes may be specific to the individual lawyer, and hence considered tolerable or even quaint. But the problem is more serious; general stereotypes are taught in law-school trial advocacy courses, as well as being passed down to neophyte lawyers on the job. Toobin (1994) described how, as a new member of the staff of federal prosecutors, he learned, "[W]e preferred jurors who were old rather than young; married rather than single; employed rather than jobless.... We sought jurors smart enough to understand the evidence but not so clever that they would overanalyze it; educated, but not to excess" (p. 42). Stereotypes also abound for the defense bar, for whom the ideal juror is a member of the helping profession—a teacher, a social worker, a psychologist—because such folks have sympathy for the underdog. Members of racial minorities are seen as prodefense jurors in criminal trials, because of their more-frequent conflicts with police and other authorities in the legal system.

Should such stereotypes be dismissed as idle folklore? Or is there some basis for their evolution? Early in the psychological study of racial stereotypes, a position was advanced that came to be called the *kernel of truth hypothesis*, which states that group stereotypes may be unwisely generalized, but that some basic distinctions exist between groups. A review by Brigham (1971) concluded that ethnic and racial stereotypes could have such a kernel of truth in the sense that different groups of respondents agreed on which traits were associated with a particular object group. (But we often lack the information to know if the object group actually possesses the traits.) Even if the kernel-of-truth proposal is accepted as a general proposition, do these stereotypes have enough predictability to be used in selecting or rejecting individual jurors? Usually not.

Psychologists have sought to determine if group differences (including racial and ethnic classifications as well as broad personality characteristics and attitudes) are predictive of verdicts. Their conclusion is not a simple one, for the verdict of an individual juror is the product of a wealth of factors, not only that juror's gender and race, attitudes and personality, but also the weight of the evidence in the case, the responses to the pressures on the juror to vote one way or another, and other factors specific to the situation. At the broadest level, we can say that jurors' verdicts can be affected by their biases, but how their biases are manifested may depend on specific aspects of the trial. For example, jurors who are relatively authoritarian *tend* to go along with the prosecution, but what if the defendant is an authority figure, such as a police officer or a physician? Then, the relationship may shift, and the authoritarian juror will side with the defense.

Two Approaches to Jury Selection

Given the fragile relationship between jurors' demographic classifications or internal qualities and their verdicts, trial consultants have followed two pathways in advising and evaluating jury selection: a general approach and a case-specific approach. After introducing each, the remainder of this chapter will focus on strategies consistent with the general approach. The case-specific approach is described in chapter 8.

Broad Attitudes and Traits: The General Approach

A fundamental principle of social psychology is that each of us perceives the world in an idiosyncratic way. It is very difficult for us to look at a stimulus without evaluating it at the same time that we perceive it. Two different jurors will interpret the same stimulus differently, based on their past experiences and training. The phenomenon of *juror bias* refers to this assumption that each of us makes interpretations based on past experience and that these interpretations can color our verdicts.

In criminal trials, jurors' biases can be classified as favoring the prosecution or favoring the defense. That is, some prospective jurors—without knowing anything about the evidence—may assume that the defendant is guilty. Proprosecution bias reflects, in some jurors, the aforementioned trust of authority figures, in others a belief in a just world, in others perhaps an acquiescent response set. In contrast, a prodefense bias often stems from a sympathy with the underprivileged or an opposition to or suspicion of those in power.

Biases can also occur when jurors are asked to decide in a civil case. Here the biases are more varied, and it may not be possible to identify a single dimension of bias that applies to every civil suit. Some plaintiffs who sue resemble defendants in criminal trials, in that they are (sometimes powerless) individuals in opposition to a powerful organization. Consider, for example, a parent with a child injured in a car wreck who is claiming that the child seat in the car was defective. A suit by an individual against a major corporation with seemingly limitless resources evokes from some jurors a sympathy bias that resembles a prodefense bias in criminal trials, but here, in civil trials, it reflects a *proplaintiff bias*. But other jurors may manifest *prodefendant biases* (or at least *antiplaintiff biases*); for example, some jurors feel strongly that there is too much litigation and that many lawsuits are without merit. By identifying with powerful corporations, some prodefendant jurors in civil cases may possess some of the authoritarian orientations that proprosecution jurors show in a criminal case.

Several instruments have been developed to attempt to measure the basic biases. A later section reviews and evaluates these instruments. But recall that some trial consultants prefer to relate jury selection to specific issues in the case at hand, rather than trying to assess general biases.

The Case-Specific Approach

If the broad-attitude/trait approach may be said to approach jury selection with a preconceived theory about dimensions of jurors that are related to their verdicts, the *case-specific approach* works in the opposite way; it looks at the particular facts and issues of the case and then tries to develop some measurable characteristics of jurors that would be related to their verdicts. In its purest form, the case-specific approach is coldly empirical; it uses the reactions of mock jurors and focus groups to identify those variables likely to be important in the actual jurors' decisions. But usually when it is used, the trial consultants have some characteristics which they hypothesize to be important. These jurors' qualities, however, are not as broad as the traits described in the other approach. For example, if a criminal defendant is a member of a minority group, the racial identifications or racial attitudes of jurors may be considered as case-specific variables. If a hospital patient is suing a surgeon for medical malpractice, attitudes toward authority figures and especially the medical profession become salient. Later, in chapter 8, we will describe the use of scientific jury selection in several actual trials, which will illustrate this approach.

Measurement of Juror Bias

As indicated earlier, the general attitudes that may be related to jurors' verdicts in criminal trials differ from those attitudes relevant to responses in civil trials; thus different instruments have been developed to assess each type of attitude.

Criminal Trials

Two types of concepts have provided the structure for measures of criminal juror bias: authoritarianism and the distinction between a proprosecution and a prodefense orientation. Attitude scales have been developed to measure each.

The Legal Attitudes Questionnaire

The Legal Attitudes Questionnaire (LAQ) was apparently the first systematic measure developed to assess jurors' biases; it was published by Virginia R. Boehm more than 35 years ago, in 1968. As a pioneering instrument, it had worth, but also some of the problems often characteristic of attitude scales of that period. The LAQ contained 30 statements, arranged in 10 sets of 3 items. In each of these triads, one statement reflected *authoritarianism*, one reflected *equalitarianism,* and one reflected, to use Boehm's term, *antiauthoritarianism.* (The instructions for the LAQ and a sample item are reprinted in Box 7-1; because the scale has been revised to reflect more contemporary measurement procedures, the entire scale is not included in this box.)

Box 7-1 LAQ Instructions and Sample Items

The Legal Attitudes Questionnaire was the first instrument to attempt systematic measurement of jurors' general predispositions. However, it was cumbersome to complete and to score, as is illustrated by its instructions below.

Instructions: On the following pages are ten groups of statements, each expressing a commonly held opinion about law enforcement, legal procedures, and other things connected with the judicial system. There are three statements in each group.

Put a plus (+) on the line next to the statement in a group that you agree with most, and minus (−) next to the statement with which you agree the least.

An example of a set of statements might be:

+ A. The failure of a defendant to testify in his own behalf should not be taken as an indication of guilt.
  B. The majority of persons arrested are innocent of any crime.
− C. Giving an obviously guilty criminal a long drawn-out trial is a waste of the taxpayer's money.

In this example, the person answering has agreed most with statement A and least with statement C.

Work carefully, choosing the item you agree with most and the one you agree with least in each set of statements. There is no time limit on this questionnaire, but do not spend too much time on any set of statements. Some sets are more difficult than others, but please do not omit any set of statements.

Set 1

−A. Unfair treatment of underprivileged groups and classes is the chief cause of crime.
−B. Too many obviously guilty persons escape punishment because of legal technicalities.
−C. The U.S. Supreme Court is, by and large, an effective guardian of the Constitution.

From Kravitz, Cutler, & Brock, 1993, p. 662; the other sets of statements may be found in Boehm, 1968.

According to Boehm (1968), the authoritarian items reflected one of three topics; they either "expressed right-wing philosophy, endorsed indiscriminately the acts of constituted authority, or were essentially punitive in nature" (p. 740). In contrast, antiauthoritarian items "expressed left-wing sentiments, implied that the blame for all antisocial acts rested with the structure of society, or indiscriminately rejected the acts of constituted authority" (p. 740). The more moderate third type, equalitarian items, "endorsed traditional, liberal, non-extreme positions on legal questions or were couched in a form that indicated the questions reasonably could have two answers" (p. 740). The questionnaire utilized a type of forced-choice procedure; for each triad, respondents assigned a + to the statement with which they most agreed and a − to the statement with which they least agreed. In scoring, these responses were treated as ratings, with the positively marked statement receiving a rating of 3, the unmarked statement a rating of 2, and the negatively marked statement a rating of 1. Then the ratings for each of the three subscales were totaled separately; no total score was determined. Thus, every respondent could have a score ranging from 30 (high) to 10 (low) on each of the three dimensions: authoritarianism, antiauthoritarianism, and equalitarianism. Boehm theorized that jurors with high scores on authoritarianism had a tendency to convict, that high scores on antiauthoritarianism were associated with verdicts of acquittal, and that scores on equalitarianism were not related to verdicts.

More recently, researchers at Florida International University—especially Gary Moran, David Kravitz, Douglas Narby, and Brian Cutler—have systematically examined the validity of the LAQ and have proposed revisions of it. As part of a meta-analysis of the effects of authoritarian attitudes on mock jurors' verdicts, Narby, Cutler, and Moran (1993) reviewed studies using the original LAQ; the results of these studies are summarized below.

Boehm (1968) gave the LAQ to 151 undergraduate respondents and then presented each with one of two written versions of a murder trial. For a case for which the weight of the evidence leaned toward innocence, those respondents who voted guilty had significantly higher authoritarian subscale scores than did respondents who voted not guilty. For a case in which the evidence was in the direction of guilt, individual subjects' antiauthoritarian subscale scores predicted the verdict in the group of respondents who were older (age 21 or over); that is, those who acquitted had significantly higher antiauthoritarian subscale scores than did those who convicted. Among younger respondents (under age 21), the difference was in the same direction but was not statistically significant. The author did not report whether the equalitarian subscale scores were related to verdicts.

Jurow (1971) asked 211 employed adults to complete the original LAQ and then listen to tapes of two simulated murder cases. An examination of the verdicts given by the respondents found that, on both trials, those who voted to convict the defendant scored higher on the authoritarian subscale. Scores on the antiauthoritarian subscale distinguished between mock jurors who voted guilty and those who voted not guilty for one case, but not for the other.

Cowan, Thompson, and Ellsworth (1984) had 288 jury-eligible adults complete the LAQ and then watch a videotape reenactment of a murder trial. The choice of verdict options by individual mock jurors was related to their scores on the authoritarian subscale; the authors did not report whether the other two subscales had any predictive validity.

These studies (plus others, to be reported later, that altered the format and scoring of the original LAQ) indicated that subscale responses (at least for the authoritarian subscale) had predictive validity, that is, they were related to eventual verdicts. But this conclusion reflected *group differences*, not results that were so precise that you could, with assurance, predict an individual's verdict on the basis of his or her authoritarian score. Furthermore, the original version of the LAQ had several problems (Kravitz, Cutler, & Brock, 1993), one of which was the cumbersome scoring structure, in which the three-forced-choice response format prevented an independent assessment of the dimensions. The format and instructions were also difficult for some respondents to understand and follow, leading to frequent invalid responses. For those and other reasons, a revised version of the LAQ was developed.

The Revised Legal Attitudes Questionnaire

The Revised Legal Attitudes Questionnaire (RLAQ) was constructed by Kravitz, Cutler, and Brock (1993), who created 30 items with statements from the original LAQ. (The items on the RLAQ may be found in Box 7-2.) Further item analyses reduced the number of scored items to 23; in Box 7-2 these items are marked with an F.) This version can be administered with the usual Likert-scale response options (strongly agree, agree somewhat, etc.).

Several types of evidence for the general validity of this revised scale are available.

Several studies converted the format of the original LAQ to that of the RLAQ, dropped some items, and related scale responses to verdicts. Using 24 of the items, Moran and Comfort (1982) administered the scale to 319 persons who had served as jurors in felony trials; they found that legal authoritarianism scores were significantly related to jurors' verdicts in female jurors but not in male jurors. Moran and Cutler (1989) dropped 3 more items and compared responses to mock-juror verdicts in another sample of persons with jury experience; again, those with higher scores on the legal authoritarianism scale were more likely to convict.

Cutler, Moran, and Narby (1992), in their second study, used all 30 items in a Likert-type response format with 61 undergraduate respondents, who also watched a videotape simulation of a murder trial in which the defendant claimed he was not guilty by reason of insanity. Again, high scorers (that is, relatively authoritarian subjects) on this revised LAQ were

Box 7-2 Items of the Revised Legal Attitudes Questionnaire

The statements in the Revised Legal Attitudes Questionnaire are the following:

1. Unfair treatment of underprivileged groups and classes is the chief cause of crime. (AA, R, F)
2. Too many obviously guilty persons escape punishment because of legal technicalities. (A, F)
3. The Supreme Court is, by and large, an effective guardian of the Constitution. (E)
4. Evidence illegally obtained should be admissible in court if such evidence is the only way of obtaining a conviction. (A, F)
5. Most prosecuting attorneys have a strong sadistic streak. (AA, R)
6. Search warrants should clearly specify the person or things to be seized. (E, R, F)
7. No one should be convicted of a crime on the basis of circumstantial evidence, no matter how strong such evidence is. (AA, R, F)
8. There is no need in a criminal case for the accused to prove his innocence beyond a reasonable doubt. (E, R, F)
9. Any person who resists arrest commits a crime. (A, F)
10. When determining a person's guilt or innocence, the existence of a prior arrest record should not be considered. (E, R, F)
11. Wiretapping by anyone or for any reason should be completely illegal. (AA, R, F)
12. A lot of recent Supreme Court decisions sound suspiciously Communistic. (A)
13. Treachery and deceit are common tools of prosecutors. (AA, R)
14. Defendants in a criminal case should be required to take the witness stand. (A, F)
15. All too often, minority group members do not get fair trials. (E, R, F)
16. Because of the oppression and persecution minority group members suffer, they deserve leniency and special treatment in the courts. (AA, R, F)
17. Citizens need to be protected against excess police power as well as against criminals. (E, R, F)
18. Persons who testify in court against underworld characters should be allowed to do so anonymously to protect themselves from retaliation. (A)
19. It is better for society that several guilty men be freed than one innocent one wrongfully imprisoned. (E, R, F)

20. Accused persons should be required to take lie-detector tests. (A, F)
21. It is moral and ethical for a lawyer to represent a defendant in a criminal case even when he believes his client is guilty. (E, R, F)
22. A society with true freedom and equality for *all* would have very little crime. (AA, R, F)
23. When there is a "hung" jury in a criminal case, the defendant should always be freed and the indictment dismissed. (AA, R, F)
24. Police should be allowed to arrest and question suspicious looking persons to determine whether they have been up to something illegal. (A, F)
25. The law coddles criminals to the detriment of society. (A, F)
26. A lot of judges have connections with the underworld. (AA, R)
27. The freedom of society is endangered as much by zealous law enforcement as by the acts of individual criminals. (E, R, F)
28. There is just about no such thing as an honest cop. (AA, R)
29. In the long run, liberty is more important than order. (E, R, F)
30. Upstanding citizens have nothing to fear from the police. (A, F)

Note: Identification of subscales (A, AA, E) is given immediately following each item. Items that were reverse-coded on the overall RLAQ scale are indicated with an R following the subscale identification. Items included in the final RLAQ23 scale are indicated with an F.

From Kravitz, Cutler, & Brock, 1993, p. 666.

significantly more likely to vote guilty than were low scorers. This version of the LAQ had greater predictive validity than did the Juror Bias Scale (to be described later in this section).

Construct validity of the RLAQ was assessed by comparing respondents of different ethnic groups (African American versus Hispanic versus White) and political parties. As expected, lower legal authoritarianism scores were found among African Americans and among Democrats.

The Juror Bias Scale

In seeking to uncover attitudes that would predict jurors' verdicts, Kassin and Wrightsman (1983) chose another dimension, the bias to favor the prosecution or the defense. They noted that virtually all models of juror decision making (cf. Pennington & Hastie, 1981) assume that in criminal cases jurors make decisions that reflect the implicit operation of two judgments. The first of these is an estimate of the *probability of commission*; specifically, how likely is it that the defendant was the person who committed the crime? While jurors will base their estimates of this probability mainly on how strong the evidence is, their previous experiences will influence their interpretation of the evidence. For example, if a police officer testifies that he found a bag of heroin on the person of the defendant, some jurors, trusting police, would use this to increase their estimate that the defendant did commit a crime, but other jurors, given the same testimony, would discount or reject it based on their prior experiences and beliefs that police witnesses are dishonest.

A second judgment by the juror concerns his or her use of the concept of *reasonable doubt*, or the threshold of certainty deemed to be necessary for conviction. Judges always instruct jurors in criminal trials that they should bring back a verdict of not guilty if they have a reasonable doubt about the defendant's guilt. But the legal system has great reluctance to operationalize reasonable doubt, and when juries, during their deliberations, ask the judge for a definition, the judge usually falls back on the prior instruction or tells them that it is a doubt for which a person can give a reason. Left to their own devices, different jurors apply their own standards for how close they must be to certainty in order to vote guilty. Some jurors may interpret "beyond a reasonable doubt" to mean "beyond any doubt," or 100% certainty. Others may interpret it quite loosely (Dane, 1985; Kagehiro & Stanton, 1985).

Kassin and Wrightsman proposed that judgments of guilt arise when a juror's probability-of-commission estimate exceeds his or her reasonable-doubt criterion; they thus used these two factors to classify jurors as having a proprosecution or prodefense bias. To determine whether bias affected verdicts, they constructed a 17-statement Juror Bias Scale (JBS). (The statements and filler items are reprinted in Box 7-3.) The JBS gives scores on each of the factors of probability of commission and reasonable doubt.

Two methods of validation of the Juror Bias Scale have been used.

Kassin and Wrightsman (1983) had college students and jury-eligible respondents complete the JBS scale and then later watch videotapes of re-enacted actual trials or read transcripts of simulated trials. Four types of criminal trials were used, dealing with offenses ranging from auto theft and conspiracy to assault and rape. After being exposed to the trial, each mock juror was asked to render an individual verdict about the defendant's guilt or innocence. These verdicts were then related to the respondents' scores on the JBS. On three of the four cases, mock jurors with a proprosecution bias significantly more often voted to convict the defendant than did mock jurors with a prodefense bias. The differences were large; the average rate of conviction for prosecution-biased jurors was 81%, compared to 52% for defense-biased ones. Thus, in most cases, scores on the JBS have predictive validity.

With regard to the trial for rape, however, those mock jurors generally predisposed to favor the defense were just as likely to find the defendant guilty as were those jurors who favored the prosecution. It is possible that prodefense jurors, who are relatively liberal in their political views, are especially sympathetic with the victim when the crime involves a sexual assault; that is, their usual bias is balanced by a concern for the victim.

Box 7-3   The Juror Bias Scale

The second measure of general juror attitudes is the Juror Bias Scale. The instructions and scale items are listed here.

Instructions: This is a questionnaire to determine people's attitudes and beliefs on a variety of general legal issues. Please answer each statement by giving as true a picture of your position as possible. (Note: On the version of the scale administered to respondents, each statement is followed by five choices: 1. Strongly agree, 2. Mildly agree, 3. Agree and disagree equally, 4. Mildly disagree, and 5. Strongly disagree. In order to conserve space, these are omitted here.)

1. Appointed judges are more competent than elected judges.
2. A suspect who runs from the police most probably committed the crime.
3. A defendant should be found guilty if only 11 out of 12 jurors vote guilty.
4. Most politicians are really as honest as humanly possible.
5. Too often jurors hesitate to convict someone who is guilty out of pure sympathy.
6. In most cases where the accused presents a strong defense, it is only because of a good lawyer.
7. In general, children should be excused for their misbehavior.
8. The death penalty is cruel and inhumane.
9. Out of every 100 people brought to trial, at least 75 are guilty of the crime with which they are charged.
10. For serious crimes like murder, a defendant should be found guilty if there is a 90% chance that he or she committed the crime.
11. Defense lawyers don't really care about guilt or innocence, they are just in business to make money.
12. Generally, the police make an arrest only when they are sure about who committed the crime.
13. Circumstantial evidence is too weak to use in court.
14. Many accident claims filed against insurance companies are phony.
15. The defendant is often a victim of his or her own bad reputation.
16. If the grand jury recommends that a person be brought to trial, then he or she probably committed the crime.
17. Extenuating circumstances should not be considered—if a person commits a crime, then that person should be punished.
18. Hypocrisy is on the increase in society.
19. Too many innocent people are wrongfully imprisoned.

continued

Box 7-3 *Continued*

20. If a majority of the evidence—but not all of it—suggests that the defendant committed the crime, the jury should vote *not guilty.*
21. If the defendant committed a victimless crime like gambling or possession of marijuana, he should never be convicted.
22. Some laws are made to be broken.

Scoring procedures: The following are filler items and are not scored: items 1, 4, 7, 18, and 22. The following are part of the Probability of Commission subscale: items 2, 6, 9, 11, 12, 13 (reversed scoring), 14, 15 (reversed scoring), and 16. These are part of the Reasonable Doubt subscale: items 3, 5, 8 (reversed scoring), 10, 17, 19 (reversed scoring), 20 (reversed scoring), and 21 (reversed scoring).

From Kassin and Wrightsman, 1983, pp. 433–434.

Lecci and Myers (1996; Myers & Lecci, 1998) sought, through the use of factor analysis, to determine if the two theoretical dimensions, reasonable doubt and probability of commission, were verified empirically. Two samples, each consisting of 301 college students, completed the JBS, and several factor analyses were done. (A *factor analysis* is a statistical procedure that examines relationships between responses to different items and thus identifies which items are related to each other; *factors* are theoretical labels for what is common to those item statements that cluster together.) The reasonable doubt concept survived the empirical analysis fairly intact; results produced a six-item empirically driven reasonable-doubt factor, but the original eight items also achieved a reasonable fit with the data in a cross-validation (Lecci & Myers, 1996, p. 6). Lecci and Myers recommend the six-item empirically based scale; the items from Box 7-3 on this scale are items 3, 5, 10, 17, 20 (reversed), and 21 (reversed).

The dimension of probability of commission was not supported empirically as one factor. Three items—numbers 2, 12, and 16—formed one factor, which could keep the probability-of-commission label. Three other items from this scale—items 6, 11, and 14—emerged on another factor, which seems to reflect cynicism about the legal system.

To determine the predictive validity of the empirically derived scales, Lecci and Myers administered the JBS scale to 406 college students and then had them watch a videotape of a simulated rape and murder trial. The videotape included opening and closing statements by the prosecution and defense, direct and cross-examination of eight witnesses, and the judge's instructions, which included an explanation of reasonable doubt; the tape lasted 60 minutes.

Subjects were classified as either prosecution-biased or defense-biased, on the basis of their responses to the original 17 items on the JBS. Consistent with previous results, the prosecution-biased respondents were more likely to find the defendant guilty than were the defense-biased ones. While the difference was statistically significant, it was not as large as in the previous validation: 54% of the prosecution-biased respondents voted guilty compared to 46% of the defense-biased respondents. A similar analysis was done with the empirically based scales—essentially, 12 of the original 17 items—and similar results were found; 52% of the prosecution-biased respondents convicted the defendant, compared to 47% of the defense-biased respondents, a difference that was also statistically significant. The reasonable-doubt items accounted for the bulk of the predictive validity, as was the case in the original validation.

Of what use are the Revised Legal Attitudes Questionnaire and the Juror Bias Scale to the trial consultant faced with aiding an attorney in jury selection for a criminal trial? Individual items can serve as the bases for questions to individual prospective jurors during the voir dire, or if there is an opportunity to administer a *supplemental juror questionnaire* (to be described subsequently), prospective jurors can be asked to respond to all of the statements. But the trial consultant should always remember that general traits, as measured here, have a very limited relationship to verdicts in specific cases. They are better than nothing, and they are probably better than most people's intuitions, but their predictive accuracy is low when it comes to verdicts by individual jurors.

Civil Trials

Most of the published work on assessment of jurors' pretrial biases has dealt with criminal trials. But it can be argued that the issue of civil law is most susceptible to the effects of bias by individual jurors. Traditionally, criminal cases come to trial because the prosecution believes there is a chance for conviction. The defendant may feel there is little chance of acquittal but, having refused to plea bargain, he or she is faced with only one last resort. In civil cases, however, it is necessary that *both* the plaintiff and the defendant be reasonably sure of a favorable decision. A litigant who is not so sure will, most likely, settle the issue out of court. Given this aspect of civil jury trials, in many cases the amount of evidence favoring each side will be nearly equal. But what are the basic dimensions or qualities of a pretrial bias in a juror in a civil trial? While such trials can differ in the nature of the claim, the types of parties involved, and other specifics, some assessment of general attitudes may be useful.

General Attitudes

Biases in civil trials may not be as easily verbalized as those in criminal cases, but they can include several possible attitudes, which together can be collapsed into a distinction between proplaintiff and prodefendant jurors. These include:

ATTITUDES TOWARD THE "LITIGATION EXPLOSION" Whether there has truly been an increase in the amount of civil litigation in recent years, there has been ample publicity for those who claim there has (Huber, 1988; Olson, 1991). Some prospective jurors—believing media claims of a litigation explosion—may have adopted beliefs that there are too many frivolous lawsuits and that people are too quick to sue, thus reflecting an antiplaintiff bias.

ATTITUDES TOWARD RISK-TAKING Risk, as a concept, is central to the content of the law (Carson, 1988), but it has not received the analysis it deserves. By *risk* is meant a danger of harm or loss from a plaintiff's action or behavior. Traditionally, the law has said that "a plaintiff who voluntarily encounters a known risk cannot recover" (Cox, 1991, p. 24). But in real life, things are not that simple, as demonstrated by the attempts to classify the allocation of blame implicit in contributory negligence. For example, in one case, a man sued Sears and Roebuck because he had a heart attack while trying to get his Sears lawn mower started (Cox, 1992), and everyone is familiar with the elderly woman's lawsuit against McDonald's for the too-hot cup of coffee.

Jurors can differ in their attitudes toward the assumption of risk. Assumption of risk can be thought of as a continuum ranging from no risk to 100% risk. Particular actions by plaintiffs can be assigned values along this continuum. For example, a person who buys a package of Tylenol and takes several tablets assumes very little risk; a patient undergoing heart-bypass surgery assumes some risk; a person who mixes drugs whose interactive effects are unknown takes a higher risk. But the same action may be rated differently by different jurors.

ATTITUDES ABOUT STANDARDS OF CARE How stringent a standard do jurors hold with regard to the manufacture of products or the providing of services? Should a drug be 100% free of serious side effects before it is approved for sale? The availability of Viagra made its use instantly popular, but it apparently contributed to the sudden deaths of several men. How much should a new car be tested to see if it has a faulty design before it is placed on the market? How risk-free should a surgical procedure be before a doctor uses it?

ATTITUDES ABOUT PERSONAL RESPONSIBILITY The public has stereotyped civil juries as proplaintiff, that is, sympathetic to claims of misfortune and willing to tap into the "deep pockets" of rich defendants. As noted in chapter 6, the empirical evidence challenges this view (cf. Vidmar, 1995) and even leads to a conclusion that an antiplaintiff bias often emerges in jury decisions. Several causes for this doubtless exist; an impression that one of the authors has from talking to jurors after civil trials is a strong belief in personal responsibility. These jurors lack sympathy for those persons with unhappy outcomes and (sometimes justified) grievances against a manufacturer, a physician, or a governmental organization. Feigenson, Park, and Salovey (1997) noted "evidence of a specifically antiplaintiff bias in responsibility judgments" (p. 600) and refer to interviews with actual jurors (Hans & Lofquist, 1992) and experimental research (Lupfer, Cohen, Bernard, Smalley, & Schippmann, 1985) that support a conclusion that jurors often attribute the behavior of plaintiffs to undesirable motives, such as greed, rather than to legitimate grievances.

Corporate Responsibility

Attitudes toward corporations are related to some of the general attitudes detailed above, but they deserve special concern (Hans, 1990). Some potential jurors are antibusiness, standing up for the powerless individual against the monolithic corporation. But others believe that businesses are hampered too much by government regulations. Should we hold corporations to higher standards of responsibility than we hold individuals? Who deserved the blame when the Exxon tanker *Valdez* ran aground off the coast of Alaska, the captain or the oil company?

Hans and Lofquist (1992) constructed an attitude scale to measure potential jurors' attitudes toward business regulation. The 16 items on this scale tap attitudes about civil litigation, the benefits and costs of government regulation of business, and standards for worker safety and product safety. After reviewing this work, Wrightsman and Heili (1992) formulated additional items that might reflect jurors' biases in civil trials. These items, called the Civil Trial Bias Scale, were administered along with Hans and Lofquist's items, to 204 undergraduate students, and the responses were factor analyzed in order to determine what constructs underlay the responses. The first factor that emerged in this analysis seemed to favor business and the easing of stringent requirements for safety. For example, the highest loading item, number 16, from the Hans and Lofquist set, states: "Requiring that products be 100% safe before they're sold to the public is just too expensive." The other factors emerging from this analysis also covered a variety of attitudes.

A separate analysis of the Hans and Lofquist items produced clearer results than did the factor analysis of the two scales together. What emerged is one set of attitudes opposed to government regulation and another dealing with what are proper safety standards. But other dimensions may also be present; the separate factor analysis of the Civil Trial Bias Scale, not detailed here, found that jurors differed on assigning responsibility for bad outcomes, the inexplicability of bad events, and the value of risk taking.

A recent instrument that shows promise here is the Attitudes Toward Corporations Scale (Robinette, 1999); it contains five subscales that measure product safety, government regulation, treatment of employees by corporations, and antiplaintiff and anticorporation attitudes. The original pool of items from which the ATC emerged capitalized on the items developed by

Hans and Lofquist (1992), described above, but other items were constructed, and then the early versions of the scale were subjected to item analyses so that a 15-item scale resulted.

Medical Malpractice

The measurement of pretrial biases of jurors in medical malpractice trials is just beginning. However, it seems plausible that jurors can be distinguished on the basis of a *tendency* to favor patients or to favor doctors. Those who favor doctors may also hold some of the attitudes about too many frivolous lawsuits illustrated in the previous section.

Conclusion

The purpose of the design of general-attitude measures for use in jury selection is to improve on lawyers' use of stereotypes and legal lore as a means of deciding which prospective jurors should be struck. For criminal trials, social scientists have applied Boehm's (1968) Legal Attitudes Questionnaire in its original and revised forms, and Kassin and Wrightsman's (1983) Juror Bias Scale. Research supports the use of both scales to predict individual jurors' verdicts in criminal cases. Several scales have been developed to measure attitudes relevant to civil litigation, and further research is needed to determine the extent of their predictive validity.

However, even when empirical evidence supports the use of measures of juror attitudes to predict jurors' individual verdict choices, there are practical concerns. It is highly unlikely that a judge would allow an attorney to administer either scale in its entirety to prospective jurors. As we have stated, it may be possible to select items from the scale and either present them orally to jurors during voir dire, or to include them on a supplemental juror questionnaire. But the validity of the scales is determined by the administration of the complete measure, and there is no research to support the contention that one or even several select items would have the same predictive strength.

Given the practical shortcomings associated with the use of general attitudes to predict juror verdicts, many trial consultants favor a case-specific approach to guide jury selection. It is to that approach that we turn in chapter 8.

8

Jury Selection
Case-Specific Approaches

Chapter 7 described how legal consultants sometimes administer sets of attitude statements that assess broad biases that many prospective jurors inevitably hold. For example, in a criminal trial, some persons called for jury service steadfastly sympathize with defendants, while others are advocates of "law and order" and may be tempted to convict every defendant. This chapter examines how trial consultants may aid in jury selection using a different framework, one built on identifying the biases of jurors that are relevant to that particular case.

Each trial is going to have its own issues and obstacles; for example, when the four Los Angeles police officers were tried for the beating of Rodney King in 1991, it was likely that every prospective juror was familiar with the videotape of the police wielding batons against King's body. The defense attorneys who represented the police officers were faced with the challenge of identifying—and dismissing—possible jurors whose focus could not be shifted away from *what* the police did to *why* they did it, specifically that (at least in the view of the officers) Rodney King was in control of the situation and posed a life-threatening risk to the officers and bystanders. Thus, attorneys not only seek to identify "ideal" jurors and keep them in the jury pool, but they also wish to "deselect" those who appear unsympathetic to their case and clients, and the distinction between these two may rest on a specific issue rather than on a general orientation toward alleged offenders.

In this chapter, two cases are described in some detail; the two cases have similarities and differences. Both led to criminal trials, and in both, the side represented by the trial consultants had rather unusual challenges in finding jurors sympathetic to its side. In both cases, the trial consultants worked on a pro bono, or unpaid, basis (which is quite atypical). In one case, the consultants assisted the prosecution, which is also atypical. As noted earlier, trial consultants most often, these days, are hired by large firms that are defendants in civil trials, and if they are used in criminal trials, it is also the defendant that tends to hire them. In each of these trials, many of the potential jurors doubtless had sympathies with the prosecution or the defense, but other, more specific, issues took prominence during the jury selection.

The Harrisburg Seven Trial

The so-called Harrisburg Seven trial in 1972 was the first in which a group of psychologists and other social scientists acted as trial consultants and systematically aided one side in seeking a desirable verdict. Before discussing what they did, we need to provide some background.

Preceding Events

Protests against the Vietnam War reached a crescendo in the late 1960s. Not all of the protesters were college students or clearly antiestablishment types; well-respected authorities such as Dr. Benjamin Spock and a significant group of Catholic priests and nuns actively opposed the war. In fact, one group, led by priests Philip and Daniel Berrigan, called themselves the Catholic "Resistance"; in October 1967 Philip Berrigan and three associates had poured blood on files in the draft-board office at the Baltimore Customs House. And this was just the beginning of more than 20 such visible, highly publicized acts of civil disobedience. During the next year, the two Berrigan brothers and others used napalm to destroy selective-service records in Catonsville, Maryland, a suburb of Baltimore. Shortly after lunchtime on May 17, 1968, as employees watched, they entered the draft-board offices, removed around 380 individuals' files to an adjacent parking lot, and then burned them with a crude form of napalm that they had manufactured from a recipe in a Special Forces handbook published by the U.S. government (Berrigan, 1970). As the fire burned, they held hands, prayed, and waited to be arrested. This protest led to a trial of the so-called Catonsville Nine; the charges were willful destruction of government property, destruction of Selective Service records, and interference with the Selective Service Act of 1967.

Interestingly, in light of the behavior of the defendants in the subsequent Harrisburg Seven trial proceedings, the attorneys representing the defendants did not participate in the jury selection in the Catonsville Nine trial, apparently feeling that one jury was as good as any other and wanting to expedite the proceedings (Bannan & Bannan, 1974). In fact, the Berrigan brothers initially did not want a jury trial; they were content to have a judge decide their case. For them, participating in jury selection might have left the implication that they thought the legal system was legitimate. Their chief defense attorney, the famed civil rights attorney William Kunstler, argued with them and they finally reached a compromise; Kunstler wrote: "We would have a jury, but the defense would not participate in selecting it and would make no challenges to any member. Any challenges would be those executed by the prosecution; we would sit mute, accepting all jurors who ended up in the box" (Kunstler, 1994, p. 189).

On the witness stand, the defendants conceded that they had defaced draft records but claimed they had no criminal intent; instead, their goal was the saving of lives. After a brief, 4-day trial and a 1-hour jury deliberation (the judge instructed the jury that they could not consider the motives of the defendants), all nine of the protesters were convicted and were sentenced to anywhere from 2 to 3 1/2 years in prison (Barkan, 1985).

While in prison, the Berrigans and others managed to recruit more people to their cause and, in the eyes of the federal government, presented a continuing risk of further antigovernment actions. In November 1970, FBI director J. Edgar Hoover warned Congress that this group was plotting to blow up tunnels under federal government buildings in Washington, DC, and to kidnap a "high government official" (who later was identified to be Henry Kissinger, then President Nixon's national security advisor). According to Hoover, if the conspirators were successful in these activities, they would demand the ending of all U.S. bombing in Southeast Asia and the release of all political prisoners (Nelson & Ostrow, 1972). The Justice Department decided to seek an indictment of the war protesters for conspiring to carry out the activities that Hoover had mentioned, as well as planning to break into other draft-board offices. Seven persons—all but one was then or had been a priest or nun—were eventually brought to trial. Only Philip Berrigan was a member of both the Catonsville Nine and the Harrisburg Seven. Daniel Berrigan, initially included, was dropped from the eventual indictment, but additional charges were made against his brother and Sister Elizabeth McAlister, for smuggling allegedly conspiratorial letters out of a Lewisburg, Pennsylvania, federal prison. The trial was scheduled to begin in January 1972.

A group of social scientists (mostly sociologists and social psychologists) who were sympathetic to war protesters offered to assist the defense team as planning for the trial began. The hurdles were great; for example, the federal government, as prosecutor, chose to try the case in Harrisburg, Pennsylvania. Among the eligible federal districts, the Middle District of Pennsylvania, containing 11 counties, was more politically conservative than the others (other possibilities included the federal districts surrounding Rochester, New York; Philadelphia, Pennsylvania; and New York City). Also, within that district, Harrisburg—the largest city—was predominantly Republican in voting pattern, had fewer Catholics, had several military installations and war-dependent factories, and even harbored an active Ku Klux Klan

(Schulman, Shaver, Colman, Emrich, & Christie, 1973). The previous protests of the Berrigan brothers—and their prison sentences—had been highly
publicized, and it was unknown how many of the 47 million other Roman
Catholics sympathized with their antigovernment activities. Furthermore,
the government had a star witness, Boyd Douglas, who, as a college student,
had infiltrated antiwar protest groups and had even smuggled letters between
Philip Berrigan and Elizabeth McAlister. These letters discussed illegal, antiwar actions; in one, McAlister even suggested that a future strategy include a
nonviolent "citizen's arrest" of a prominent government official. Interviews
with jurors in recent trials of war protesters and draft evaders had evoked a
common response: sympathy with the defendants and detesting the Vietnam
War and yet a recognition that the defendants had broken the law and hence
had to be found guilty (Barkan, 1985).

Not only was the case against the defendants seemingly a strong one,
but at the time social scientists had little experience in assisting in trial
advocacy, including jury selection. The account of their activities, by the
participants, first published in 1973 (and the source of much of the specific
information in this section) describes a few change-of-venue surveys done
by social scientists prior to this case, but the Harrisburg Seven trial stands as
the first systematic effort by social scientists to assist in the selection of a jury
sympathetic to one side.

Pretrial Activities

The activities of the social scientists can be divided into those done prior to the
trial, with regard to the adequacy of the jury pool, and those done at the
beginning of the trial, with regard to jury selection. Early on, the social scientists began to form provisional profiles about the kinds of persons they
preferred on the jury, as well as the kinds they sought to avoid. They decided to
conduct a telephone poll of persons whose names were in the jury wheel (the
jury pool), to determine its demographic characteristics, especially age, gender,
education, occupation, and race. Did their characteristics match those of a
random sample of persons registered to vote, which was then the criterion for
eligibility for federal jury service? Given that the money for such a survey was
limited (nowadays, a marketing firm would charge about $40,000 for such a
telephone survey), the social scientists were benefited by the presence of vol-
unteers from the Harrisburg Defense Committee. After almost 1,000 phone
calls, they found that members of the random sample of registered voters
were significantly younger than members of the actual jury pool, leading the
judge to order that a new jury pool be drawn before the actual jury was chosen.

Emboldened by this early success, the social scientists decided to do
another set of interviews, this time in-home interviews with a representative
sample of potential jurors. Time was limited, but 252 people from the
original sample were interviewed, with the focus on their attitudes as well as
their ability to be impartial. Among the topics were:

1. Contact with the media, specifically what magazines, newspapers, and radio and television stations they paid attention to.
2. Knowledge of the defendants; the names of Philip Berrigan and Elizabeth McAlister were sprinkled among prominent names (Johnny Carson, Spiro Agnew, Joe Namath, etc.) in a recognition quiz.
3. Trust in government, tested by employing three questions developed by the University of Michigan's Survey Research Center.
4. The ages and activities of the respondent's children.
5. The respondent's religious affiliation and commitment.
6. The respondent's spare-time activities and organizational memberships
7. The respondent's attitudes that were potentially related to the trial, including attitudes toward government property, the police, and patriotism, as well as proprosecution attitudes.
8. Finally, a set of seven questions that assessed the respondent's degree of support of antiwar activities. These questions were, of course, intended to indicate the respondent's potential reaction to the alleged plans of the Harrisburg Seven.

This decision to try to assess potential jurors' attitudes prior to the trial was a ground-breaking action. The researchers were able to see if any demographic characteristics or attitudes were related to the potential jurors' support or antipathy toward the defendants' actions. And some surprises emerged for the analysis. A higher amount of education and exposure to metropolitan news media—usually assumed to reflect more liberal attitudes—was associated, at least in this sample, with more conservative positions, such as support of the government and rejection of antiwar protests. The respondents' religion was also related to all of the attitudes relevant to the trial issues. The researchers wrote: "We therefore recommended that the lawyers should ask prospective jurors about religion, which they had been reluctant to do; and that certain religious categories—for example, Episcopalians, Presbyterians, Methodists, and fundamentalists—were 'bad' enough from our point of view to warrant exclusion from the jury unless there were strong reasons to the contrary. (The 'better' religions were Catholic, Brethren, and Lutheran)" (Schulman et al., 1987, p. 21).

As expected, and consistent with the federal government's apparent reasons for choosing the Middle District of Pennsylvania for the trial, the sample was unusually conservative and trusting in government. Responses to specific items reflected these beliefs: 65% thought that one should support the government, whether it was right or wrong; 81% approved of the police using violent tactics if they were necessary to maintain order. The social scientists found that about 80% reflected a trust in government, compared to 45–50% in national samples at that time; they recommended to the defense attorneys that they try to assess the prospective jurors' degree of trust in the federal government. But the sample showed little awareness of the trial participants; while 93% could identify Johnny Carson, only 37% had heard of Philip Berrigan.

Was It Wrong to Conduct Pretrial Interviews
With Members of the Jury Pool?

The term *jury pool* refers to all of the persons who are eligible for jury service, based on whatever criterion is used (in this case, persons registered to vote). In many jurisdictions, the names of these people are literally placed in a large wheel and drawn out by random. A small percentage of those people is chosen to form the *jury panel* for a particular trial; the percentage is dependent on the size of the panel and characteristics of the trial; if the trial is a highly publicized one or one anticipated to last a long time, more prospective jurors' names are drawn for the jury panel, in anticipation of more persons being excused from service. Thus some probability existed that some of the 252 people interviewed by the social scientists' team could have been called in to serve on the Harrisburg Seven jury. The issue at hand is: is there anything illegal or improper in interviewing prospective jurors before they have been called for jury service? Is this jury tampering? The legal system has apparently not dealt with the specific issue posed here. Once people have been chosen for the jury, however, it is illegal to communicate with them, even if it is unclear that the goal of the communication was to influence them (*Kelly v. United States*, 1918). A defendant was held in contempt of court for hiring a detective agency to follow jurors during a trial, even though the detective did not speak to any juror—in fact, no jurors were aware that they were being shadowed (*Sinclair v. United States*, 1929).

It is certainly possible that someone from the 252 interviewees could have ended up in the jury panel. (A total of 465 persons were chosen for the panel.) In their report of their activities, the social scientists state that none of these prospective jurors had been interviewed by them and furthermore, "[W]e agreed before the trial that if anyone from our survey sample was called as a prospective juror, we would not provide defense lawyers with specific information about that person" (Schulman et al., 1987, p. 45). But, of course, the social scientists, in advance, could not guarantee there would be no overlap, and if there were, it is legitimate to ask if the questioning of these persons beforehand might have affected their jury service or somehow "contaminated" them. There is no way of knowing. But even if this question remains unanswered, some would propose—as discussed in chapter 4—that when such interviewing is initiated, an early question should ask if the respondent has received a jury summons, and if the answer is yes, the interview should be politely terminated.

Procedures During Voir Dire

By the time the trial was scheduled to begin, on January 24, 1972, the team of social scientists had developed a profile of the "ideal juror" that was specific to this particular case and its dominant issues:

[A] female Democrat with no religious preference and a white-collar job or a *skilled* blue-collar job. Furthermore, a "good" defense juror would sympathize with some elements of the defendants' views regarding the Vietnam War, at least tolerate the rights of citizens to resist government policies nonviolently, and give signs that he or she would presume the defendants to be innocent until proven guilty. (Schulman et al., 1987, p. 21; italics in original)

Furthermore, based on the interviews, the social scientists concluded that such ideal jurors would be hard to find; they expected that four out of every five prospective jurors would not sympathize with the defendants.

But how easy would it be to determine the attitudes of each prospective juror? In federal trials, judges exert more control over the questioning of prospective jurors than state judges traditionally do. The federal judge initiates the questioning of each prospective juror, and the degree to which the judge then permits the attorneys for each side to question the jurors is a matter of discretion. One of us observed a federal trial in Oklahoma in which the judge had asked lawyers from each side to furnish questions, but then he had refused to ask any of them. Beyond the traditional questions about the prospective juror's demographic characteristics and any possible conflicts of interests, the only question this judge asked was about the hobbies of each prospective juror. And the attorneys were not permitted to ask any questions.

Federal judge R. Dixon Herman, presiding at the Harrisburg Seven trial, was more agreeable to letting the attorneys ask questions after he had completed his. In fact, he permitted the attorneys to address individual jurors, to follow up, and to probe, with only occasional interruptions. Furthermore, he liberally granted the defense 28 peremptory challenges and the prosecution only 6. (In federal trials, the defense is traditionally given 10 peremptory challenges, or prospective jurors they can dismiss without cause, but in trials with multiple defendants, the judge has the discretion to increase the number of peremptory challenges given to the defense.)

On the first day of jury selection, the judge questioned the prospective jurors as a group, superficially assessing if any biases existed, as well as determining any reluctance to serve. Many prospective jurors were excused because they had read about the defendants and had already formed opinions about their guilt. Others were unable to serve for an anticipated 4–5 months of the trial. Most of these were well informed and well educated. While the defense attorneys were disappointed—still clinging to stereotypes that better-educated and -informed jurors would side with the defense—the social scientists were happy to see them go. But, to reconfirm, they telephoned 20 of these dismissed prospective jurors; 14 acknowledged they were biased against the defense, 5 refused to answer, and only 1 expressed support for the defendants.

Once the judge turned over the questioning of individual prospective jurors to the attorneys, the strategy of the prosecution differed strikingly from that of the defense. The prosecuting attorney spent only about 5 minutes questioning each; the defense team spent much more time—as much as an hour on each—and four different defense attorneys questioned each prospective juror. Thus it took 3 weeks to thin down the 465 in the panel to 46. Of these 46, 6 would be dismissed by the use of the prosecution's peremptory challenges, and 28 by the defense, leaving 12 for the actual jury.

For each of these 46, the defense team (some 15 or so lawyers, defendants, and social scientists) discussed and gave ratings; a rating of "1" signified a very good juror for the defense; a "2" a good defense juror; "3" a juror who showed both desirable and undesirable attributes, or a juror who could not be classified; and "4" and "5" were jurors whom the defense wanted to avoid. This rating system has come to be used by many trial consultants in jury selection. The procedure of having each lawyer and consultant provide an individual rating makes clear where differences exist and provokes useful discussion and articulation of reasons for the ratings.

After discussion of each of the 46 and a rating of each, the defense team found that it had the following:

Rated as a 1: 8 prospective jurors
Rated as a 2: 6 prospective jurors
Rated as a 3: 15 prospective jurors
Rated as a 4 or 5: 17 prospective jurors.

Thus, only 14 were considered favorable to the defense, and of course it was likely that the prosecution would use its 6 peremptory challenges to dismiss at least some of those. But things turned worse even before that. An elderly woman had been rated a 2 because she had announced in court that her 90-year-old mother had told her, "Daughter, you go down to the court and do justice to both the defendants and the government." But the defense team learned that she had told an acquaintance that really, she wanted to get on the jury to "show those Catholic priests and nuns" (Schulman et al., 1987, p. 24). So her classification was changed to a 5. The acquaintance had passed this information to Thomas Menaker, a local attorney on the defense team. The advantage of having someone who is a local resident participate in the jury selection process will be illustrated again in the second trial to be described in detail in this chapter, one in which the jurors all came from a small town.

As expected, the prosecution dismissed six of the defense's eight favorites, leaving them with two 1's and five 2's. Thus, the defense had to select from among the remainder whom to dismiss and whom to keep. One consideration was the composition of the jury. For example, what was the right mix of young and old, men and women? Shouldn't there be at least one Catholic on the jury, to deter any anti-Catholic expressions? Who was likely to be chosen as the jury foreperson?

The survey data had led to a profile of the ideal juror as possessing certain demographic characteristics, but the team's choices had to be between flesh-and-blood individuals. A prospective juror who fit the demographic profile might not be as impressive as someone else who did not. Members of the defense team had to remind themselves that the main value of the survey results was to indicate trends that differentiated *types* of persons, not individuals.

After intensive discussion of the pro's and con's of each of the 15 rated as a 3, each member of the defense team ranked the prospective jurors; then the group resolved discrepancies, and told the judge of their peremptory challenges. The final jury was composed of nine women and three men, ranging in age from the mid-20s to 68, only one of whom was a Catholic (however, the spouse of another juror was a Catholic). One juror was an African American; the rest were White. (This discussion makes the process of what is casually called "jury selection" to appear to be a positive selection process. But the great imbalance between the number of peremptory challenges given each side in the Harrisburg Seven trial has left the wrong impression. Generally, the process remains one that is better described as "jury deselection" in that one cannot guarantee the presence of any individual, but can only guarantee that a certain subset will *not* be on the jury.)

The Trial and Its Outcome

After several months of testimony, the closing arguments, and the judicial instructions, the jury was left to decide. The jurors deliberated for more than 60 hours over a period of 7 days before the foreperson informed the judge that they were "hopelessly deadlocked" with regard to the most important charge, that a conspiracy had existed which planned to carry out the bombings and kidnapping. They had unanimously agreed that Philip Berrigan and Elizabeth McAlister were guilty of a lesser charge, smuggling letters in and out of a federal prison. The judge then declared a mistrial, and the federal government decided not to prosecute the defendants a second time.

Was this then a victory for scientific jury selection? Answers of "yes," "no," and "can't say" are all defensible. Pragmatists would say that the defendants were not convicted and that is enough to say that scientific jury selection could count this trial in the success column. While we do not have the control group necessary to isolate cause and effect (a control group here would mean the very same trial, in a parallel universe, with the jurors selected only by the attorneys or at random), the social scientists did carry out a procedure that supports a conclusion that their decisions made a difference in the outcome. While the trial was going on, they attempted to reinterview 96 of the earlier 252 respondents, who were selected to match the actual jurors; 83 of these were contacted by telephone. A total of 63 of these gave usable responses to three questions: "Do you think the defendants really (1) intended to kidnap Henry Kissinger? (2) planned to blow up tunnels? (3) conspired to raid draft boards?" (Schulman et al., 1987, pp. 38–39). Slightly more than half of these respondents had what the social scientists classified as a "high presumption of guilt," while 28 had a "low-to-moderate presumption of guilt." The social scientists themselves recognize that this is not proof that their procedures made a difference:

> It is difficult to compare these respondents with the actual jury since the questions we asked did not correspond perfectly to the task set for the real jurors. The jurors had to decide whether all of the evidence taken together indicated a conspiracy and whether the government had actually *proven* its case against the defendants. Also, we cannot separate the effects of the trial itself from effects due to the jurors' personal characteristics. Nevertheless, the over-whelming majority of our respondents presumed some guilt on the part of the defendants, whereas the real jury voted 10 to 2 for ac-quittal. (Schulman et al., 1987, p. 39; italics in original)

In contrast, a case could be made that other factors were the major determinants of the inability to achieve consensus. First of all, conspiracy is a charge that is always difficult to prove. The judge's explanation of the def-inition of conspiracy was complicated, and jurors initially did not agree as to what constituted a conspiracy. Most jurors concluded that the defen-dants should be found guilty of conspiracy only if they were guilty of all three counts: conspiring to raid draft boards, conspiring to kidnap Henry Kissinger, and conspiring to blow up the underground tunnels (Schulman et al., 1987). Furthermore, the charges had claimed that the defendants proposed to do violent acts, while their history had always emphasized nonviolent protest.

Second, some of those whom the prosecution thought to be their best trial witnesses were ineffective or even counterproductive. We know this because Paul Cowan, a journalist, interviewed seven of the jurors after their deadlock was announced and a mistrial was declared. For example, the prosecutor placed heavy emphasis on the testimony of Boyd F. Douglas, Jr., the courier who transported letters between Philip Berrigan and Elizabeth McAlister. Douglas, who was in prison, claimed that he was there because of an antiwar act in California and that he was sympathetic to the protesters, but he actually was an FBI informant and was in prison for assaulting an FBI agent and forging checks which he transported across state lines. He had an extensive criminal record and had violated his parole that had resulted from a previous offense. But despite that, he ingratiated himself with the trusting group, all the while betraying them and even tape recording phone calls he made to Elizabeth McAlister. He read many of the letters he was given to transmit and, while on released time, he even copied a number of them. On the stand, Douglas came across as an arrogant braggart who had duped several girlfriends as well as the war protesters, and doubtless the impact of his testimony was not what the prosecution had hoped.

For example, on cross-examination, defense attorney Ramsey Clark got Douglas to admit that he had committed bank fraud in several states, that he had impersonated an army officer, and that he had stolen cars in two different states, escaped from five different jails, and had numerous prison violations, including theft, gambling, and lying to an official (Nelson & Ostrow, 1972). Douglas even seemed somewhat proud of his escapades. He boasted of misleading several college women while he was on released time from prison; here is an exchange that was part of his cross-examination regarding a student named Betsy Sandel, whom he had courted:

Q. And did you point out Betsy Sandel as being one of the demonstrators? Did you identify her photograph to the FBI?
A. I am sure I did, if she was there.
Q. And did you describe her as a student at Bucknell to the FBI?
A. The FBI knew that.
Q. Did you ask her to marry you?
A. (Pause, and then a laugh.) Possibly.
Q. Was it before or after you pointed out her picture to the FBI?
A. (Head bowed.) I don't recall. (Nelson & Ostrow, 1972, p. 269)

According to court observers, most of the jurors appeared shocked at this acknowledgment.

Whether or not the scientific jury selection in this case is considered an overall success, the expectations of the social scientists were completely in error with regard to a few jurors, including the two who became holdouts and consistently voted that the defendants were guilty. One of these jurors, a man in his 50s who owned two grocery stores, a Lutheran, had expressed antiwar attitudes during the jury selection. But as soon as the deliberations began, it became clear that his true feelings were far from sympathetic with war protesters. The other, the 68-year-old woman, belonged to a pacifist church; four of her sons were conscientious objectors on religious grounds. The defense team had accepted her immediately on hearing that. But in the deliberations, she showed that she did not share her sons' feelings.

Both of these jurors had initially been rated as favorable jurors; the social scientists' account does not indicate whether they were classified as 1's or 2's; probably the man was rated as a 2 because his occupation as the owner of a business was considered somewhat detrimental. It does appear that this juror deliberately misrepresented his feelings during the jury selection, as he made statements at that time that included, "More could be done and should be done to end the war," and he "couldn't be against hippies because I have some sons who look like that" (Schulman et al., 1987, p. 26). But during the first day of the deliberations, he pronounced the defendants guilty by the will of God. He

began to shout that it was necessary to find the defendants guilty to satisfy God's will and to save the children and grandchildren of America. [He] asserted that the defendants had to be guilty if the government had brought them to trial; he banged on the table for emphasis.... He appealed to their religious convictions, threatening them with the wrath of God. Not once, said the other jurors, did he offer reasons to support his assertion of the defendants' guilt. (Schulman et al., 1987, p. 33)

If a prospective juror decides to misrepresent his or her true feelings during the voir dire questioning, in order to get selected for the jury (or for whatever reason), little can be done by trial consultants who cannot detect the deception. But we believe that the defense team can be faulted for their other wrong guess; they acknowledged that when the older woman mentioned that she had four sons who were conscientious objectors to the war, they stopped questioning her. She made it clear that her sons made their own decisions, but the defense team failed to pursue the issue further.

As noted, another possible response to the question of whether scientific jury selection was successful in the Harrisburg Seven trial is to acknowledge that we cannot say. This is the conservative response, as we lack the resources to control the effects of other variables. However, short of that ideal, and given the atmosphere in the country and especially in that federal district, we believe that the procedures used by the social scientists in this trial provide a model for increasing the chances of obtaining a favorable verdict. Indeed, the jury was clearly more liberal and younger than was expected. Three of the jurors expressed antiwar views, and the other nine were ambivalent or reserved their opinions. And even though this was the first comprehensive application of scientific jury selection, its procedures remain a model even today.

The Retrial of Byron de la Beckwith

In preparing for jury selection, trial attorneys and legal consultants need to ask what are the salient issues for the jurors who will decide the outcome of the trial. In the retrial of Byron de la Beckwith, some of the most salient issues were unique—it was a retrial 30 years after the crime—but still the trial serves as a generally applicable example of the case-based approach to jury selection.

The Crime

In June 1963, Medgar Evers was spearheading the drive in Mississippi to get African Americans registered to vote. It wasn't easy, as throughout the South, county clerks and registrars had set up outrageous obstacles to Blacks who sought to vote, for example, requiring them to answer a set of difficult questions or quote long sections of the U.S. Constitution from memory. While he did not have the visibility of Martin Luther King, Jr., Medgar Evers was the field secretary of the Mississippi branch of the National Association for the Advancement of Colored People (NAACP) and was recognized beyond the boundaries of Mississippi as an up-and-coming leader among African Americans who sought justice. In addition to pushing for voter registration, he documented the appalling nature of Mississippi's Black schools, still segregated almost a decade after the *Brown v. Board of Education* decision; he organized sit-ins that sought equal accommodations at restaurants, movies, and other public places (Morris, 1998).

Returning home in Jackson, Mississippi, about 12:45 A.M. on June 12, 1963, Evers parked his car in the driveway and started toward the front door of his house. As his wife and children watched (the children had been permitted to stay up to watch President John F. Kennedy's speech on civil rights on television and to welcome their father home), he was ambushed from behind. A single bullet struck Evers in the back, came out through his chest, went through the front window of the house, and even penetrated a wall separating the living room and kitchen before it spent itself. Medgar Evers died shortly after the shooting, from internal injuries and loss of blood.

Based on the bullet's trajectory, police concluded that it had come from a gun fired about 200 feet away from the Everses' house, in a honeysuckle thicket near a drive-in restaurant. They found a gun, suspended about a foot above the ground, hidden in a kind of sniper's nest among these bushes and trees; it was a 1917 .30-caliber Enfield rifle, a seven-shot, bolt-action repeater. The chamber contained one empty casing and six live bullets. One fingerprint was found on the Golden Power riflescope attached to the rifle; otherwise, the gun appeared to have been wiped clean. Employees of the drive-in restaurant reported that a car had been parked in an isolated part of the back parking lot of the restaurant, near the cluster of trees. The car was identified as a white Plymouth Valiant, with a long, whiplike antenna on the back.

The gun and the scope were traced to a man named Byron de la Beckwith, who lived in Greenwood, Mississippi. He also drove a 1962 white Valiant, actually a company car assigned to him. Beckwith told the police that the gun had been stolen from him several weeks earlier, but he had not reported its theft to the police. Concurrently, police learned that several cab drivers in Jackson reported that on the day before the shooting, a man fitting Beckwith's description had asked them where Medgar Evers lived. The fingerprint found on the scope was Beckwith's. The police believed there was enough evidence to arrest Beckwith. (Actually, the FBI made the initial arrest of Beckwith, for violating Medgar Evers's civil rights, not for murder, as the latter was a state crime. But then the Justice Department dropped the federal charges.) On July 2, 1963, Beckwith was indicted for the murder of Medgar Evers.

Byron de la Beckwith's Background

Byron de la Beckwith was born on November 9, 1920; thus he was 42 years old when Medgar Evers was killed. Beckwith was born in Colusa, California (a Mississippi newspaper proclaimed, "California Man Charged With Evers Murder"), but his roots were in the South and he bragged that Jefferson Davis, the president of the Confederacy, was one of his ancestors. He was active in the White Citizens Council, a militant segregationist organization, and it was authenticated that he was also a speaker at rallies of the Ku Klux Klan. A biography of Beckwith by his own nephew (Massengill, 1994) documents how Beckwith saw that his God-given mission was to uphold the racial purity of the antebellum South. As far back as 1956, in a letter to President Dwight D. Eisenhower published in the Greenwood, Mississippi, *Morning Star*, Beckwith wrote, "We shall not be integrated and therefore mongrelized. We shall walk away from the field of honor avenged. Behind us shall lie the remains of all those responsible for the crime of promoting integration" (Massengill, 1994, p. 8). The next year, in a letter to the Memphis *Commercial Appeal*, he wrote, "I believe in segregation just as I believe in God. I shall oppose any person, place or thing that opposes segregation. I shall combat the evils of integration and shall bend every effort to rid the United States of America of the integrationists, whosoever and wherever they may be" (Massengill, 1994, p. 8). He compared Blacks to a boll weevil and the segregationist White South to a cotton boll, stating, "[T]hey must be destroyed lest the pure, white cotton boll be destroyed" (Smothers, 1994, p. A12).

Beckwith's rampant anti-Semitism was also no secret. He viewed Jews as children of the devil, and when his nephew Reed Massengill initially contacted him about writing his biography, Beckwith demanded that the book document the perceived injustices he had received from Jews (Massengill, 1994, p. 13). He propagated the myths that Jews managed an international financial cartel and that they controlled both the Federal Reserve System and the national news media. It was reported that he once said that "most of the Jews in the world are living in the United States" and that he was ready to "get some of them" (Massengill, 1994, p. 261).

The Initial Trials of Byron de la Beckwith

On January 27, 1964, Beckwith's trial on the charge of murdering Medgar Evers began in Jackson, Mississippi. Things were different then; racial segregation still was the operative procedure, although in this trial, the 30 or so Blacks who attended the first day of the trial were permitted by the judge to sit anywhere they wanted and to use the "Whites Only" restrooms down the hall (Massengill, 1994). The jury pool was male and almost entirely White (of the 109 summoned, only 7 were Black). Race was the predominant theme of the jury selection. William Waller, then the Hinds County district attorney (and later a governor of Mississippi) reflected the race-based customs of the time; he addressed those prospective jurors who were White as "mister," while calling Blacks by their first names only. Yet he appeared to seek an impartial jury; he asked, for example, "if you go into the jury room and somebody says, 'I can't convict a White man for killing a Negro; let's go home,' would you agree?" (Massengill, 1994, p. 181). He pushed prospective jurors as to their ability to look at the evidence impartially "even if Evers' work was obnoxious to you" (Massengill, 1994, p. 181). District Attorney Waller's language would be considered offensive today, but 40 years ago it passed without judicial recognition or reprimand: "Did you hear that the niggers might want Mr. Beckwith acquitted so that they can go north and raise more money [for civil rights activities]? . . . Day after day you may sit here and see this room jammed with nothing but niggers. Would that influence you in your deliberations?" (Massengill, 1994, p. 181).

After 4 days of voir dire, a jury of 12 White males was chosen. By no means was it an impartial jury: one juror's brother was a police officer and another juror's labor union had contributed money to Beckwith's defense fund. Beckwith himself, during the jury selection, appeared cocky; he chatted with newspaper reporters and mugged for the television stations' sketch artists. The assumption of court watchers was that there was no way Beckwith would be found guilty.

The prosecution's main evidence in this first trial consisted of the facts described above: that his rifle had been found at the crime scene with one of his fingerprints on the scope, that a car resembling his had been close to the crime scene (several witnesses testified to seeing the car in the neighborhood that day), and that he had been inquiring about Medgar Evers's address. The man who traded the gun to Beckwith and the man who sold him the scope testified. The fingerprint expert not only identified the fingerprint as Beckwith's, but also testified that when he lifted it from the scope, the morning of the murder, it could not have been more than 12 hours old because of the amount of perspiration present. Furthermore, an FBI fingerprint expert testified that the fingerprint could have come from "no one else in the world" (Massengill, 1994, p. 190). A total of 36 witnesses testified for the prosecution, and 60 items of evidence were introduced.

Beckwith's defense provided an alibi, in the form of testimony of three Greenwood police officers, who stated that they had seen Beckwith that night, one at 11:45 P.M., two at 1:05 A.M., in Greenwood, 90 miles away from Jackson. (None of these officers had come forward until 8 months after Beckwith's arrest.) Another defense witness testified that he had seen Beckwith the morning before Evers's murder and that he had a noticeable cut over his eye (the prosecutor had argued that the cut was a result of the recoil of the rifle).

The defense also tried to discredit many of the prosecution's witnesses and tried to portray the victim as such an "integrationist" that he posed a threat to many White Mississippians. Beckwith also took the stand in his own defense, acknowledging his views proudly and denying that he had shot Medgar Evers or that he had been in Jackson at the time. He conceded that the murder weapon was "similar" to one that he had possessed, but reaffirmed that it had been stolen several weeks before. In his cross-examination of Beckwith, District Attorney Waller produced a letter Beckwith had written to the National Rifle Association, in which he said, "For the next fifteen years, we here in Mississippi are going to have to do a lot of shooting to protect our wives, our children, and ourselves from bad Negroes" (quoted by Massengill, 1994, p. 197). Beckwith continued to deny that he advocated violence, claiming that, in defending the cause of segregation, he was only "a writer."

After several days of deliberations and 20 ballots, the jury foreman informed the judge that the jury was deadlocked, and the judge declared a mistrial. Apparently, about half of the jurors (five, according to one account; six, according to another) held out for the conviction of Beckwith. In light of the predominant attitudes of White Mississippians at the time, a jury's vote that was almost evenly divided was a testimonial to the strength of the evidence against Beckwith, for the charge of murder against him had even made Beckwith an object of some respect in the White community (Smothers, 1994). Even the prosecuting attorney, in his opening statement, had said, "I am a segregationist. I don't believe any good can come from a forced mixing of the races" (Associated Press, 1994, p. A-8). An example of the support for Beckwith was the appearance of the then-governor of Mississippi, Ross Barnett, who came to shake his hand and sit with him as the jurors in the first trial began their deliberations.

The prosecution decided to retry Beckwith, and a second trial was begun barely more than 3 months later, on April 6, 1964. A panel of 310 men was called. The prosecution took 4 days to present the same evidence it had in the first trial; the defense offered one new witness, James L. Hobby, who testified that he had parked his 1960 Valiant in the drive-in's parking lot on the night of the killing. Again, the jury deliberated for 2 days and then reported that it was irrevocably split. After the judge once again declared a mistrial, it was reported that the final vote was eight for acquittal and four for conviction. Beckwith was released from jail.

The Next 30 Years

All of the above happened in 1963 and 1964. The retrial of Beckwith, which serves as an example of case-based jury selection, occurred *30 years later*. What happened in the interim, and why did the prosecutors decide to reinitiate a trial?

It is rare, almost unique, for a person to be tried 30 years after a crime. (The trials of aging Nazi war criminals and the recent trial of Michael Skakel are the only equivalent ones that come to mind.) Two types of factors led to the decision to retry Byron de la Beckwith. First was the behavior of Beckwith himself. On September 27, 1973, Beckwith was arrested by police in New Orleans after they found a time bomb and a small arsenal of weapons in his car. Beckwith was charged with planning to bomb the residence of a leader of the Anti-Defamation League, a Jewish organization, in

New Orleans. (An informant within the Ku Klux Klan had notified the authorities of Beckwith's plan.)

The next May, he was convicted of transporting dynamite without a permit and sentenced to 5 years in the Louisiana state prison at Angola. After numerous appeals and, finally, an arrest on a fugitive warrant while in Washington, DC, Beckwith began his prison term on May 16, 1977; he remained in prison for 3 years. (In 1992, long after he had been released from prison, a judge in Orleans Parish, Louisiana, threw out his conviction.)

More relevant was the fact that Beckwith began to brag about the killing of Medgar Evers. For example, a minister who had infiltrated the Ku Klux Klan said that Beckwith had told a Klan group: "Killing that nigger gave me no more inner discomfort than our wives endure when they give birth to our children. We ask them to do that for us. We should do just as much. So, lets [*sic*] go in there and kill those enemies, including the President, from the top down" (quoted by DeLaughter, 2001, p. 100). Prosecutors also received a letter from a woman who wrote: "During the summer of 1967, Byron De La Beckwith was introduced to me in a Greenwood restaurant as the man who killed Medgar Evers. He openly bragged that he had killed Medgar Evers. . . . I had the thought of a murderer going free, regardless of his age. If my testimony will be helpful at this late date, I will gladly offer it" (quoted by DeLaughter, 2001, p. 162). A jail inmate in Louisiana also reported that Beckwith had admitted the murder; "he was not worried about being prosecuted because he had been tried twice and found not guilty," he reported (quoted by DeLaughter, 2001, p. 180). Eventually, the prosecution found three other witnesses who reported that Beckwith had bragged to them of the murder.

The second reason for reopening the case was pressure from the media, from civil rights activists, and from Myrlie Beasley Evers, the widow of Medgar Evers. For example, in late 1989, the Jackson *Clarion-Ledger* reported that, prior to Beckwith's second trial in 1964, a state agency had investigated potential jurors in order to eliminate those who were not sufficiently in favor of segregation. The Mississippi State Sovereignty Commission, originally established in 1956 by the state legislature, had as its original purpose the perpetuation of racial segregation in the state—it even financed activities of the White Citizens Councils—but it evolved, in the words of prosecutor Bobby DeLaughter, into a "state-operated spy corps" (2001, p. 20). The commission hired investigators to uncover inflammatory information about civil-rights activists and maintained files on such individuals and groups (Trillin, 1995). (Ironically, soon after its formation, Beckwith applied to become an investigator with the commission, but he was not hired.) The commission stopped its activities in the early 1970s, and its records were sealed, but in 1989 a reporter for the Jackson newspaper gained access to them and revealed the allegation that prospective jurors had been screened by the state. It claimed that Beckwith's defense attorney had enlisted the help of an investigator for the commission, who provided information about prospective jurors' backgrounds, affiliations, and racial beliefs.

By this time, in 1989, the staff of the Hinds County prosecutor's office had changed; Ed Peters was the district attorney and Bobby DeLaughter was one of his assistants. (DeLaughter's book *Never Too Late*, published in 2001, provides many details about the investigation and retrial.) They decided that sufficient evidence existed to consider initiating a retrial of Beckwith. But many obstacles stood in the way. For example, the district attorney's office was unable to locate a transcript of the first trial in 1964; finally, a newspaper reporter provided the prosecutors with his copy. More important, significant evidence could also not be found in the office files or those of the police department. The murder weapon could not be located; someone told Assistant District Attorney DeLaughter that after the trial, "the judge had taken it." DeLaughter thought that referred to the trial judge, but later he came to realize that his own father-in-law, who was so eminent a jurist in Jackson that clerks referred to him as "The Judge," was a gun collector and that he had even mentioned having the gun. DeLaughter was able to retrieve the gun from the top of a closet in his in-laws' house.

Other obstacles included an effort by Beckwith, who now lived in Tennessee, to avoid extradition to Mississippi and an appeal to the Supreme Court of Mississippi by the defense, claiming that Beckwith had been denied the right to a speedy trial and that, also, the possibility of a retrial violated the principle of double jeopardy. On December 16, 1992, the court rejected the double-jeopardy claim outright and decided not to decide the speedy-trial issue (by a slim 4–3 vote). On the latter issue, the court, in effect, said, wait until after the trial is over to raise this objection. (In 1997, the Mississippi Supreme Court was required to face the issue and ruled that the delay did not conflict with the right to a speedy trial.) After further delays, the trial was scheduled to begin in January 1994.

The 1994 Retrial

When someone is tried or retried 30 years after a crime, trial consultants— regardless of which side they are representing—have unique challenges in identifying ideal jurors and jurors to avoid. The prosecution had to overcome what seemed an overwhelming feeling of "why bring this up now?" Many Mississippians, White and Black, felt that the state had made much progress with respect to racial relations in 30 years, and old issues should be left alone. Another problem was sympathy for Beckwith, who was by then more than 70 years old, frail, hard of hearing, and in other ways not in good health. But the district attorney's office also believed that it was essential that justice be done. The trial went forward.

Because of the heavy publicity involving the retrial, upon the request of the defense, the judge ordered a change of venue. Instead of coming from Jackson and the surrounding Hinds County, jurors were to be drawn from

Panola County, a smaller county 140 miles north of Jackson. Panola County had a population of about 30,000; the county seat, Batesville, had fewer than 6,500 residents, but its racial composition—about 51% Black—was similar to that of Hinds County. After the jurors were selected in Batesville, they were to be brought to Jackson for the actual trial; they would be sequestered there until they reached a verdict.

A number of social scientists and trial consultants also felt that it was essential that Beckwith be brought to justice, and they offered their services pro bono to the prosecution to assist in trial preparation and jury selection. Chief among these was Dr. C. K. "Pete" Rowland, a political science professor at the University of Kansas and a partner in a trial-consulting firm located in Overland Park, Kansas. Dr. Rowland had testified in several trials in Mississippi and knew the prosecuting attorneys. Dr. Rowland was assisted in the assembly of voir dire questions by the two authors of this book. He spent several weeks in Mississippi in preparation for the trial and during jury selection. Andrew Sheldon, a trial consultant from Atlanta, also participated in the jury selection, assisting the prosecution pro bono; Dr. Sheldon was particularly skilled at observing the nonverbal behavior of prospective jurors, whom he observed before each participated in the sequestered voir dire. Another member of the prosecution team was Dr. Lee Maril, a sociology professor from Oklahoma State University, who collected impressions from the community. Which prospective jurors should be deselected? Those with racist attitudes, for one, but would they express them during the voir dire? The jury questioning found that older Whites were reluctant to talk about their racial attitudes, but some of the younger Whites were quite open; some simply said, "I don't like integration" (C. K. Rowland, Personal communication, February 28, 1994).

Pete Rowland, Lee Maril, and some helpers had talked to residents of Batesville and learned of an issue that split the county along racial lines. The southern part of the county was predominantly White, while the northern part was mostly Black. A bond issue to improve and expand North Panola High School had generated opposition from some voters in the southern part of the county. The district attorney asked prospective jurors from the southern part of the county how they felt about the bond issue. The consultants also discovered that there were two softball leagues in the county; one was all-White but the other was racially integrated. Similarly, after racial desegregation was instituted in the public schools, a number of White parents removed their children from these schools and enrolled them in "private academies" (a code term for all-White schools). Political party membership had some value; if a White person was a Republican and fairly well off, it told little about his or her racial preferences, but those who were Republican and poor tended to be racist. Each of these pieces of information was potentially helpful in classifying White jurors as possessing prodefense attitudes. The most diagnostic question for White jurors, it was later found, was: Where did your kids go to school?

What about African Americans as potential jurors? Certainly, the defense did not want any on the eventual jury; when the pool was reduced to 36 and each side was to indicate the 12 for whom it would exercise its peremptory challenges, there would still remain a number of Blacks as potential jurors. But not all Blacks were ideal jurors for the prosecution. Some of the young Blacks had not heard of Medgar Evers. Some African Americans, active in their churches, declared that they were uncomfortable passing judgment about guilt; that was "God's role." One told the court, "Judge not, that ye be not judged." But some Blacks wanted to be jurors; they waived the automatic exemption whereby anyone over the age of 65 could be excused from jury service. Some in the community advised the prosecutors and jury consultants that older Blacks, if on the jury, would be intimidated by younger Whites, but the trial consultants believed that the desire of these African Americans to serve on this jury was a strong indication of their eventual contribution, and they proved to be correct. (Eventually, two older jurors, ages 67 and 70, were among the Blacks chosen.)

The jury selection began on January 18, 1994. Five hundred juror summonses were issued; about half of those people showed up. Only one of these indicated that she had not heard of the case.

In preparation for the voir dire, the trial consultants had prepared a series of questions for the prospective jurors to answer in writing; these included questions about due process and racial attitudes, as well as some of the questions assessing juror bias described in chapter 7. The consultants had hoped that the judge would permit the administration of this supplemental juror questionnaire, but the county clerk vetoed its use, claiming the county did not have the resources to make copies and collate them (even though the prosecution team had offered to do so). But, perhaps in compensation, the judge instituted a sequestered voir dire, in which each prospective juror was questioned individually in the judge's chambers, and during this voir dire, the judge did permit a number of the questions from the supplemental juror questionnaire to be asked.

A number of prospective jurors asked the judge to be excused because of employment or medical problems. Others—some White, some Black—questioned the wisdom of the retrial; among prospective jurors' comments were the following (the last two were made by Black prospective jurors):

> "This trial is not about justice; it's about politics."
> "The whole thing was senseless."
> "He's what, 70 years old?"
> "I think if Mr. De La Beckwith were Black, we wouldn't be having this trial."
> "Why prosecute someone after all these years, regardless of what the evidence may show?"

"Why bring it back up, whether he's guilty or innocent? You know,
wherever he's at, just let him stay, and I feel he's guilty."
(DeLaughter, 2001, pp. 223–224)

One of the tasks of the trial consultants, in their assistance to the
prosecutors, was to determine, at least among White jurors, their sympathy
with prosegregation forces. Rowland and Sheldon suggested to District
Attorney Peters that he ask: "What was your first impression or feeling when
you heard that the case was reopened and going to trial after 30 years?" This
often elicited candid answers that were very helpful in the decision whether
to retain the juror. Similarly, the question "What does fairness mean to you
in this case?" was helpful.

The jury selection process took 6 days. While the original pool of 250
was about evenly divided between Blacks and Whites, more Whites were
given exemptions or successfully challenged for cause. The final group of 49
potential jurors was composed of 28 Blacks and 21 Whites. The final result
of the jury selection process was a jury of 8 Blacks (3 males and 5 females)
and 4 Whites (2 males and 2 females). They tended to be old (in their 60s or
70s) or young (in their late 20s or 30s). The most educated had only 1 year
of college, and several lacked a high-school degree. The prosecution team
had doubts about several of the White jurors, but did not have enough
peremptory challenges to strike them. (During the second day of the trial,
the Jackson *Clarion-Ledger* reported that an alternate juror, a White woman,
once threatened a Black woman she supervised and told her that her husband was a member of the Ku Klux Klan.)

Amazingly, almost all of the witnesses from the 1964 trials were still
alive and able to testify; prosecution witnesses included the pathologist, the
men who traded the gun and sold the scope to Beckwith, some of the
neighbors who heard the shot, and the Jackson police detective. But during
its 4 days of testimony, the prosecution also presented the new evidence that
had reopened the case: six witnesses (acquaintances, a tenant of Beckwith's
in Tennessee, an FBI informant, a prison guard, and a fellow prisoner) who
said that Beckwith had made incriminating remarks about his role in the
killing. In his closing argument, prosecutor DeLaughter told the jury the
reasons that they should find Beckwith guilty: "It was his gun, his scope, his
fingerprint, his car—and lastly, but certainly not least—his mouth" (Associated Press, 1994, p. A-8).

For the defense, one of the police officers who located Beckwith in
Greenwood that night also testified. A second witness from the first trials
was now dead, and a third police officer was infirm, but his testimony from
the first trial was read to the jury. Beckwith did not testify; although he was
present in the courtroom, his attorney stated that the 73-year-old defendant was "unavailable" because of his failing memory. (A request to read
Beckwith's testimony from the first trial to the jurors was denied by the
judge.) In contrast to the prosecution, which presented 39 witnesses, the

defense only had 5; the prosecution's case took 4 days, the defense's 1½. The judge refused to admit the testimony of the man who, in the second trial, had testified that his car, similar in appearance to Beckwith's Valiant (it even had the same whiplike antenna), was parked in the drive-in lot the night of the murder. The defense attorneys had waited until the last day of the trial evidence to disclose their plans to introduce this witness, leading the judge to conclude that this was unfair to the prosecution.

The jurors were sent to begin their deliberations at 1:30 on a Friday afternoon. After deliberating for 5 hours, they were excused for the evening and sequestered, to begin their deliberations again the next morning. On their first vote on Friday they split, eight voting for conviction and four for acquittal (including two of the Blacks). But by 9:35 on Saturday morning, February 5, 1994, they had a unanimous verdict. Beckwith was found guilty of murder and immediately sentenced to life in prison. The jury foreperson, who was 70 years old, Black, and a minister, later told the media that the first thing the jury had done that morning was to join hands and pray for guidance from the Almighty; "after only one hour of prayer, we were certain the man was guilty," he said (C. K. Rowland, personal communication, February 28, 1994).

Did the Jury Consultants Make a Difference?

A retrial led to a unanimous guilty verdict, while two trials 30 years before had led to split verdicts, with most jurors favoring acquittal; it is impossible to identify a single cause for the difference in outcome. Mississippi was a different place in 1994 than it was in 1964. Medgar Evers was killed as he sought to have Blacks register to vote; in 1994 Mississippi had 825 elected officials who were Black, more than any other state (Ferris, 1994). Many possible reasons exist for the shift in verdicts; while the evidence favoring conviction was strong in 1964, it was even stronger in 1994. Some research evidence exists that in retrials, the prosecution wins three out of every four times, but that piece of information comes from federal cases (Cox, 1995). Did the activities of the trial consultants contribute to the difference? We think so. They posed questions for the attorneys to use in jury selection, and the lawyers listened to them and adopted them. The district attorney had a tendency to ask closed-ended questions; the consultants persuaded him that open-ended questions provided more diagnostic information. Information about community activities (private-school enrollment, softball teams, etc.) assisted in eliciting information relevant to prospective jurors' attitudes. But how much difference did all of this make? How different would the actual jury have been without the input of the consultants? The prosecuting attorneys certainly were aware of racial differences in attitudes and had a great deal of experience in jury selection. Like the Harrisburg Seven trial described above, the side assisted by the trial consultants had some obstacles to overcome and yet emerged successfully, but any outcome is a product of many causes.

Conclusions

The purpose of this chapter has been to illustrate that each trial is different in the sense that special issues exist which can color the eventual verdicts of the jurors. Litigation consultants, in preparing for voir dire, need to identify these salient issues and encourage attorneys, to the extent they can question prospective jurors, to try to elicit these jurors' positions on these issues. In the Harrisburg Seven trial, a basic issue was the legitimacy of protest against the Vietnam War; in the Beckwith retrial, issues included the acceptability of retrying a man who was now near his death, as well as the overriding issue of racial attitudes. We believe that the consultants did an effective job in bringing these to the forefront during voir dire. Whether the presence of the trial consultants and their input had any effect on the outcome is impossible to answer, although we believe it is more likely that they did than that they didn't.

9

Jury Selection
Effectiveness and Ethics

First came, in the fall of 2001, the Enron Corporation scandal—a loss of $142 million and the dismissal of thousands of Enron employees, many of whom had their pensions built on their employer's assurances of Enron's stability. Then came the allegations of the role of the accounting firm Arthur Andersen in this debacle. And in the spring of 2002, this company—one of the nation's leading accounting firms, with 28,000 employees—was placed on trial for obstructing justice by shredding evidence, hence impeding a Securities and Exchange Commission's inquiry into Enron's finances. The federal government claimed that Arthur Andersen, as Enron's auditor, had signed off on financial statements that obscured billions of dollars of debts and losses by Enron. Most commentators believed that the government would have a tough job proving a criminal act in this case, for it had to show that Arthur Andersen, as a company, had the intent to deceive the government (Hoeflich, 2002). While the defendants conceded that they had destroyed documents, they claimed that this was simply a routine business procedure, done by all large corporations that seek to avoid being overwhelmed by their own paperwork.

The jury in the Arthur Andersen trial deliberated for 74 hours over a period of 10 days; on several occasions the foreperson reported to the judge that the jury was not able to reach agreement, but the judge urged the jury to try to reach a unanimous verdict. Finally they did, finding Arthur Andersen guilty as charged.

Not only was the verdict surprising, but the reason for it was even more so. As reporters pursued the jurors to learn about their deliberations, it became clear that the jury based its verdict not on what prosecutors believed to be the most incriminating evidence—testimony by the lead auditor, who had plea bargained and agreed to testify for the prosecution. Instead, the jury concentrated on a single e-mail from an Andersen staff attorney, Nancy Temple, that asked to delete references to Andersen's legal group and remove her name from an Andersen internal memo that detailed a disagreement between the accounting firm and Enron about the use of the term "non-recurring" to describe a $1 billion charge. In her memo Ms. Temple had recommended "deleting some language that might suggest that we have concluded the release is misleading" (quoted by Gillers, 2002, p. A18). Observers had seen this memo as routine legal advice—in the words of a prominent legal ethicist, "the kind of advice that lawyers give clients all the time" (Gillers, 2002, p. A18)—and it would have been covered by the attorney-client privilege had not Andersen waived it (Bartley, 2002). But in the minds of the jurors, this became the "smoking gun" that helped to break the jury's deadlock. One of the jurors later told the press that this was the memo that convinced him that Andersen employees intended to keep information from the SEC (Rozen & Jeffries, 2002). The jury foreperson, a computer-science professor, told the media, "Arthur Andersen set about to change things, to alter documents; it's against the law to alter the document with the intent to impair the fact-finding ability of an official proceeding" (quoted by Hart, 2002, p. 8A).

The Difficulty in Predicting Jury Outcomes

On occasion in this book, we have described trials in which the jury's verdict either was difficult to predict or surprising, in that it differed from the expected outcome. As noted earlier, many experienced trial attorneys throw up their hands when asked to predict a given jury's decision. But still they try, and trying means doing everything they can to compose the jury of persons sympathetic to their position. And they hire trial consultants to aid them in achieving this goal. Sometimes it works, sometimes not.

The purposes of this chapter are twofold: to examine the effectiveness of what is referred to as "jury selection" and to evaluate the ethics of such a procedure. In describing the viewpoints of some of the critics of the process, we will find that sometimes discussions of ethics and effectiveness are confounded. Some critics seem to be saying, "Jury selection by outsiders shouldn't be done, and it doesn't work anyway." We will try to separate these issues, but in regard to each, the answer is not clear.

Effectiveness of Lawyer-Conducted Jury Selection

As noted earlier, many attorneys, including some prominent ones, believe that the trial can be won or lost during voir dire. Certainly, attorneys believe that jury selection works, to a degree at least. A book titled *The Chosen Ones* (Davis, 1971) contains laudatory endorsements by prominent trial attorneys F. Lee Bailey and Melvin Belli. Most trial attorneys in the United States would be upset if suddenly they no longer had the opportunity to use peremptory challenges to dismiss seemingly unsympathetic prospective jurors. Chapter 7 described some of the stereotypes and beliefs held by trial attorneys in selecting the jury. Psychologists and other social scientists, more grounded in an empirical basis for decision making, doubt that such stereotypes have much usefulness.

Not only do many trial attorneys believe that jury selection works, but they take pride in their ability to select a "winning jury." A number of years ago the president of the American Association of Trial Lawyers in America wrote, "Trial attorneys are acutely attuned to the nuances of human behavior, which enables them to detect the minutest traces of bias or inability to reach the appropriate decision" (Begam, 1977, p. 3). Yet in their classic book on jury behavior, Kalven and Zeisel (1966) proposed that trial attorneys generally overestimate their own abilities to select sympathetic jurors or to persuade them successfully. What do observations of jury selection and empirical studies conclude?

In an early observational study, Broeder (1965) was in the courtroom for the jury selection phase of 23 consecutive trials in a federal court in the Midwest; he concluded that "the voir dire was grossly ineffective not only in weeding out 'unfavorable' jurors but even in eliciting the data which would have shown particular jurors as very likely to prove 'unfavorable'" (pp. 505–506).

More recently, more sophisticated procedures have been used. Johnson and Haney (1994) observed the jury selection process in four felony trials. They were permitted to administer Boehm's (1968) Legal Attitudes Questionnaire (described in chapter 7) to prospective jurors. By comparing the attitude scores of those persons who were retained as jurors with those who were dismissed by the prosecutors or defense attorneys, the researchers were able to determine just how effective were the decisions of each side in the use of their peremptory challenges. This analysis led to two findings: (1) prospective jurors who were dismissed by prosecutors held stronger prodefense attitudes than those prospective jurors dismissed by the defense, and likewise, those dismissed by the defense favored the prosecution more than those excused by the prosecution; (2) yet, the attitudes of those jurors who were *not* dismissed by either side did not differ significantly from the first 12 jurors questioned nor from a group of prospective jurors sampled at random.

Do trial attorneys' selections differ from laypersons' choices? Experienced trial attorneys were compared with inexperienced college undergraduate students and law students (Olczak, Kaplan, & Penrod, 1991). Participants in each group were given demographic information about each of 36 possible jurors and the facts of the case, then asked to represent the defense and choose the 12 best and 12 worst possible jurors. (The jurors had participated in earlier trial simulations, so their verdicts were known.) The strategies used by the attorneys were no more effective than those of the other two groups. Both the lawyers and the students made more mistakes than correct choices when asked to choose which prospective jurors would favor their side. Similarly, when a separate set of researchers presented lawyers with videotapes of the voir dire in actual trials, the lawyers selected jurors at an accuracy rate below chance; i.e., they selected jurors who had voted against their client and rejected jurors who had favored their client (Kerr, Kramer, Carroll, & Alfini, 1991).

Another, equally impressive approach to the question of lawyers' effectiveness was used by Zeisel and Diamond (1978). They chose 12 federal criminal trials, and after prospective jurors had been dismissed by one side or the other, they asked these people to remain in the courtroom, watch the trial from the spectator section, and provide verdicts as "shadow jurors." Zeisel and Diamond estimated that in 3 of the 12 trials, the defense attorney's use of peremptory challenges influenced the verdicts in a direction favorable to the attorney's side. Thus they concluded that attorneys do win *some* of their cases because of decisions made in voir dire.

As an aside, we note Zeisel and Diamond's (1978) observation that defense attorneys seem to exercise more peremptory challenges than do prosecutors, even when the number granted to each side is equal. This is also our impression, based on our reading about some highly publicized trials (Bernhard Goetz; the Los Angeles police officers charged with beating Rodney King), and the conclusion has been replicated in a survey of 13 trials; the prosecution did not exhaust its peremptory challenges in 10 of these, while the defense did not in only 2 (Rose, 1999).

Psychologists' Views on the Effectiveness of Jury Selection

Those psychologists who are knowledgeable about jury selection differ in their views about its effectiveness. Some also serve as trial consultants and have a vested interest in believing that jury selection can be helpful, although even they acknowledge the complexity of the task. Other psychologist-observers are more dubious.

Michael Saks

Michael Saks, a social psychologist who is a professor of law at Arizona State University, is one of the leading scholars in the psychology-and-law field. In a treatise titled "Social Scientists Can't Rig Juries" (Saks, 1976b, 1977), he offered the following as his reactions to the claim that the techniques of scientific jury selection are so powerful as to be a threat to the jury trial system and to justice.

First, he noted, prospective jurors sometimes lie. They may wish to appear open-minded when, in actuality, they are consumed with prejudices. They may claim they have not formed an opinion when they have. In the Harrisburg Seven trial, as noted in chapter 8, the store owner who became a juror appeared, during voir dire, to be sympathetic to war protesters, only to reveal opposite feelings when the deliberations started.

Along with this, Saks argued that sometimes prospective jurors are willing to reveal information that reflects a predisposition or a conflict of interest, but they are not asked. Thus, the voir dire procedure often is ineffective in doing what it is supposed to do. The average jury selection in a civil trial takes only 1 hour; in a criminal trial, 2 hours. Our impression of the questioning done by attorneys is that it is usually quite superficial and often does not uncover real biases. One of us observed a civil trial in which an affluent couple from Kansas City was suing the Internal Revenue Service. The couple had donated an expensive piece of property to a charitable organization, but the Internal Revenue Service had valued the contribution to be substantially less than the couple's claim. When the couple sued the IRS, as is the standard procedure in such disputes, the Internal Revenue Service sent one of its attorneys from Washington, DC, to represent the government. After the prospective jurors had been assembled in the jury box and the judge had asked them some preliminary questions, the IRS attorney asked the jurors, en masse, "Has anyone ever been audited by the IRS?" No one put up a hand. Then he dropped this line of questioning. He failed to ask, "Does anyone hate the IRS? Does anyone have strong feelings about the IRS?" Granted, some prospective jurors might have been reluctant to reveal their true feelings, but even nonverbal reactions to this question might have been a trigger to question a juror or two individually.

Another reason that, in Saks's view, juries can't be rigged is the difference between group differentiation and prediction of the individual. Take, for example, the Juror Bias Scale described in chapter 7. Jurors who reflect proprosecution attitudes are, as a group, more likely to convict the defendant than are jurors who reflect prodefense attitudes. The differences in the verdicts between these two groups are impressive, sometimes as much as a 20% or 30% difference. But this does not mean that every individual with a proprosecution attitude necessarily will find the defendant guilty. Researchers are often content to demonstrate group differences, but trial consultants and attorneys need to predict the behavior of individuals. That, of course, is much more difficult.

Saks also pointed out that some of the fears about the power of scientific jury selection stem from the fact that it has been successful in all of the highly publicized trials in which it has been used, starting with the Harrisburg Seven trial and including other political trials in the 1970s and 1980s, such as the Gainesville Eight, the Angela Davis trial, and the trial of the Native American militants from Wounded Knee. (More recently, scientific jury selection was used successfully by the defense in O. J. Simpson's criminal trial and in the trial of William Kennedy Smith.) But he noted the absence of well-controlled studies that manipulate the effect of this type of jury selection. Ideally, a series of cases would be tried before a number of juries, some chosen through scientific jury selection and some chosen through traditional methods (Diamond, 1990). Only one study exists that had this general goal—we will discuss it subsequently—and it used mock jurors and was limited in other ways.

Shari Seidman Diamond

Shari Diamond (1990), another distinguished legal psychologist and, like Michael Saks, a former president of the American Psychology-Law Society, also has reviewed the evidence for the effectiveness of scientific jury selection.

One of her conclusions is that even if attitudes and other intra-individual characteristics have some relationships to jurors' verdicts, it is infrequent that a full range of questions will be permitted to be asked in court. Questions asked during voir dire must appear logically relevant to the case, and "attorneys who use the results of scientific jury selection in the courtroom must thus decide which jurors to excuse based on abbreviated tests of attitudes distorted by the public arena in which they are expressed" (Diamond, 1990, p. 181).

A second conclusion of Diamond's focuses on the lack of general characteristics which predict in a breadth of cases:

> A second implication of the research on jury selection is that there is no profile of the good defense (or prosecution or plaintiff) juror that can be used across cases. Characteristics that emerge as predictors on one case do not show the same pattern on another case. Jurors who are most favorable to the defense in one trial will not necessarily make the best defense jurors in another trial. This is not particularly surprising. Psychologists have spent years trying to predict behavior and the results have revealed only modest levels of consistency across situations. The jury consultant who provides a profile of the good defense juror suitable for all cases and applicable to all communities is offering the most blatant voodoo voir dire advice. (p. 181)

Diamond also asserted that conclusions drawn from scientific jury selection do not always trump those of the trial lawyer:

> Research on jury selection indicates that the survey efforts of scientific jury selection will not improve the accuracy of jury selection in every case. In some cases, a jury consultant may even be less accurate than the trial attorney operating without consultant advice. Statistical prediction is usually, but not always, more accurate than clinical prediction. The trial attorney knows the evidence in

the case, both on the client's and on the opposition's side, better than does the consultant. In addition, the attorney operating in a familiar court may be able to use the incidental information that emerges during voir dire (e.g., the strike of a local business where a prospective juror is employed). The attorney can eliminate some hostile jurors without expert advice. Accordingly, the attorney should accept advice from a survey formula for jury selection only when provided with hard evidence that the advice offers the genuine prospect of improved prediction. (p. 181)

Empirical Study of the Effectiveness of Jury Selection

The above viewpoints lead to a conclusion that the association between identified juror variables and verdicts is weak. But what does the empirical research indicate as the specific relationship? Several studies are relevant.

Hastie, Penrod, and Pennington (1983) showed a total of 828 jurors a videotape reenactment of an actual murder trial. Of 12 background characteristics, 4 were significantly related to the jurors' individual verdicts; these were employed versus unemployed, gender, number of previous criminal trials as a juror, and number of previous cases (civil and criminal) as a juror. These accounted for a very small percentage of the variance in verdicts, 3.2%. A number of other attitudinal and background characteristics were examined for a sample of 269 jurors from this larger group; with these, Hastie et al. (1983) were able to explain 11% of the variance in the jurors' verdicts. Among the useful variables were residence in a wealthy suburb, attitude toward punishing someone who causes another's death, marital status, and newspaper read. Accounting for 11% of the variance means that the verdicts of 61% of the jurors could be correctly classified, above the 50% rate achievable by sheer guessing, but not by much.

Steven Penrod (1979), for his doctoral dissertation, had 367 jurors respond to 21 attitude and background characteristic questions before they rendered individual verdicts in three criminal cases and one civil case. (They listened to 30-minute audiotape summaries of each case.) No single variable had a high correlation with verdicts, the highest correlation being +.18. The percentage of variance in verdicts accounted for by the combination of best predictors differed from case to case: 16% in the rape case, 14% in the murder case, less than 10% in the negligence case, and less than 5% in an armed robbery case; the average across the four trials was 11%. The best predictors of the verdict were not consistent from case to case. But despite the seemingly low correlations and percentage of variance accounted for, they reflect an improvement of 15–20% above chance.

Michael Saks (1977) assessed 27 background characteristics and attitudes of 461 jurors prior to their watching the videotape of a trial for the charge of burglary. The best predictor of verdicts was whether the juror believed that crime was mainly a product of "bad people" or "bad social conditions," but it accounted for only 9% of the variance. The four best predictors, combined, accounted for 13% of the variance.

Several studies have examined the relationship between attitudes toward the death penalty and verdicts in capital murder cases. A meta-analysis revealed a small but significant relationship; over 19 studies, the correlation was $+.11$, but attitudes had a higher relationship with severity of punishment ($+.24$) (Nietzel, McCarthy, & Kern, 1999).

Among contemporary psychologists who have studied the effectiveness of scientific jury selection, Gary Moran is probably the strongest advocate of the usefulness of the procedure. Moran, Cutler, and DeLisa (1994) reviewed findings like those cited above, as well as others which conclude a lack of relationship, but Moran and his colleagues argued that these conclusions are mostly based on jury simulations and that "[w]hen real juror verdicts are at issue, scientific jury selection has been shown to increase the predictability of juror verdicts appreciably, especially if the evidence in the case is at all equivocal" (p. 312). They reported four studies in which attitudes toward tort reform accounted for up to 30% of the variance in verdicts.

A Laboratory Study of Two Approaches

The question of whether scientific jury selection is effective might seem to be easily answered. For example, Nietzel and Dillehay (1986) sought to evaluate the defense's use of trial consultants in 31 death penalty trials. They found that juries recommended the death penalty in 61% of those trials in which a trial consultant was not used, compared to only 33% of the trials when the defense attorney used a trial consultant. While this difference is impressive, these cases differed on many variables besides the use of a consultant, and it is hence not possible to say that the consultant's participation *caused* the difference.

For other reasons, too, the effectiveness of the contributions of a consultant to jury selection are difficult to assess. For instance, we may ask, the choices made by consultants are effective compared to what? To dismissing jurors by chance? To the traditional methods used by attorneys? A further difficulty is that real-life trials are not susceptible to an experimental manipulation, in which they are repeated with a different method of selecting the jury. The study by Zeisel and Diamond (1978), described above, that used shadow jurors who stayed in the courtroom provides one of the best procedures, and it would be interesting to replicate it, using trial consultants' choices rather than those by attorneys, but this methodology still suffers from the fact that the shadow jurors—even while watching the same trial unfold—know that they are not determining the actual verdict.

One study did attempt to provide a contrast between two methods, but it was a laboratory study that used mock jurors recruited from the community and law students as those charged with selecting the jury. The purpose of the study, by Irwin Horowitz (1980), was to compare scientific jury selection with the traditional method; in the latter, the law students acting as attorneys used their past experience, conventional wisdom, and beliefs about jurors to make their choices, which were probably more intuitive than analytic. Four different criminal trials were used. The results indicated that scientific jury selection was more effective in some trials, but not in all four. In fact, its effectiveness seemed to be limited to trials in which a strong relationship existed between jurors' personality or demographic variables and their votes. This study was a noble effort, but its conclusions are limited by its artificial situation, its use of law students instead of experienced trial attorneys and consultants, and its lack of assurance that those in the scientific-jury-selection condition fully followed the instructions. Perhaps the fact that this study was done more than 20 years ago and has not been redone is testimony to the difficulty in accurately assessing the efficacy of scientific jury selection.

Conclusions About Jury Selection Effectiveness

Some of the examples of trials described in this book—Marcia Clark rejects a trial consultant's advice and her side loses; in the Harrisburg Seven and Beckwith trials the side using the trial consultants wins—may leave the impression that jury outcomes can routinely be successfully "rigged" by the use of trial consultants' techniques. And some consultants are not reluctant to claim high rates of success (Strier, 1999); recall the promises by the firm Litigation Sciences, described in chapter 1.

As we have seen, legal psychologists remain divided about the effectiveness of scientific jury selection. Strier (1999), in a review, concluded that "empirical studies testing the predictive value of scientific jury selection have produced inconclusive findings" (p. 101). Reid Hastie's (1991) review of his own and other studies observed:

> It remains unclear exactly what types of cases will yield the greatest advantage to "scientific" selection methods. . . . "Scientific" jury selection surveys or attorney intuitions occasionally identify a subtle, case-predictor of verdicts. It is difficult, however, to cite even one convincingly demonstrated success of this type, and these methods frequently suggest the use of completely invalid, as well as valid, predictors. . . . The predictive power of these [juror] characteristics invariably turned out to be subtly dependent on specific aspects of the particular case for which they proved valid. Due to their subtlety, prospective identification of any of these factors under the conditions that prevail before actual trials remains doubtful. (pp. 720, 723–724)

We believe that while the empirical studies show a limited degree of relationship, the findings are consistently better than chance, or guessing, and without them, the real-world decision often reflects a guess. However, we also recognize that a number of conditions affect the likelihood of success; Kressel and Kressel (2002) have summarized them:

> The best conclusion is that there are some cases where jury selection consultants can make a critical difference but that such cases are few and far between. Scientific jury selection will be most likely to matter when: (1) cases are publicized, or unusual; (2) the facts of the case are likely to activate, inflame, or polarize jurors' attitudes; (3) the evidence does not strongly favor one party; (4) juror leanings are strongly related to observable demographics or otherwise discernible characteristics; (5) the attorney's case strategy depends heavily on certain assumptions made about jurors; (6) the predictors of juror leanings are not obvious, or better still, they are counterintuitive; (7) attorneys are permitted to conduct voir dire, ask many questions, and distribute comprehensive juror questionnaires; (8) the jury pool is diverse; (9) the court permits many peremptory challenges; (10) the other side is not using jury selection; (11) the attorney lacks familiarity with the jurisdiction; and (12) the budget permits well-designed pretrial research. (p. 134)

Ethical Issues in Jury Selection

We have had occasion to refer to one of John Grisham's novels earlier in this book. His highly entertaining novel *The Runaway Jury* (1996) begins with the surveillance of a young man who works in a computer store in a shopping mall. Observers note that he apparently doesn't smoke—at least he doesn't during his breaks from work. They also discover that he has falsified information about himself, as he has reported being a part-time college student but is not enrolled in any college in the vicinity.

Why is he being watched? Because he has reported for jury duty, and the case is an important one involving a lawsuit against tobacco companies; the observers are from a trial-consulting firm hired by the defendants. In the fall of 2003, a film based on Grisham's book was released; the defendants were now gun manufacturers, not tobacco companies, but the activities of the trial consultants were similar to those portrayed in the book. While reviews of the movie said that these activities were probably exaggerated and unrealistic, how many of the viewers now believe the portrayal?

Invasions of Privacy of Jurors

Exaggerations or not, the activities of trial consultants sometimes invade the privacy of the ordinary citizens who are called for jury duty. The courts have recognized the rights of trial attorneys and their associates to obtain information about prospective jurors to determine if they possess any biases. But how far should the inquiry go? As described in chapter 8 regarding the retrial of Byron de la Beckwith, trial consultants, on occasion, go outside the court to uncover indications of the attitudes and values of prospective jurors. Public records such as declarations of bankruptcy, divorces, financial liens, or house appraisals are fair game; the trial consultant's team may drive by the prospective juror's house, note the quality of the neighborhood and the condition of the house, and search for any information—such as bumper stickers on the juror's car—that they consider to be diagnostic. Friends and neighbors have even been interviewed (Farrell & Bunch, 1999). But such intrusive activities and spying are not the norm.

Are such activities unethical? The Code of Professional Standards of the American Society of Trial Consultants does not yet include a set of ethical standards and guidelines for jury selection. However, one of the nine current ethical principles of social responsibility states, "The trial consultant does not provide services with the intent of jeopardizing the integrity of the jury pool" (American Society of Trial Consultants, 2003, p. 6). Of course, some activities would not merely violate professional ethics; they would also be a violation of the law. Those who have been called for jury selection cannot be contacted outside the courtroom; jury tampering is illegal, and the courts have held persons to be in contempt of court for communicating with those persons in the jury pool who have already been selected to serve on the jury. But would such punishments be assigned to those who investigate *prospective* jurors? Herbsleb, Sales, and Berman (1979) thought not; they wrote, "[I]t seems unlikely [that such jury tampering laws as the above] will be applied today to hold social scientists in contempt for gathering jury information, unless some communication with the sworn jurors has occurred in or near the courtroom" (p. 206). As long as the consultant's activities are limited to the perusal of public documents and other information that is publicly accessible, such as the exterior condition of a juror's home, no legal or ethical violation has technically occurred.

That does not mean, however, that across-the-board approval exists for such activities. We would expect, for example, that most judges would not be happy with these investigative practices; judges are quite protective of their jurors and resent any intrusion on the sanctity of the trial. In recent high-profile trials, such as those of Robert Blake and Martha Stewart, the presiding judge took unusual steps to protect the privacy of jurors; for example, in Blake's case, the judge started the voir dire a month earlier than announced, to try to diminish the publicity (Mauro, 2004).

If prospective jurors were to learn that they were being investigated in this way for jury-selection purposes, we suppose it would make them, at the very least, uncomfortable. Such discomfort does not constitute an ethical violation, though. But what if jurors are not aware that such investigations are taking place? Some might argue that this is an ethical violation, as federal guidelines for research conducted with human participants require that researchers obtain the informed consent of their participants (Title 45, 1991). Are prospective jurors "research participants"? The answer is no, as long as the information gathered about them is used solely for the purposes of jury selection. And even if they were research participants, perusal of their public records would not require their consent, as long as their identities were protected.

Although the tactics we have described do not constitute ethical violations, it must be acknowledged that dangers exist. As Herbsleb et al. (1979) suggested:

> Suppose that as social scientists are establishing their network, one of the people contacted becomes suspicious of the investigator's motives and of the propriety of their actions. . . . [H]e may contact the prospective juror to inform him that persons of questionable character and motives are conducting an investigation of his personal affairs. The prospective juror in turn may well feel threatened or intimidated by the knowledge that someone is "checking up" on him. (pp. 207–208)

What is the solution to this problem? Should outside-of-court inquiries be approved by the presiding judge before they commence? We doubt that many judges would approve. It has been suggested that the judge announce the presence of social scientists and ask jurors if they object to investigations into their backgrounds. "If objections are voiced, the judge orders the social scientists to discontinue their research; if no objections are voiced, it is assumed that the jurors are participating voluntarily" (Herbsleb et al., 1979, p. 211). Although "compliance" in this context seems rather coerced, this might at least allay jurors' fears if they should learn that they are being investigated.

Use of Supplemental Juror Questionnaires

One solution to the above problem is to avoid out-of-court investigations and substitute for them the use of a supplemental juror questionnaire, which is an extensive set of questions that prospective jurors answer in writing before the voir dire begins. Such questionnaires can assess the broad, potentially predictive attitudes described in chapter 7. They can cover many of the topics that might have been answered through out-of-court investigations, such as what newspapers and magazines the prospective jurors read, whether they rent or own a house, whether they own any guns. Typically, both sides contribute questions to the survey, and the judge must approve them. Given the time constraints in some courts, it is often a challenge to get a final, acceptable draft prepared, but something is better than nothing.

The validity of the information now rests on the honesty of the jurors; some invasion of their privacy remains, but this seems inevitable, given defendants' rights to have their outcomes determined by impartial jurors. But what if prospective jurors feel that some questions are too personal?

Their informed consent has not been obtained—the judge has, in effect, ruled in their stead—and jurors can be punished if they refuse to answer. This happened to a Texas juror who refused to answer 12 questions (out of 100) that dealt with her religion, her income, and her political party affiliation. The judge cited her for contempt and sentenced her to 3 days in jail.

The rules in most jurisdictions do not specifically address the use of questionnaires prior to voir dire, and so the judge has the discretion to permit them. However, the federal courts have recommended the use of prescreening questionnaires in highly publicized cases, and they were used in the trials of O. J. Simpson, Martha Stewart, William Kennedy Smith, General Manuel Noriega, and Susan Smith (Fargo, 1994). While attorneys for each side are permitted to examine the responses (or even have copies of them) prior to voir dire, sometimes the time to peruse them is quite brief (overnight, or even less). However, responses not only help the attorneys and trial consultants to identify possible peremptory challenges, but also help to identify the prospective jurors who might be challenges for cause. Thus their use saves some time in the courtroom and also adds to achieving the goal of fairness by giving both sides equal access to the information.

An experienced trial consultant, Marjorie Fargo (1994), has suggested the following in the preparation and administration of supplemental juror questionnaires:

1. Keep the questionnaires as short as possible. It is suggested that four to six pages will suffice. Follow-up questions may be allowed during voir dire.
2. The introduction to the questionnaire should explain its purpose. Fargo suggested the following:

> This questionnaire will be used only to assist the judge and the attorneys in the jury selection process. The information requested is strictly confidential and will not be used for any other purpose. Please read all questions carefully, answer them fully, and notify court personnel if you need any assistance or have any questions. Do not discuss the questions or answers with fellow jurors. It is very important that your answers be your own. You are sworn to give true and complete answers to all questions. (Fargo, 1994, p. 1)

3. Questions should be clustered by topic and arranged in logical sequence.
4. Topics to be covered should include the prospective juror's experience with legal matters and the courts, his or her experiences related to the case at hand, and the juror's exposure to media coverage about the case. On all of these topics, the experiences of the juror's immediate family and close personal friends are also relevant. Questions on those topics often work better as open-ended ones, rather than as yes-or-no types.

5. At the end of the questionnaire, statements reflecting general attitudes and opinions, such as those from the instruments described in chapter 7, may be included.

Fargo's initial recommendation—that the questionnaire be brief—is sometimes violated; the O. J. Simpson criminal trial was an example. The supplemental juror questionnaire covered more than 60 pages and included almost 300 questions (Gordon, 1997). Both sides contributed questions. For the prosecution, the questions were developed by the district attorney's office. Marcia Clark (1997) has stated that their trial consultant, Donald Vinson, submitted only one question. Jo-Ellan Dimitrius, the defense team's trial consultant, supervised the preparation of questions for the defense. Prospective jurors must have wondered about the relevance of some questions to the issues at hand, but one side or the other (or both) could have provided a rationale. For example, one question asked: Have you ever written a letter to the editor of a newspaper or magazine? An affirmative response might indicate an individual who has strong opinions and is likely to assert them. Another asked: Have you ever asked a celebrity for an autograph? A yes answer might indicate a prospective juror who would be sympathetic to the defendant.

Trial Consultants and the Matter of Discovery

When legal consultants work for one side, should it be required that their reports be made available to the other side? A basic rule of courtroom procedure is that attorneys are required to provide to the other side any evidence in their possession that is relevant to the case. For example, if a defense attorney asks a clinical psychologist to evaluate the intelligence level of the defendant, a copy of the report is made available to the prosecution. But anything that can be classified as attorney work product is not discoverable, and this usually includes legal research, correspondence, reports, and memoranda that contain opinions and conclusions by the attorneys. What about the written recommendations of trial consultants to the lawyers as to the desirability of certain prospective jurors, based on an analysis of supplemental juror questionnaires? Commentators have suggested that such material is protected from discovery because it can be considered an attorney work product, even though it is not produced by the attorney (Davis & Beisecker, 1994; Herbsleb et al., 1979).

Fairness in Jury Selection

The issue of fairness was raised as a criticism of the use of trial consultants in chapter 1. Fairness is a concern here, in that one side may have more resources, such as trained observers or investigators, thus giving that side an advantage in identifying biased jurors. Are the courts concerned if one side employs a litigation consultant and the other does not? The position of the courts is that no legal violation has occurred when one side and only one side uses a consultant. A generally recognized principle of the law is that the counsel for the two sides are "never perfectly equal in abilities or resources" (Herbsleb et al., 1979, p. 201, who cite the case of *Hamer v. United States*, 1958, which concluded, on p. 281, that "perfect equality of counsel can never be achieved"). Recall that a justification of the participation of social scientists on the defense team in the Harrisburg Seven trial was that the federal government, as prosecutor, had many unfair advantages in its efforts to convict war protesters. In some cases, this claim seems irrefutable. For example, in one case (*United States v. Costello*, 1958), the federal government, in prosecuting the case, obtained the income-tax returns of prospective jurors and used information from them in its ratings of them as favorable or unfavorable jurors. The defendant, Costello, was convicted; his appeal was rejected on the basis that the exercise of peremptory challenges is a process of the rejection of biased jurors, not the selection of a "specially conditioned" jury (p. 884). Franklin Strier (1998) has summarized the current situation as follows:

> [U]ntil clear and convincing evidence of the ability of scientific jury selection to affect verdicts surfaces, there appears no sustainable argument that its use threatens the Constitutional right to an impartial jury or the court-mandated injunction to seek cross-sectional juries. The law seeks jury representativeness. Scientific jury selection will still result in unfairly excluding some Americans from jury service: it will merely substitute exclusion based on scientific analysis for those derived from stereotypes and intuition. (p. 11)

Conclusions

The purpose of this chapter has been to evaluate jury selection by trial consultants in the broadest sense of "evaluation," that is, by considering both its effectiveness and its ethics. No simple answer is possible to the question: Does jury selection work? Whether we like it or not, the proper answer here is the one that social scientists—infuriatingly to some—often use in response to complex questions: it depends. Consider all of the sources of variability in this task: the nature of the case, the nature of the procedures used to select jurors, the extent of questioning allowed (including whether questioning by lawyers or supplemental juror questionnaires are permitted), the composition of the jury pool, and the nature of individual jurors.

We support the use of trial consultants in jury selection for a basic reason: two heads are better than one. The consultant may be sensitive to responses and qualities of the prospective jurors that the trial attorney overlooks (the opposite may also be true, of course). The rating procedure first systematically used by the defense in the Harrisburg Seven trial forces attorneys and other jury selectors to quantify and defend their choices. But still it is no guarantee of success. Here we agree with Kressel and Kressel's listing—reprinted earlier in this chapter—of the 12 factors that increase the likelihood of successful prediction.

But *should* psychologists and other social scientists participate in activities that intrude on the privacy of prospective jurors? Do they violate their professional ethical principles when they do so? We accept the court's need to violate the privacy of potential jurors to some degree, in order to increase the likelihood that the trial is fair and the outcome is just.

10

What Needs to Be Changed?

One goal of this book has been to illustrate the variety of activities done by legal consultants in the United States. It should be recognized that many of the activities described in earlier chapters, such as witness preparation or change-of-venue evaluations, are infrequent in other countries, at best, or even prohibited by them. Furthermore, some countries—Israel is an example—do not have trial by jury. The litigation consultant in the United States has far greater freedom than in any other country, not only because of the breadth of allowable activities but because of the way the jury trial system has evolved in the United States.

The purpose of this chapter is to provide our evaluation of the contributions of litigation consultants to the functioning of the legal system. We will offer our conclusions about each of several activities described in previous chapters. But before we do so, we consider it necessary to evaluate how the jury system operates in the United States. Are some of the public's criticisms of trial consultants really criticisms of the system in which the consultant operates? In order to determine that, we believe it is fruitful to compare the jury system in the United States with its counterparts in other countries.

The Jury System in Other Countries

The legal system in the United States was inherited from Great Britain, as were the legal systems of other British Commonwealth countries, including

Canada, Australia, and New Zealand. It is thus useful and even provocative to compare the rules for jury service and jury selection currently employed in the United States with those of England and Wales, Scotland, Ireland, and the Commonwealth countries. The extreme variation, given the common progenitor, is surprising; as we have noted before, the procedures in the United States give much greater latitude to attorneys (and trial consultants) than do those of the other countries.

In some respects, procedures in the United States stand in sharp contrast to those of all of the other countries based on the English common law. For example, pretrial publicity is severely restricted in the United Kingdom and in Canada. If a newspaper publishes details of an arrest and the suspect's name, it may be cited for contempt. With the strict limits on what the media can say about criminal investigations and court proceedings prior to trial, change-of-venue requests are unusual.

A Concern for Jury Representativeness

The activities ordinarily done by trial consultants are quite circumscribed in these other countries. For example, in England and Wales, there is no jury selection (Hans, 1982). The goal of a representative jury, given lip service in the United States, is more strongly sought in the United Kingdom. Everyone on the voting rolls between the ages of 18 and 70 who has lived in the United Kingdom for a continuous period of 5 years since the age of 13 is liable for jury service, with only a few categories of exemptions or exclusions. Anyone sentenced to prison within the last 10 years is not allowed to serve. Exemptions are given to lawyers, judges and justices of the peace, prison governors, members of Parliament, clergy, and doctors (Bresler, 2003; Graham, 1983). The goal of representativeness is carried over through the process of selecting actual jurors from the pool—absolute randomness is assumed. From a panel of more than 12, the clerk selects 12 by random.

Questioning Prospective Jurors and Use of Peremptory Challenges

The opportunity to question prospective jurors is quite restricted in England, Wales, and Scotland. Apparently this is limited to certain types of trials, and even there, "the questions are relatively narrow in scope and closely linked to the case at hand [but] the existence of this sort of limited questioning is by all accounts quite rare" (Hans, 1982, p. 286). Jury questionnaire forms, needless to say, are not used in Great Britain.

Defense barristers in England, Wales, and Scotland have seen the number of peremptory challenges reduced from seven, to three, and then to zero. (Parliament abolished them in 1988.) The prosecution has had a similar right, in which prospective jurors not acceptable to the prosecution could be told to "stand by for the Crown," which meant that they were to be part of the jury only if all other panel members had been chosen or dismissed. But nowadays, although still technically an option, "standing by for the Crown" seldom occurs (Bresler, 2003).

All challenges by trial lawyers to dismiss prospective jurors must be for cause, but that also seldom happens (Bresler, 2003) and, if attempted, is not likely to be successful. For a favorable challenge for cause, the defense must have a priori reasons, and ordinarily only very limited information is available about the background and beliefs of prospective jurors. One English judge commented, "I have never seen this done" (Clarke, 1975, p. 47). What if some prospective jurors are racially prejudiced? The English courts reject the possibility; an appellate decision in 1989 stated:

> It appears to have been suggested that there is a "principle" that a jury
> should be racially balanced. . . . In our judgement [*sic*] such a principle
> cannot be correct, for it would depend on an underlying premise that
> jurors of a particular racial origin or holding particular religious be-
> liefs are incapable of giving an impartial verdict in accordance with
> the evidence. (quoted by Bresler, 2003, p. A13)

The fundamental principle of obtaining a representative jury is reflected in a dictum in 1980 by Lord Denning: "Our philosophy is that the jury should be selected at random, from a panel of persons nominated at random. We believe that 12 persons selected at random are likely to be a cross-section of the people as a whole and thus represent the views of the common man. . . . The parties must take them as they come" (quoted by Bresler, 2003, p. A13).

"Take them as they come" means, in Great Britain, taking them with very little knowledge about them. Each side has access to the jury list before the trial begins, but this list contains only the prospective jurors' names and addresses. (Their occupations, at one time included on the list, are no longer there.) Only in special cases may the prosecution undertake, with authorization, the investigation of potential jurors. Called "jury vetting," the prosecution might consult with the police to determine if prospective jurors have been in trouble with the law. But the defense is always limited to only names and addresses.

The process which we in the United States call voir dire takes, in Great Britain, about 5 minutes. In some countries that have the British model as their heritage—specifically New Zealand and the Republic of Ireland—peremptory challenges are allowed, but lawyers cannot question prospective jurors. This would seem to encourage the use of stereotypes based on demographic characteristics or folklore (Greene & Wrightsman, 2003).

While Scotland, Canada, Northern Ireland, the Republic of Ireland, Australia, and New Zealand all derive their legal traditions from the English common law, they reflect surprising and often unique variations. Northern Ireland, although a part of the United Kingdom, differs from England and Wales in that it permits defendants the use of peremptory challenges—up to 12 per trial (Jackson, Quinn, & O'Malley, 1999). A survey found that in

more than one third of the cases, defendants use their full rights of peremptory challenge, and furthermore, the right of the prosecutor to defer
the use of certain prospective jurors (the above-described procedure of
"standing by for the Crown") was employed between four and five times per
trial (Jackson et al., 1999).

The Procedures in Scotland

Scotland is a part of the United Kingdom and has representation in the
Parliament, yet it differs from England and Wales (and all of the other
countries described here) in several important respects. First, there are no
opening statements in trials in Scotland and, even more extreme, barristers
may have had little or no opportunity to interview witnesses prior to the
trial. Equally striking are the size of the jury and the decision rule used in
criminal trials in Scotland. Uniquely, 15 jurors comprise the criminal jury in
Scotland, and a simple majority—8 out of 15—is sufficient for a verdict. The
verdict options may be described as follows:

> The Scottish jury is offered three verdict options: guilty, not guilty, or
> not proven (Duff, 1999). Although the intermediate, "not proven"
> option counts as an acquittal, it does not function as a positive dec-
> laration of innocence. Rather, it conveys the notion that the defen-
> dant's guilt has not been conclusively demonstrated. . . . Scottish
> juries frequently select this verdict option, as we suspect would be
> true in many other jurisdictions if juries were given that option. . . .
> Yet one feature of Scottish law—the requirement that the prosecu-
> tor's case be corroborated—may make it an especially attractive
> alternative in this locale. A Scottish Office study showed that the not-
> proven verdict option comprised a slightly higher proportion of
> acquittals in rape and sexual assault cases, where there is typically
> only one victim, than in other cases where there are likely to be
> multiple witnesses or victims. (Greene & Wrightsman, 2003, p. 411)

It has been suggested that the not-proven option is sometimes used
when the jury is convinced that the accused is guilty but wishes to extend
mercy to that particular defendant; in so doing, the jury effectively nullifies
the law (Duff, 1999). Equally of concern is the one-vote margin necessary
for conviction. Although this procedure eliminates hung juries, observers
have questioned whether the procedure encourages a thorough evaluation of
the evidence and extensive debate during the deliberations (Greene &
Wrightsman, 2003).

Canada's Unique Lay "Trier" Procedure

Canada, like Ireland, also permits peremptory challenges, up to 20 per side
in a murder trial, with fewer in less-serious offenses, but always at least 4 per

side (Vidmar, 1999a). In that respect, Canada resembles the United States, but in some ways it emulates the British system, and in one respect, Canada has a unique procedure. This deals with the way that prospective jurors are assessed to determine if they have been influenced by pretrial publicity:

> In Canada, the impartiality of jurors is deemed a question of fact, not a question of law. Therefore, the decision about whether a juror can be impartial is made by two lay "triers" selected from the pool of potential jurors, rather than by the judge. At the commencement of voir dire, lay triers selected at random from the jury pool listen to a prospective juror's answers to the questions posed and render a verdict on whether that prospective juror is "impartial between the Queen and the accused." After the first two jurors are selected, they assume the role of triers and determine the impartiality of juror number three. This rotation occurs until 12 jurors are seated. (Greene & Wrightsman, 2003, p. 404)

Summarizing the Differences

Thus in several important ways, the jury system in the United States differs significantly from each of the British Commonwealth jurisdictions; these include other aspects not described above.

It is against the law in Great Britain and Canada for jurors to discuss the case after it is over or to disclose anything about their deliberations. In Canada, a juror can be punished for doing so with 6 months' imprisonment and a fine of up to $5,000. This obviously discourages trial consultants—as well as losing attorneys or intrepid newspaper reporters—from learning anything about the process of deliberations.

The use of juries in civil trials has almost disappeared in all countries except Canada and the United States (Vidmar, 1999b). In England and Wales, the judge has the right to refuse a civil defendant the right of trial by jury (Lloyd-Bostock & Thomas, 1999). In Canada, civil juries are prohibited in Quebec and federal trials and allowed in only certain types of cases in other provinces (Bogart, 1999). They are most frequently used in Ontario, but even there in only about 20% of the trials.

In a criminal trial, the accused does not sit with his or her defense counsel, as in the United States but instead sits in what is referred to (in Canada, at least) as the "prisoner's box" throughout the trial.

A staple of the trial consultant's contributions—witness preparation—is generally not viable, as defense attorneys are not permitted to have contact with witnesses prior to the trial.

The decision rule varies from country to country, and in Australia even from state to state; most Commonwealth nations require unanimous verdicts in criminal trials, but Scotland, as we have seen, requires only a bare majority. In England and Wales, a unanimous verdict is not absolutely required, even in the more serious of cases. If the jury has deliberated for at least 2 hours (or a longer period if, in the opinion of the judge, the case is sufficiently complex), the judge will accept a verdict held by at least 10 of the 12 jurors. (In the United States, the states of Louisiana and Oregon do not require unanimous verdicts in criminal trials.)

The judge plays a more active role in the jury trials of most Commonwealth nations than he or she does in the United States. In Canada, for example, the judge can ask witnesses questions to clear up a misunderstanding and can express an opinion about the credibility of some witnesses (Vidmar, 1999a).

Reforming the Jury System

Jurors and juries in the United States have been criticized for making capricious and invalid decisions. With millions of jury trials in the United States each year, it cannot be expected that every juror and every jury will comply with the judgments of observers as to the "correct" verdict, and we acknowledge that some errors occur. But we believe that one source of the problems is the system—the ground rules—under which the jury has to operate. Supreme Court justice Sandra Day O'Connor (2003) has written:

> The world is a very different place now than it was in 1220, or in 1789, or fifty years ago. We therefore should not be surprised to learn that aspects of the jury system that worked well in those times work less well today and need some repairs. What *should* surprise us is that so little of the necessary repair work has been done.
>
> There are three aspects of the jury system that need particular attention. First, *the conditions of jury service.* When citizens are called for jury service, they often view it as a burden rather than a privilege. And for good reason: when they arrive at the courthouse they frequently are treated more like sheep than people, and the system can seem designed to disrupt their lives to a maximum degree. Second, *jury selection.* The process of selecting a jury out of the citizens called for jury service on a particular day has changed from a necessary safeguard against potentially biased jurors to a way for highly paid jury consultants to attempt to ensure a jury favorable to the side paying their fees. And third, *the conduct of the trial itself.* Too often jurors are allowed to do nothing but to listen passively to the testimony, without any idea what the legal issues are in the case, and without being permitted to take notes or participate in any way, finally to be read a virtually incomprehensible set of instructions and sent into the jury room to reach a verdict in a case they may not understand much better than they did before the trial began. (2003, pp. 217–218)

We agree with much of what Justice O'Connor has said. We will have little to say about her first concern, because we believe it speaks for itself and extends beyond the role of trial consulting. Her second concern, the emergence of trial consultants as a powerful influence, we have assessed in previous chapters, and we take a somewhat different perspective on that concern. We believe that many of their activities further the cause of justice and that some of their excesses are the result of a permissive system. It is the third concern, the conduct of the trial itself, for which we look to reforms. In the next sections, we describe and evaluate a number of current procedures and innovations that affect the conduct of trials.

Peremptory Challenges

As we have seen, the greatest criticism of legal consultants stems from their alleged attempts to rig juries; the greater the number of peremptory challenges available, the greater the concern about this activity. States vary in the number of peremptory challenges they grant, ranging from as many as 20 to as few as 4 per criminal defendant. In civil trials, the number is smaller, with each side typically having only 3.

The provision for a certain number of "free" challenges derived from the English system, although, as we indicated above, the provision was abolished in England almost 20 years ago. Doubtless, the original purpose was to increase the chances of a defendant having an impartial jury. But the procedure can also be used to eliminate certain segments of the community from being on the jury, which harms the achievement of representativeness. Thus the use of peremptory challenges has always had a questionable status and has been periodically subjected to scrutiny by the courts.

In 1965, in the case of *Swain v. Alabama*, the Supreme Court reaffirmed the right of attorneys to remove prospective jurors "without a reason stated, without inquiry, and without being subject to the court's control" (p. 220). But in actuality, the prosecution had used its strikes to destroy the representativeness of the jury. In that trial, Robert Swain, the defendant, was a 19-year-old Black man charged with raping a 17-year-old White woman in Talladega, Alabama. Six African Americans were among the prospective jurors, but each was dismissed by the prosecutor. The resulting all-White jury convicted Swain and sentenced him to death. Swain lost his appeal in 1965, even though no African American had ever served on a jury in Talladega County. The Supreme Court, incredibly, concluded that no proof existed that Blacks had systematically been excluded from the jury system nor that Swain had been denied his rights under the Equal Protection Clause of the Constitution. The endorsement of the use of peremptory challenges was extreme; the majority opinion of the Court, written by Justice Byron White and endorsed by six of the nine justices, stated that it "provides justification for striking any group of otherwise qualified jurors in any given case, whether they be Negroes, Catholics, accountants, or those with blue eyes" (*Swain v. Alabama*, 1965, p. 220).

In the next 20 years, the provision for peremptory challenges continued to be used to exclude minority-group members, in the North as well as in the South. In 1985, two African American men were convicted of assault and robbery by an all-White jury in Michigan. A total of 22 of the prospective jurors were Black; each was dismissed by the prosecutor, who privately acknowledged that his actions were based on racial considerations (Davis & Graham, 1995). (The defense was equally blatant, using its peremptory strikes to dismiss 37 White prospective jurors.)

But in the mid-1980s, things began to change. In the above Michigan case, the Sixth Circuit Court of Appeals overturned the decision on the grounds that the defendants' rights to an impartial jury had been violated. Other appellate court decisions were critical of defense attorneys for dismissing all members of "cognizable groups."

In 1986, in the case of *Batson v. Kentucky*, the Supreme Court in effect reversed its decision in *Swain v. Alabama*. James Batson, an African American, was charged with second-degree burglary and receipt of stolen goods. In his trial, the prosecutor used his peremptory challenges to dismiss all four Black persons in the venire, and the resulting all-White jury convicted Batson. By a 7–2 vote, the Supreme Court stated that if a defendant is of a cognizable group (such as race) and the prosecutor excludes all prospective jurors of that race, then the prosecutor must show that the basis for exclusion of each prospective juror was some other reason than his or her race. For example, let us say that in a jury panel of 30 persons, 6 are African American. If the prosecutor uses his or her peremptory challenges to remove these 6 persons from the jury, the judge must question the prosecutor. The latter may say, "I struck Mr. Burton because his brother is in prison; I struck Ms. Ashton because she has filed a suit against the police," and so on. It is up to the judge to decide if these nonracial reasons are legitimate.

The effect of the *Batson* decision was to shift the burden of proof onto the state, which now has to prove that what it is doing is not discrimination. More recent decisions have extended the principle. In *Holland v. Illinois* (1990), the Supreme Court ruled that a White defendant could complain about the exclusion of Blacks because the principle of representativeness was violated by the exclusion of a racial group, regardless of the race of the defendant. The principle was extended to civil juries in the decision in *Edmonson v. Leesville Concrete Company, Inc.* (1991) and to the actions of defense attorneys in *Georgia v. McCollum* (1992).

The Supreme Court has also extended this rule to one other cognizable group—gender. The case of *J.E.B. v. Alabama ex rel. T.B.* (1994) dealt with a paternity suit, in which the alleged father had refused to pay child support, claiming that he was not the father. At the trial, one side used all but one of its peremptory challenges to remove women; the other side used all but one of its challenges to remove men. The resulting jury—because of a larger number of women in the venire—was composed of 12 women, who concluded that the alleged father was, in fact, the father and must pay child support. In this case, the Supreme Court ruled that if peremptory challenges were used to eliminate one gender, this process was as unacceptable as one seeking to dismiss members of one race, and hence such actions must be justified on other grounds than simply the gender of the potential juror.

Will the *Batson* rule be extended to other classifications, specifically to religion? In the last months of 2003, two circuit courts considered this issue and came up with different rulings in *United States v. DeJesus* (2003) and *United States v. Brown* (2003). The Supreme Court, at this time, has not yet considered this specific issue, but we expect that it will in the near future.

Jury Instructions

As Justice O'Connor noted, another problem with the jury system is the instructions given to the jury. In this section, we describe two problems: their incomprehensibility and their timing.

Wording of Instructions

Jury instructions are written for lawyers, not for jurors. For more than 20 years, research studies have consistently found that these instructions are unnecessarily complex, technical, and wordy (Lieberman & Sales, 1997). One study found that jurors given the standard instructions of the definition of negligence did no better in understanding the term than did uninstructed jurors (Elwork, Sales, & Alfini, 1982). Another study found that when juries interrupted their deliberations to request a clarification of the instructions from the judge, typically the judge refused to amplify or clarify, but instead told the jurors to reread them (Severance & Loftus, 1982).

Is the jury not competent to understand? We think it is; in the words of Kassin and Wrightsman, "The problem is not jury comprehension, but the comprehensibility of judges' instructions" (1988, p. 149).

Timing

Even if the instructions were comprehensible, another problem is present. Typically, jurors are not instructed about many central aspects of the procedure until *after* they hear the evidence. For example, if they are jurors in a criminal trial, the judge often does not tell them about the standard of "beyond a reasonable doubt" before they hear the evidence. (The lawyers may attempt to define the term during the voir dire, however.) As discussed in chapter 6, Justice O'Connor (2003) has argued that jurors should be provided general instructions at the beginning of the trial, before the evidence is presented.

Trial judges have discretion to instruct jurors at the beginning of the trial, and some advocate such a procedure (cf. Dann, 1993). In Arizona, judges are required to give both oral and written instructions at both the beginning and the end of the trial. A committee of the Supreme Court of Missouri has recommended a similar procedure. And psychological research demonstrates that preinstruction leads to a variety of benefits, including better memory for the evidence (Kassin & Wrightsman, 1979), a clear differentiation between those plaintiffs who had been injured to a greater or lesser degree (ForsterLee, Horowitz, & Bourgeois, 1993), increased satisfaction with serving on a jury (Heuer & Penrod, 1989), and a greater ability to integrate the facts of the case and the law (V. L. Smith, 1991).

Treatment of the Jurors as Passive Information Processors

As suggested above, in many courtrooms jurors are expected to sit through the trial and absorb everything, without the opportunity to use memory aids and without the recognition that they might have questions about the case. But some judges are beginning to recognize the limitations in the traditional way of running things; jurors are permitted to take notes in a number of jurisdictions, and a few judges permit jurors to ask questions. The latter innovation is more extreme and more controversial, but if the questions are submitted in writing at the end of the testimony of a particular witness, if they are screened by the judge, and if the attorneys have a chance to object, our feeling is that the only cost is some extra time. Justice O'Connor has summarized our view:

> Juries are a great institution, with a proud history. But we need to make sure we do not remain wedded to practices haling from the twentieth century, or the eighteenth, or the thirteenth, that we make it difficult for juries to do their job well. We need to take this issue seriously, to think hard about ways that juries can be made to work better, and not to fear change simply because it is different. (O'Connor, 2003, p. 224)

Summary Evaluation of Trial-Consulting Techniques

In the remainder of this chapter, we provide a brief review of the research support for each of the trial-consulting techniques discussed in prior chapters and take a look at the ethical issues associated with each technique. We pay special attention to the ethical concern that trial consultants' involvement in the legal system has merely exacerbated the inequity that characterized the system before they arrived. Next, we discuss the struggle by trial consultants, and especially by the membership of the ASTC, to carve a professional identity out of a very diverse foundation. Finally, we identify and discuss some future directions for the field.

Witness Preparation

Many trial consultants assist lawyers in preparing their witnesses to testify at trial, and the practice is empirically supported. As discussed in chapter 2, research has shown that the amount of emotion displayed by a witness influences jurors' judgments about the witness's testimony; this is especially true regarding the testimony of criminal defendants when the evidence against them is weak. In addition, research has revealed that there is an inverse relationship between the perceived nervousness of a witness and perceptions of his or her credibility, that those who use a powerful speaking style are generally more persuasive than those using a powerless style, and that certain nonverbal behaviors are often perceived to be indications of lying. Finally, there is research support for the notion that witnesses who receive some amount of pretestimony instruction are more confident on the witness stand than those who do not.

The real issue with witness preparation is an ethical one. Consultants do not work with witnesses as much on the content of their testimony as they do on the way in which witnesses present themselves in court. This might include advising the witness on such matters as attire and posture, as well as on stylistic elements like grammar, enunciation, and the use of a more powerful speaking style. In taking steps to increase the credibility of the witness, the consultant sometimes walks a fine line and runs the risk of changing the meaning of the testimony by changing the style in which it is delivered. However, without some degree of witness preparation, an otherwise honest witness might be disbelieved by a jury who discounts the testimony because it is characterized by powerless features or is delivered by a nervous witness. In the end, witness-preparation techniques employed by trial consultants have the potential to increase the credibility of any witness, honest or dishonest. As long as witness-preparation techniques are empirically and theoretically sound and do not encourage witnesses to change the content of their testimony in order to better convince the jury, we feel that they are ethically acceptable.

Change of Venue

Given the thousands of civil and criminal trials annually, pretrial publicity, as a threat to fairness, is infrequently a problem. However, in those relatively few cases that do receive extensive media coverage or that become the primary topic of conversation within a small town, the defendant's right to a fair and impartial jury is jeopardized. In such cases, the likelihood of inclusion of jurors who have already formed an opinion justifies the use of a trial consultant to conduct a survey to determine the extent of knowledge of the case and the likelihood of preformed conclusions regarding guilt.

As discussed in chapter 3, there is sound empirical support for the use of a change-of-venue survey by consultants. Research reliably has shown that pretrial publicity does increase bias against the defendant in criminal cases, and prospective jurors do not always admit to that bias during voir dire, due either to demand characteristics in the courtroom or to a genuine belief in their ability to set aside what they have learned about the case.

Detailed guidelines have been created by the ASTC for the construction and administration of the survey, and those guidelines represent the state of the art for survey methodology. As a consequence, this activity of trial consultants is effective in the fundamental way that it provides a fairly accurate portrayal of judgments about the case among prospective jurors.

However, if the effectiveness of a trial-consulting method is measured by whether it achieves the desired outcome for the client, assessment of the change-of-venue survey becomes trickier. Survey results might reveal that no change of venue is needed. Alternatively, a judge may decide not to grant a change of venue even if the lawyer and the trial consultant feel that one is warranted. In that situation, the survey results may be used to convince the judge to allow an extended voir dire, in which case the survey might be considered to be a partial success.

We see few ethical problems associated with the change-of-venue survey. Consultants need to take steps to protect the integrity of the jury pool and to ensure the confidentiality of respondents, which require special vigilance when conducting surveys in small jurisdictions. The benefits of a properly conducted survey far outweigh the costs, in that the survey can be used as a tool to enhance the likelihood that a case will be tried before a fair and impartial jury as guaranteed under the Sixth Amendment of the U.S. Constitution.

Small-Group Research

Small-group research techniques, including primarily focus groups and trial simulations, make up the most common practice area of trial consultants. Although any given participant's responses may not accurately represent his or her true feelings about the case, the methods have good ecological validity, in that they closely resemble the true dynamics of a jury deliberation. To increase confidence in the validity of conclusions drawn from small-group research, participants should be randomly selected and jury-eligible, and enough groups should be conducted to allow for saturation of the topic, that is, to the point where information obtained from the groups becomes redundant. In addition, it is recommended that consultants run their conclusions by participants before dismissing them to make sure that they do not misrepresent the feelings of the group as a whole. Whenever possible, consultants should also conduct posttrial interviews with actual jurors to determine whether small-group research findings were predictive of jurors' responses to the case.

As for the ethics of small-group research in the context of trial consulting, the greatest threat lies in the use of sloppy methodology. Although the ASTC's Standards for Small Group Research include the requirement that consultants not overstate the applicability of their findings, the methodological guidelines lack detail, and we have some concern that consultants who are not trained in the use of small-group research methods will be unaware of the boundaries and therefore uncertain as to what constitutes an overstatement. We also have some concerns about the use of online focus groups; it is impossible to know that participants are acting on their own as they work from their home computers, and in some cases, participants do not ever interact with each other. The latter rendition should not even be referred to as a focus group, as member interaction is a defining criterion.

Trial Strategy

In our perusal of legal periodicals, we found abundant recommendations regarding construction of the perfect opening statement and closing argument, the most effective direct examination, and the most damaging cross-examination. Many of these were written by lawyers, some by trial consultants. Although a few of these recommended practices contradict research findings (such as the suggestion that lawyers should memorize, word for word, their opening statements), most were consistent with existing basic and applied research. Opening statements should provide jurors with a cognitive framework in the form of a story; they should focus jurors' attention on the actor or action that is deemed to be most blameworthy; and they should steal their opponent's thunder. Many of those same findings hold true for direct examination of witnesses. The closing argument should provide an expository, as opposed to a story model, and should take steps to reduce the hindsight bias.

More research is needed in the areas of cross-examination and attorney style. It is not yet clear under what circumstances an especially aggressive cross is likely to be effective, although various forms of aggressive cross-examination are recommended in the literature by lawyers and consultants alike. There are also many recommendations having to do with such stylistic factors as an attorney's body language during trial and the amount of interpersonal space an attorney should allow between him- or herself and a witness or the jury; however, there is very little in the way of empirical research to allow for an analysis of the validity of those recommendations.

Even if the research shows that the recommendations are valid, is it ethical to advise an attorney to engage in practices that will influence the jury in ways of which that jury is unaware? It is our position that these methods are ethical. If it turns out that a closing argument is more influential when delivered from directly in front of the jury box than from behind a podium, that will be true whether the attorney trying the case knows it or not. The fact is that jurors are influenced by extralegal factors throughout the trial, and those factors will have an influence even when the lawyers, witnesses, and judge are not aware of them and are therefore doing nothing to control them. Opening statements that told a story were more compelling than those that did not before any social scientist conducted research to determine that such was the case.

We see no reason to conclude that a jury's decision will be less just when the attorneys for one or both sides in the case have been educated about these extralegal issues. It is equally plausible that jurors would reach an unjust conclusion in the absence of a well-constructed opening statement, for example, because they might erroneously recall certain important facts or focus their attention on matters of little relevance. We imagine that critics would have less of a problem with this if the attorneys were educating themselves about the relevant research, rather than being advised by paid trial consultants, or if each side could afford to employ trial consultants. We revisit the matter of resource inequity later in this chapter.

Jury Selection

In 1964, the Mississippi State Sovereignty Commission secretly investigated prospective jurors in the trial of Byron de la Beckwith, in order to identify those who were liberals or Jewish. In 1994, in the retrial of the same individual, trial consultants combed neighborhoods and questioned citizens in order to identify those prospective jurors who harbored racist or segregationist views. The Sovereignty Commission was financed by the state's taxpayers and—ironically—was working against the state's interests in convicting someone against whom enough evidence existed to warrant a trial. The trial consultants in 1994 were assisting the prosecution for free because of their strong desire to achieve racial justice. But are there any differences in the ethics of what they did?

In a speech before the National Press Club in July 2001, the noted author Dominick Dunne decried the use of trial consultants who make inferences about a potential juror's leanings by the way he or she gestures or appears during jury selection. Dunne is not the only critic of the intrusion of litigation consultants into the process of jury selection, as previous chapters have shown. But as long as peremptory challenges exist, someone must make decisions as to which prospective jurors to reject. While a few trial attorneys boast that "any 12 jurors" are fine with them, they still seek to have as decision makers those people who are sympathetic to their viewpoint.

Thus, as long as peremptory challenges are granted, jury selection, as defined as considering the pool of possibilities and selecting some, will always exist, whether trial consultants are involved or not. The ethical question for us is where to draw the line regarding trial consultants' level of involvement. The extreme viewpoint is to prohibit trial consultants from participating in jury selection. We believe that trial consultants are sometimes blamed for the excesses that really are the result of some states and the federal government permitting a high number of peremptory challenges. Defendants should have the right to dismiss, without cause, a small number of prospective jurors who seem biased, even if the judge cannot be convinced that they are. But the granting of 20 or 25 peremptory challenges is excessive and justifiably has drawn fire from critics.

The Supreme Court has toyed with the idea of eliminating peremptory challenges; in her book Justice O'Connor wrote:

> Some commentators, as well as the late Justice Thurgood Marshall, have argued that the benefits of peremptory challenges are not worth the costs and have recommended that we follow England's lead. I am not prepared to abolish *all* peremptory challenges; the person whose life or property is at stake must have the assurance that the jurors selected can render a fair, impartial verdict. But thoughtful debate about this issue is overdue. (O'Connor, 2003, p. 223; italics in original)

Let us assume that any change will still permit at least a few. Given that, what should be the role of the trial consultant? Two principles seem salient— the privacy of prospective jurors and the goal of achieving justice. We recommend some ground rules. The first is that the investigation of prospective jurors should be limited to the courtroom. Taking the list of jury pool members and questioning their neighbors, peering at their bumper stickers, and rummaging through their garbage should not be allowed. Prospective jurors surrender enough of their privacy during the voir dire without losing it outside of the courtroom. But inside the courtroom, what should be the limits on the questioning of prospective jurors? Here we believe the goal of achieving justice should be paramount. We should remember that the basic purpose of questioning prospective jurors is to determine whether they have any biases that prevent them from evaluating the evidence objectively. The goal of obtaining unbiased jurors is a challenging one, and the task of distinguishing whether someone is biased is equally difficult. But we believe the trial consultant has a place in the courtroom, advising the attorney as to what questions to ask and which jurors to strike.

The Money Issue

In addition to the ethical issues relevant to each of the specific activities of trial consultants, there is the overarching issue of equity: to the extent that trial consultants do not work for free, doesn't their presence in the legal process simply increase the edge that the wealthy have over the poor? As discussed in chapter 1, Hans and Vidmar (1986) pointed to this as the "major ethical problem with social science in the courtroom" (p. 94). Of course, the entrance of trial consultants into the adversarial system did not create the imbalance; people with more money have always been in a position to hire the best attorneys and benefit from the advantages that come with greater financial resources. But trial consultants do represent yet another weight that tips the scale of justice in favor of the rich.

We don't believe that it is fair to completely disparage the profession on that point. First of all, the blanket statement that all trial-consulting activities favor the rich is inaccurate. We have discussed the role of trial consultants in change-of-venue surveys, which are most often conducted in criminal cases with indigent defendants. When that occurs, the consultant usually works for a much-reduced rate of pay. The same is true when trial consultants assist in the jury selection in death penalty cases. When one considers that the jury selection process in those cases can go on for months, one sees that consultants who provide that service not only work at a reduced rate during that time, but often necessarily turn down much higher-paying jobs in order to do it. Most work in the criminal arena, with the exception of the truly rare case involving the celebrity defendant, is done by consultants in an effort to narrow the gap between rich and poor in our justice system. In our survey of ASTC members, the median percentage of respondents' practice that was dedicated to criminal cases was 5%; not very impressive, but laudable nonetheless. And for 16% of our respondents, work in the criminal arena represented at least 50% of their trial-consulting practices.

In addition, many trial consultants provide some of their services pro bono; for example, the consultants who assisted the prosecution with jury selection in the Byron de la Beckwith trial discussed in chapter 8 were not paid for their services. In a recent *Court Call* article, trial consultant Andy Sheldon (2004) noted that members of his Atlanta firm had donated their time to the Georgia Justice Project, a capital defense organization, and to the Lawyers' Committee for Civil Rights Under Law. In addition, they lecture to law students about the benefits of trial consulting and participate in continuing legal education for attorneys (although the latter activity is considered more a marketing strategy than philanthropy by some). Chair of ASTC's Pro Bono Committee, Sheldon encouraged his colleagues to engage in more pro bono work by citing its benefits. He reported that, for every hour of pro bono work, his firm received 2 hours of paid work in the following month and that members of the firm felt better about themselves as a result of their pro bono initiatives.

In addition to the more traditional forms of trial-consulting pro bono work, a service we would like to see consultants provide is to periodically combine their research findings and disseminate their results within the academic and legal communities. For example, as discussed in chapter 3, judges do not have much to guide them in deciding whether to grant motions to change venue. Even when survey data are presented, there is no existing standard that indicates how much prejudice is too much. We agree with the recommendation of Nietzel and Dillehay (1983) that surveys be conducted even when a change of venue is not being sought, which would allow judges to compare the degree of prejudice in a contested case versus that in the majority of other cases. This would provide some guidance in evaluating the merits of the change-of-venue motion to judges who might otherwise have no benchmark for comparison.

Even in the absence of such a database, consultants who have conducted change-of-venue surveys are collectively in a position to contribute to the scientific study of judicial decision making in change-of-venue cases. Most surveys measure similar variables, such as degree of familiarity with the case and judgments of guilt, and these could be combined with other variables, including the size of the community and whether the judge is elected or appointed. By combining data from the venue surveys they have conducted, trial consultants could determine whether there are reliable predictors of judges' decisions to change venue.

Similar collaborative efforts might be used to contribute to research findings concerning jury selection in specific types of cases, such as identifying predictors of jurors' decisions in product liability cases, or the circumstances under which a particular trial strategy, such as the use of day-in-the-life videos, is likely to be successful. We are encouraged by a recent *Court Call* article in which trial consultant Gary Giewat (2004) briefly describes a recent initiative of ASTC's Research Committee, the Piggy Back Research Project. According to Giewat, the project is a collaborative effort to gather data on important research questions, such as jurors' attitudes relevant to tort reform, and to share those data with the ASTC membership, clients, and the media.

The Identity (Crisis) of the Profession

In chapter 1, we discussed the fact that the trial-consulting profession has no certification or training requirements; virtually anyone can practice as a trial consultant. The possible creation of certification requirements has been hashed and rehashed by the membership, always ending with the conclusion that such requirements are all but impossible to create for a group with such a diversity of backgrounds, training, and professional activities. Is it reasonable to expect that the graphics expert obtain a social science Ph.D., or that the social scientist receive theatrical training? To require certification is to necessarily exclude some from membership and to place limits on allowable practices. The profession has repeatedly concluded that it is prepared to do neither. As a consequence, however, the profession is left to struggle somewhat with its identity.

Standards and Practice Guidelines

One attempt to reduce the variance has been the development of a set of standards and guidelines. According to Andrew Sheldon (2000), the standards allow the profession to define itself. Yes, there are many areas of practice under the trial-consulting umbrella, but as long as everyone engaging in each of those areas is following the same general set of rules, the practice achieves definition. Sheldon argues that standards are necessary not only to define trial consulting, but to distinguish it as a profession as distinct from a trade, an industry, or a business. Because trial consultants work among professionals who are guided by standards, it is important for trial consultants to have their own standards in order to achieve equal footing. Of course, the standards for trial consultants are written by members of the ASTC, and therefore are only applicable to those trial consultants who are ASTC members, but they do represent a positive attempt by trial consultants to guide and regulate themselves.

Practice areas for which standards and guidelines currently exist include change-of-venue surveys, small-group research (i.e., focus groups and mock trials), and witness preparation. In addition, a draft of proposed standards and guidelines for jury selection was recently introduced to the membership for review. Identification of practice areas for which guidelines should be created is probably not based as much on the frequency with which members employ the practice (most trial consultants do not conduct change-of-venue surveys) as on the ease with which guidelines can be developed for it. We expect that the practice guidelines will become increasingly difficult to develop as the practice areas become less clearly defined or even begin to defy acceptable standards.

Recall from our discussion in chapter 4 that there is not an agreed-upon definition of a focus group versus a mock trial, or even a mock trial versus a trial simulation, and the distinct objectives of each method are not clear, either. To the extent that there is definitional fuzziness for other practice areas, we anticipate more difficulties to come. For example, one practice area listed in the ASTC membership directory is variously referred to as "attorney persuasiveness," "presentation strategy," and "communication strategy." If we are correct in assuming that these refer roughly to the same activity, we are concerned that it may prove difficult for the membership to agree on the specific behaviors in which consultants engage while working with attorneys to increase persuasiveness, making the creation of guidelines an arduous task.

All of this raises the question: Are there some practice areas in which the majority of the membership feels that trial consultants should *not* engage and for which they could never agree on a set of guidelines? One practice that stands out for us as questionable is juror profiling through handwriting analysis, or graphology. Some of the consultants who engage in this practice claim that they can make inferences about prospective jurors' personalities from handwriting samples, including whether they are "introverted or extroverted, passive or aggressive, slow or fast thinkers, conservative or liberal and decisive or indecisive" (Holmes & Holmes, 2003, p. 43). Therefore, they assist in jury selection and case preparation by analyzing prospective jurors' handwriting on juror questionnaires, or by comparing handwriting samples taken from focus-group or mock-trial participants to those of prospective jurors (Holmes, 1999).

Of course, there is no empirical evidence that inferences about the personality can reliably be made based on handwriting samples. If a significant segment of the ASTC membership agrees that it is inappropriate to use handwriting analysis for juror profiling, will it be possible to construct guidelines for this practice area? Is it even ethical to charge people money for this based on the claim that it is effective? One solution is for the ASTC to establish a requirement that all trial-consulting practices be empirically supported. However appealing this may be at first glance, it is nearly impossible to put into practice. There is likely to be much debate as to what constitutes empirical support and how much support is enough. Possibly, consultants could adopt a standard similar to that established in *Frye v. United States* (1923) for the admissibility of expert testimony: as long as the practice is generally accepted by the relevant experts (i.e., the membership of ASTC), the practice is allowable.

Pressure to use only empirically supported techniques is currently being felt by clinical and counseling psychologists, who run the risk of forfeiting reimbursement for their services from insurance companies if their techniques are not empirically supported (see, e.g., Deegear & Lawson, 2003; Herbert, 2003). A key component in that debate is the art versus the science of therapeutic techniques; we imagine that a similar debate might emerge relevant to techniques used by trial consultants. Particularly for techniques whose purpose is to enhance the persuasiveness of the attorneys, and where the background of the consultant often lies in the arts, such as theater, versus the sciences, we envision resistance to an emphasis on empirical support.

As difficult as it may be, however, we believe that a move in that direction would pave the way for the profession to identify practices that are fully without merit and that run the risk of giving trial consulting a charlatan image. As the profession works to define itself, standards will allow it to say, "This is what we are," and that definition can include a diversity of activities. However, standards also allow the profession to define what it is *not*, and although that will be difficult, we see it as critical to the credibility of the field.

Consequences of Violating the Standards

The ASTC's standards and practices guidelines are a critical step in the direction of establishing trial consulting as a true profession; the problem, however, is that the guidelines have no teeth. The organization's board recently made available on the ASTC Web site the procedure for filing a grievance against another member and the due process granted to the member who is the subject of the complaint (American Society of Trial Consultants, 2004). In the end, the Grievance Committee of the board has the authority to apply sanctions ranging from written admonishment to suspension or expulsion from ASTC. However, a member who is expelled from the organization can continue to practice as a trial consultant, along with the many trial consultants who have chosen not to join ASTC and who have never been bound by the organization's standards and guidelines. In short, there are currently no formal professional costs associated with a violation of the code.

At its June 2004 conference, the members of ASTC discussed and debated the merits of certification for trial consultants. No decision regarding certification was reached at that meeting, and the ASTC Certification Task Force planned to administer a survey in the spring of 2005 to determine how the membership feels about moving forward with the certification process. However, in preparation for the discussion at the 2004 conference, position papers arguing for and against certification were published in the spring 2004 issue of *Court Call*. Arguing in favor of certification, Lisko and Barker (2004) noted that the only "disincentive for violating [the] standards is our grievance procedure." Rather than taking a punitive approach to educating members who might not otherwise have the necessary training required to comply with the guidelines, certification requirements that include continuing education could accomplish that goal in a more positive, proactive fashion. Lisko and Barker also argued that certification would enhance the credibility of trial consulting in the eyes of other professions, provide prospective clients with a gauge for judging the competence of consultants, establish a demand for excellence in training for consultants, and prevent other bodies, such as state legislatures, from establishing guidelines that are based more on media portrayals of the profession than on reality.

Arguing against certification for trial consultants, Feldhake and Keele (2004) noted the difficulty that the ASTC has faced in trying to agree on the wording of practice standards and the resultant watering-down of the standards in order to satisfy a diversity of training and practice methods. They posit that certification will not solve the diversity problem and will do no more than the current standards and guidelines to ensure consistency of practice. Any attempt to establish certification will cause rifts within the membership; for example, will the persistent nod given to social science methodology in the standards render the non–social scientists unqualified for certification? Feldhake and Keele further argued that, without state licensure requirements, certification status will be as irrelevant as ASTC membership currently is— clients are generally unaware of and unconcerned about membership status. What is important to them is that the consultant is someone they trust and with whom they have had good experiences in the past.

Feldhake and Keele also asserted that consultants are not in a position to judge the qualifications of their colleagues to practice trial consulting. Here, they argued, "If given clients perceive they are getting a quality service, who is qualified to deny that perception? Do we need to protect attorneys from those who some might say are selling a less than acceptable service?" We believe that the membership of ASTC is in a position to identify poor practices and does have an obligation to protect prospective clients. It is dangerous for a profession made up of people who claim to be expert at what they do to profess an inability to judge the quality of work of others who are doing the same thing. We further believe that it is professionally unethical to fail to take any steps to educate prospective clients about practices that most consultants would agree are not valid. However, we do not believe that certification is necessary in order to identify and address poor trial-consulting practices.

On the issue of whether trial consultants, and more specifically the ASTC, should establish certification, we tend to believe that they should not, simply because we don't see certification in this particular profession accomplishing much beyond what a code of standards and guidelines can do. In spite of the potential benefits of certification identified by Lisko and Barker (2004), as well as by us in chapter 1, in the absence of any requirement that one must be certified in order to legally practice trial consulting, we feel that certification is probably more trouble than it's worth. However, we do believe that the ASTC could take steps to strengthen its membership criteria and standards and guidelines, and then, as recommended by Feldhake and Keele (2004), elevate what it means to be an ASTC member.

First, we agree with Lisko and Barker (2004) that continuing education is important for the profession, and we see no reason that the ASTC cannot include a minimum amount of continuing education as a criterion for membership. Second, in order for a practice to be included in the standards and guidelines, we recommend that it be deemed generally acceptable by some majority of the membership. To avoid ambiguity, any practice that is voted down by the membership should be explicitly identified in the code. Third, we would like to see the ASTC revisit the current standards and guidelines, making them more stringent; at the very least, some of what are currently listed as guidelines (i.e., recommended best practices) could be converted into required standards. If that were the case, membership in ASTC, with its requisite compliance with the standards and guidelines, would be more meaningful. Finally, the ASTC must make it a priority to educate current and prospective clients about its code and to promote the value of membership status as an important credential.

Future Directions and Conclusions

In this book, we have attempted to provide an overview of the field of trial consulting, with a specific examination of its most common practice areas. However, there are many trial-consulting activities that we have not discussed. Some of those practice areas have been around for several years, such as preparing trial graphics and conducting posttrial interviews of jurors. Other areas might be described as emerging practices, such as mock bench trials, mock arbitration panels, and the use of mock appellate judges for clients who are preparing to argue before an appeals court (Lisko, personal communication, October 13, 2003).

In addition to adding to the arsenal of consulting activities, the new generation of trial consultants is changing the way they do things. For example, we discussed in chapter 1 the tendency for consultants to protect their personal trade secrets; even when they make presentations at conferences, they are hesitant to share much beyond that which is already common knowledge within the field. However, this trend appears to be changing, as shown by the Piggy Back Research initiative discussed earlier in this chapter, in which consultants will share their research findings on similar topics. Perhaps the increased collaboration among trial consultants is due to the increased success of the field. Many consultants at least occasionally must turn away work, referring jobs to their colleagues, and often consultants in the smaller firms will invite a colleague to collaborate on a sizable project. Increased availability of work renders less important the guarding of trade secrets, and increased collaboration renders it nearly impossible. We see this ultimately as a good thing; establishing best practices necessitates knowledge of the universe of practice options, and whenever a consultant learns a better way of doing something, the profession benefits from an improved reputation.

Another emerging trend is that consultants are becoming more specialized in their work (Lisko, personal communication, October 13, 2003). Although many consultants still advertise by practice area (e.g., indicating that they conduct mock trials, witness preparation, and jury selection), some are focusing their advertisements on the type of case. For example, a consultant's entire practice might consist of working for the plaintiff's side in medical malpractice cases. The work might include the use of focus groups, witness preparation, and jury selection, but what is most important is that the consultant's expertise centers on that type of case. Therefore, the client benefits from the insights the consultant has gained specific to matters that are likely to arise in medical malpractice cases, as opposed to more general knowledge relevant to civil cases.

As the profession grows and changes in these and other directions, it will be necessary for it to continue to monitor itself, to create new guidelines, and to revisit those that have been created. There is great potential for trial consulting to make positive contributions to the legal system. Practice methods that are consistent with empirical research findings can be used to increase the credibility of an honest witness, improve information processing by jurors, and reduce the likelihood that juries will be selected on the basis of stereotyped beliefs. We believe that if the profession focuses its efforts on cultivating practices with the greatest potential to promote justice, as well as on educating its members and its clients about those practices, it will achieve an identity in which its diverse membership will thrive.

References

Abell, J. (1991, March 17). "Black widow" trial titillates New Hampshire. *San Francisco Examiner,* p. A-6.

"About *Court Call.*" (2001, Fall). *Court Call, 17*(4), 2.

Adler, S. J. (1989, October 21). Consultants dope out the mysteries of jurors for clients being sued. *Wall Street Journal,* p. 1.

Adler, S. J. (1994). *The jury: Trial and error in the American courtroom.* New York: Random House.

Albrecht, T. L., Johnson, G. M., & Walther, J. B. (1993). Understanding communication processes in focus groups. In D. L. Morgan (Ed.), *Successful focus groups: Advancing the state of the art* (pp. 51–64). Newbury Park, CA: Sage.

Allen v. United States, 164 U.S. 492 (1896).

Allison, W. (1998, September). Tell your story through opening statement. *Trial, 34,* 78–85.

American Association of Public Opinion Research. (1986). *Code of professional ethics and practices.* Retrieved July 20, 2004, from http://www.aapor.org/default.asp?page=survey_methods/standards_and_best_practices/code_for_professional_ethics_and_practices.

American Bar Association. (1971, 1980, 1993). *Standards for criminal justice: Prosecution function and defense function.* Washington, DC: Author.

American Bar Association, Project on Minimum Standards for Criminal Justice. (1968). *Standards relating to trial by jury: Standard 5.4.* Chicago: Author.

American Greetings Corp. v. Dan-Dee Imports, Inc., 619 F. Supp. 1204 (S.D. N.Y.) (1985).

American Society of Trial Consultants. (1998, Spring). Proposed minimum standards for survey research in connection with motions to change venue. *Court Call, 14*(2), 1–6.

American Society of Trial Consultants. (2002, June). Conference materials booklet for the American Society of Trial Consultants annual conference, Westminster, CO.

American Society of Trial Consultants. (2003). *Code of professional standards.* Retrieved June 16, 2004, from http://www.astcweb.org/code.lasso.

American Society of Trial Consultants. (2004). *Board grievance model.* Retrieved June 12, 2004, from http://www.astcweb.org/aboutus/code.lasso.

American Society of Trial Consultants, Small Group Research Sub-Committee. (2002, May 7). *Proposed small group research (SGR) standards and practice guidelines.* Timonium, MD: Author.

Anonymous. (1998, January). Accidental exposure. *Harper's Magazine, 296,* 20–24.

Arnold, M. (1974, May 5). How Mitchell-Stans jury reached acquittal verdict. *New York Times,* p. 1.

Aron, R., & Rosner, J. L. (1998). *How to prepare witnesses for trial* (2d ed.). St. Paul, MN: West.

Asch, S. E. (1946). Forming impressions of personality. *Journal of Abnormal and Social Psychology, 41,* 258–290.

Associated Press. (1994, February 5). Jury considers evidence in Evers murder. *Kansas City Star,* p. A-8.

Associated Press. (2000, December 21). Shooter in Carruth's trial says murder was planned. *New York Times,* p. C26.

Austin, W., & Utne, M. K. (1977). Sentencing: Discretion and justice in judicial decision making. In B. D. Sales (Ed.), *Psychology in the legal process* (pp. 163–194). New York: Spectrum.

Austin, W., & Williams, T. (1977). A survey of judges' responses to simulated legal cases: A research note on sentencing disparity. *Journal of Criminal Law and Criminology, 68,* 306–310.

Baldwin, J., & McConville, M. (1979). *Jury trials.* Oxford: Clarendon.

Ball, D. (2002, June). Story and structure for plaintiffs. Paper presented at the meeting of the American Society of Trial Consultants, Westminster, CO.

Ballew v. Georgia, 435 U.S. 223 (1978).

Bannan, J. R., & Bannan, R. S. (1974). *Law, morality and Vietnam: The peace militants and the courts.* Bloomington: Indiana University Press.

Barkan, S. E. (1985). *Protesters on trial: Criminal justice in the southern civil rights and Vietnam antiwar movements.* New Brunswick, NJ: Rutgers University Press.

Barnett, K. E. (1999, April). Letting focus groups work for you. *Trial, 35,* 74–75.

Bartley, R. L. (2002, June 24). Andersen: A Pyrrhic victory? *Wall Street Journal,* p. A17.

Batson v. Kentucky, 476 U.S. 79 (1986).

Begam, R. (1977). Voir dire: The attorney's job. *Trial, 13,* 3.

Beisecker, T. (1995, Spring). The role of change of venue in an electronic age. *Kansas Journal of Law and Public Policy, 4,* 81–88.

Belli, R. F., Lindsay, D. S., Gales, M. S., & McCarthy, T. T. (1994). Memory impairment and source misattribution in postevent misinformation experiments with short retention intervals. *Memory and Cognition, 22,* 40–54.

Bergman, P. (1989). *Trial advocacy in a nutshell.* St. Paul, MN: West.

Berman, G. L., & Cutler, B. L. (1996). Effects of inconsistencies in eyewitness testimony on mock-juror decision making. *Journal of Applied Psychology, 81,* 170–177.

Bernstein, C. (1994). Winning trial nonverbally: Six ways to establish control in the courtroom. *Trial, 30,* 61–66.

Berrigan, D. (1970). *The trial of the Catonsville nine.* Boston: Beacon.

Bertrand, J. T., Brown, J. E., & Ward, V. M. (1992). Techniques for analyzing focus group data. *Evaluation Review, 16,* 198–209.

BMW of North America, Inc. v. Gore, 116 S.Ct. 1589 (1996).

Boccaccini, M. T. (2002). What do we really know about witness preparation? *Behavioral Sciences and the Law, 20,* 161–189.

Boehm, V. (1968). Mr. Prejudice, Miss Sympathy, and the authoritarian personality: An application of psychological measuring techniques to the problem of jury bias. *Wisconsin Law Review, 1968,* 734–750.

Bogart, W. A. (1999). Guardian of civil rights . . . medieval relic: The civil jury in Canada. *Law and Contemporary Problems, 62,* 305–319.

Bornstein, B. H. (1999). The ecological validity of jury simulations: Is the jury still out? *Law and Human Behavior, 23,* 75–91.

Bornstein, B. H., Whisenhunt, B. L., Nemeth, R. J., & Dunaway, D. L. (2002). Pretrial publicity and civil cases: A two-way street? *Law and Human Behavior, 26,* 3–17.

Bothwell, R. K., & Abbott, W. F. (1999). The primary processes: Majority effects, factionalism, and negotiating. In W. F. Abbott & J. Batt (Eds.), *A handbook of jury research* (pp. 21-1–21-9). Philadelphia: American Law Institute/American Bar Association.

Bothwell, R. K., & Jalil, M. (1992). The credibility of nervous witnesses. *Journal of Social Behavior and Personality, 7,* 581–586.

Bower, G. H. (1978). Experiments on story understanding and recall. *Quarterly Journal of Experimental Psychology, 28,* 511–534.

Boyll, J. R. (1989). Enhancing juror comprehension and memory retention. *Trial Diplomacy Journal, 12,* 194–199.

Boyll, J. R., & Parshall, D. R. (1998, July). Using early jury focus research. *For the Defense, 40,* 25–28.

Bradac, J. J., Hemphill, M. R., & Tardy, C. H. (1981). Language style on trial: Effects of "powerful" and "powerless" speech upon judgments of victims and villains. *Western Journal of Speech Communication, 45,* 327–341.

Branscombe, N. R., Owen, S., Garstka, T. A., & Coleman, J. (1996). Rape and accident counterfactuals: Who might have done otherwise and would it have changed the outcome? *Journal of Applied Social Psychology, 26,* 1042–1067.

Bray, R. M., & Kerr, N. L. (1982). Methodological considerations in the study of the psychology of the courtroom. In N. L. Kerr & R. M. Bray (Eds.), *The psychology of the courtroom* (pp. 287–323). Orlando, FL: Academic.

Bresler, F. (2003, March 17). Picking juries—or not. *National Law Journal,* p. A13.

Brewer, W. F., & Nakamura, G. V. (1984). The nature and function of schema. In R. S. Wyer, Jr., & T. K. Srull (Eds.), *Handbook of social cognition: Vol. 1* (pp. 119–160). Hillsdale, NJ: Erlbaum.

Brigham, J. C. (1971). Ethnic stereotypes. *Psychological Bulletin, 76,* 15–38.

Brodsky, S. L. (1991). *Testifying in court: Guidelines and maxims for the expert witness.* Washington, DC: American Psychological Association.

Brodsky, S. L., Hooper, N. E., Tipper, D. G., & Yates, S. B. (1999). Attorney invasion of witness space. *Law & Psychology Review, 23,* 49–68.

Broeder, D. (1965). Voir dire examinations: An empirical study. *Southern California Law Review, 38,* 503–528.

Broeder, D. E. (1958). The University of Chicago Jury Project. *Nebraska Law Review, 38,* 744–761.

Brooks Shoe Manufacturing Co., Inc., v. Suave Shoe Corp., 533 F. Supp. 75 (S.D. Fla.) (1981).

Brown, K. R. (1991). Additional reflections on cross-examination. *Utah Bar Journal, 4,* 14–15.

Burgoon, J. K. (1991). Relational message interpretations of touch, conversational distance, and posture. *Journal of Nonverbal Behavior, 15,* 233–259.

Calder, B. J., Insko, C. A., & Yandell, B. (1974). The relation of cognitive and memorial processes to persuasion in a simulated jury trial. *Journal of Applied Social Psychology, 4,* 62–93.

Carey, M. A. (Ed.). (1995). Issues and applications of focus groups [Special issue]. *Qualitative Health Research, 5,* 413–530.

Carey v. Saffold, 122 S.Ct. 2134 (2002).

Carroll, J. S., Kerr, N. L., Alfini, J. J., Weaver, F. M., MacCoun, R. J., & Feldman, V. (1986). Free press and fair trial: The role of behavioral research. *Law and Human Behavior, 10,* 187–201.

Carson, D. (1988). Risk: A four letter word for lawyers. In P. J. Hessing & G. Van den Heuvel (Eds.), *Lawyers on psychology and psychologists on law* (pp. 57–63). Amsterdam: Swets & Zeitlinger.

Chaiken, A. L., & Derlega, V. J. (1974a). Liking for the norm-breaker in self-disclosure. *Journal of Personality, 42,* 117–129.

Chaiken, A. L., & Derlega, V. J. (1974b). Variables affecting the appropriateness of self disclosure. *Journal of Consulting and Clinical Psychology, 42,* 588–593.

Chaiken, S. (1980). Heuristic versus systematic information processing and the use of source versus message cues in persuasion. *Journal of Personality and Social Psychology, 39,* 752–766.

Chaiken, S., & Maheswaran, D. (1994). Heuristic processing can bias systematic processing: Effects of source credibility, argument ambiguity, and task importance on attitude judgment. *Journal of Personality and Social Psychology, 66,* 460–473.

Chapman, G. B., & Bornstein, B. H. (1996). The more you ask for, the more you get: Anchoring in personal injury verdicts. *Applied Cognitive Psychology, 10,* 519–540.

Chelune, G. J. (1976). Reactions to male and female disclosure at two levels. *Journal of Personality and Social Psychology, 34,* 1000–1003.

Chi, M. T. H., Glaser, R., & Farr, M. J. (Eds.). (1988). *The nature of expertise.* Hillsdale, NJ: Erlbaum.

Chopra, S. R., Dahl, L. M., & Wrightsman, L. S. (1996, August). *Sequestered-juror syndrome.* Paper presented at the meetings of the American Psychological Association, Toronto.

Clark, M. (1997). *Without a doubt.* New York: Viking Penguin.

Clarke, E. (1975). The selection of juries, qualifications for service, and the right to challenge. In N. Walker (Ed.), *The British jury system* (pp. 19–27). Cambridge: Cambridge Institute of Criminology, Cambridge University.

Cole, A. H. (1999, Spring). From the president. *Court Call, 15*(2), 10.

Coleman v. Kemp, 778 F.2d 1487 (1985).

Corboy, P. H. (1986). Cross-examination: Walking the line between proper prejudice and unethical conduct. *American Journal of Trial Advocacy, 10,* 1–13.

Costantini, E., & King, J. (1980). The partial juror: Correlates and causes of prejudgment. *Law and Society Review, 15,* 9–40.

Cotchett, J. W., & Rothman, R. (1988). *Persuasive opening statements and closing arguments.* Berkeley: California Continuing Education of the Bar.

Cowan, C. L., Thompson, W. C., & Ellsworth, P. C. (1984). The effects of death qualification on jurors' predispositions to convict and on the quality of deliberation. *Law and Human Behavior, 8,* 53–79.

Cox, G. D. (1991, October 28). Assumption of risks. *National Law Journal,* pp. 1, 24–25.

Cox, G. D. (1992, August 3). Tort tales lash back. *National Law Journal,* pp. 1, 36–37.

Cox, G. D. (1995, April 17). Retrials and tribulations. *National Law Journal,* pp. A1, A24–A25.

Craig, M. (1998, June). He talked too much. *American Spectator, 24,* 48–50.

Crawford, R. J. (1989). *The persuasion edge.* Eau Claire, WI: Professional Education Systems.

Creyer, E. H., & Gürhan, Z. (1997). Who's to blame? Counterfactual reasoning and the assignment of blame. *Psychology and Marketing, 14,* 209–222.

Crowley, A. E., & Hoyer, W. D. (1994). An integrative framework for understanding two-sided persuasion. *Journal of Consumer Research, 20,* 561–574.

Cutler, B. L., Moran, G., & Narby, D. J. (1992). Jury selection in insanity defense cases. *Journal of Research in Personality, 26,* 165–182.

Dane, F. C. (1985). In search of reasonable doubt: A systematic evaluation of selected quantification approaches. *Law and Human Behavior, 9,* 141–158.

Daniels, S., & Martin, J. (1995). *Civil juries and the politics of reform.* Evanston, IL: Northwestern University Press/American Bar Association.

Dann, B. M. (1993). "Learning lessons" and "speaking rights": Creating educated and democratic juries. *Indiana Law Journal, 68,* 1229–1279.

Davis, A. L., & Graham, B. L. (1995). *The Supreme Court, race, and civil rights.* Thousand Oaks, CA: Sage.

Davis, J. H., Bray, R. M., & Holt, R. W. (1977). The empirical study of decision processes in juries: A critical review. In J. L. Tapp & F. J. Levine (Eds.), *Law, justice, and the individual in society: Psychological and legal issues* (pp. 326–361). New York: Holt, Rinehart, & Winston.

Davis, R. W. (1986). Pretrial publicity, the timing of the trial, and mock jurors' decision processes. *Journal of Applied Social Psychology, 16,* 590–607.

Davis, S. D., & Beisecker, T. (1994). Discovering trial consultant work product: A new way to borrow an adversary's wits? *American Journal of Trial Advocacy, 17,* 581–591.

Davis, W. J. (1971). *The chosen ones.* New York: Vantage.

Deegear, J., & Lawson, D. M. (2003). The utility of empirically supported treatments. *Professional Psychology: Research & Practice, 34,* 271–277.

DeLaughter, B. (2001). *Never too late: A prosecutor's story of justice in the Medgar Evers case.* New York: Scribner's.

DePaulo, B. M., Charlton, K., Cooper, H., Lindsay, J. J., & Muhlenbruck, L. (1997). The accuracy-confidence correlation in the detection of deception. *Personality and Social Psychology Review, 1,* 346–357.

Deutsch, M., & Gerard, H. B. (1955). A study of normative and informational social influence upon individual judgment. *Journal of Abnormal and Social Psychology, 51,* 629–636.

Devine, D. J., Clayton, L. D., Dunford, B. B., Seying, R., & Pryce, J. (2001). Jury decision making: 45 years of empirical research on deliberating groups. *Psychology, Public Policy, and Law, 7,* 622–727.

Dexter, H. R., Cutler, B. L., & Moran, G. (1992). A test of voir dire as a remedy for the prejudicial effects of pretrial publicity. *Journal of Applied Social Psychology, 22,* 819–832.

Diamond, S. S. (Ed.). (1979). Simulation research and the law [Special issue]. *Law and Human Behavior, 3*(1–2).

Diamond, S. S. (1990). Scientific jury selection: What social scientists know and don't know. *Judicature, 73,* 178–183.

Diamond, S. S. (1995). Reference guide on survey research. In J. M. McLaughlin (Ed.), *Weinstein's evidence special supplement 1995: Reference manual on scientific evidence* (pp. 221–272). New York: Matthew and Bender.

Diamond, S. S., Casper, J. D., Heiert, C. L., & Marshall, A. (1996). Juror reactions to attorneys at trial. *Journal of Criminal Law and Criminology, 87,* 17–47.

Dillehay, R. C., & Nietzel, M. T. (1985). Juror experience and jury verdicts. *Law and Human Behavior, 9,* 179–191.

Dillehay, R. C., & Nietzel, M. T. (1999). Prior jury service. In W. F. Abbott & J. Batt (Eds.), *A handbook of jury research* (pp. 11-1–11-17). Philadelphia: American Law Institute/American Bar Association.

Dimitrius, J., & Mazzarella, M. (1998). *Reading people.* New York: Ballantine.

Duff, P. (1999). The Scottish criminal jury: A very peculiar institution. *Law and Contemporary Problems, 62,* 173–201.

Early v. Packer, 537 U.S. 3 (2002).

Edmonson v. Leesville Concrete Company, Inc., 111 S.Ct. 2077 (1991).

Eisenberg, T., Hannaford-Agar, P., Hans, V., Mott, N., & Munsterman, T. (2004, March). *Judge-jury agreement in criminal cases: A replication of Kalven and Zeisel's The American Jury.* Paper presented at the meetings of the American Psychology-Law Society, Scottsdale, AZ.

Ekman, P. (1989). Why lies fail and what behaviors betray a lie. In J. C. Yuille (Ed.), *Credibility assessment* (pp. 71–81). Boston: Kluwer.

Ekman, P. (1992). *Telling lies: Clues to deceit in the marketplace, politics, and marriage* (2d ed.). New York: Norton.

Ekman, P., & O'Sullivan, M. (1991). Who can catch a liar? *American Psychologist, 46,* 913–920.

Ellis, L. (2002, March). *Don't find my client liable, but if you do... Defense award recommendations.* Paper presented at the meetings of the American Psychology-Law Society, Austin, TX.

Ellsworth, P. C. (1988). Unpleasant facts: The Supreme Court's response to empirical research on capital punishment. In K. C. Haas & J. A. Inciardi (Eds.), *Challenging capital punishment: Legal and social science approaches* (pp. 177–211). Newbury Park, CA: Sage.

Elwork, A., Sales, B. D., & Alfini, J. J. (1982). *Making jury instructions understandable*. Charlottesville, VA: Michie.

Estes v. Texas, 381 U.S. 532 (1965).

Etzioni, A. (1974a, September). On the scientific manipulation of juries. *Human Behavior, 15,* 10–11.

Etzioni, A. (1974b, May 26). Science: Threatening the jury trial. *Washington Post,* p. C3.

Evans, C., & Van Natta, D. (1993, May 3). The verdict on juries: Only human. *Miami Herald,* pp. A1, A24.

Faber, T. (1973). Change of venue in criminal cases: The defendant's right to specify the county of transfer. *Stanford Law Review, 26,* 131–157.

Fargo, M. (1994, April). Using juror questionnaires to supplement voir dire. *Court Call,* 1–3.

Farrell, D., & Bunch, W. T. (1999). Using social science methods to improve voir dire and jury selection. In W. F. Abbott & J. Batt (Eds.), *A handbook of jury research* (pp. 4-1–4-43). Philadelphia: American Law Institute/American Bar Association.

Feigenson, N. (2000). *Legal blame: How jurors think and talk about accidents*. Washington, DC: American Psychological Association.

Feigenson, N., Park, J., & Salovey, P. (1997). Effects of blameworthiness and outcome severity on attributions of responsibility and damage awards in comparative negligence cases. *Law and Human Behavior, 21,* 597–617.

Feild, H. S. (1978). Juror background characteristics and attitudes toward rape: Correlates of jurors' decisions in rape trials. *Law and Human Behavior, 2,* 73–93.

Feldhake, R. J., & Keele, L. M. (2004, Spring). Or not to certify: Avoiding a distinction without a difference and a raft of practical problems. *Court Call, 20.* Retrieved June 9, 2004, from http://www.astcweb.org/courtcall/story_display.lasso?pub_id=10000028&article_id=20000135.

Ferris, W. (1994, July 24). The battle for Mississippi. *New York Times Book Review,* pp. 16–17.

Finkel, N. (1995). *Commonsense justice*. Cambridge, MA: Harvard University Press.

Finkel, N. (1997). Commonsense justice, psychology and the law: Prototypes that are common, senseful, and not. *Psychology, Public Policy, and Law, 3,* 461–489.

Finkel, N. (2001). *Not fair! The typology of commonsense unfairness*. Washington, DC: American Psychological Association.

Finkel, N. J., Meister, K. H., & Lightfoot, D. M. (1991). The self-defense defense and community sentiment. *Law and Human Behavior, 15,* 585–602.

Finlay, B., & Cromwell, T. A. (1999). *Witness preparation manual* (2d ed.). Aurora, Ontario: Canada Law Book.

Fischhoff, B. (1975). Hindsight ≠ foresight: The effect of outcome knowledge on judgment under uncertainty. *Journal of Experimental Psychology: Human Perception and Performance, 1,* 288–299.

Fiske, S. T., & Taylor, S. E. (1991). *Social cognition* (2d ed.). New York: McGraw-Hill.

Follingstad, D. R. (1984, January). Preparing the witness for courtroom testimony: Modifying negative behavior through employment of psychological principles. *Trial, 20*(1), 50–58.

ForsterLee, L., Horowitz, I. A., & Bourgeois, M. J. (1993). Juror competence in civil trials: Effects of preinstruction and evidence technicality. *Journal of Applied Psychology, 78,* 14–21.

Frank, J. (1949). *Courts on trial: Myth and reality in American justice.* Princeton, NJ: Princeton University Press.

Franklin, B. (1994, August 22). Gender myths still play a role in jury selection. *National Law Journal,* A1, A25.

Frederick, J. (2003, Spring). Report from the jury selection standards and practice guidelines committee. *Court Call, 19*(2), 5–7.

Freedman, M. H. (1966). Professional responsibility of the criminal defense lawyer: The three hardest questions. *Michigan Law Review, 64,* 1469–1484.

French, T. R. (1992, November). KISS in the courtroom: Keep it short and simple. *Trial, 28,* 130–136.

Frisch's Restaurant Inc. v. Shoney's Inc., 759 F.2d 1261 (1985).

Frye v. United States, 293 F.1013, 34 A.L.R. 145 (DC Cir. 1923).

Fulero, S. M., & Penrod, S. D. (1990a). Attorney jury selection folklore: What do they think and how can psychologists help? *Forensic Reports, 3,* 233–259.

Fulero, S., & Penrod, S. (1990b). The myths and realities of attorney jury selection folklore and scientific jury selection: What works? *Ohio Northern University Law Review, 17,* 229–253.

Gallagher, F. (1995, August 13). Advising the lawyers. *Roanoke Times,* pp. D1, D12.

Gannett Co., Inc., v. DePasquale, 443 U.S. 368 (1979).

Geders v. United States, 425 U.S. 80 (1976).

Geimer, W. S., & Amsterdam, J. (1988). Why jurors vote life or death: Operative factors in Florida death penalty cases. *American Journal of Criminal Law, 15,* 1–54.

Genard, G. (2000, Fall). Through the looking glass: The mirror images of trials and theater. *Court Call, 16,* 8–9.

Genard, G. (2001a, Spring). How to create a powerful presence in the courtroom. *Court Call, 17,* 14–15.

Genard, G. (2001b, Summer). Speaking smart: Harnessing the power of your voice to convince others. *Court Call, 17,* 10.

Genard, G. (2002, Winter). Making yourself a "worthy adversary" in the minds of jurors. *Court Call, 18,* 8–9.

Georgia v. McCollum, 112 S.Ct. 2348 (1992).

Gerbasi, K. C., Zuckerman, M., & Reis, H. T. (1977). Justice needs a new blindfold: A review of mock jury research. *Psychological Bulletin, 84,* 323–345.

Gershman, B. L. (2002). Witness coaching by prosecutors. *Cardozo Law Review, 23,* 829–863.

Gibbs, M. S., Sigal, J., Adams, B., & Grossman, B. (1989). Cross-examination of the expert witness: Do hostile tactics affect impressions of a simulated jury? *Behavioral Sciences & the Law, 7,* 275–281.

Giewat, G. (2004, Spring). Research notes: See poster on Piggy Back Research at Memphis convention. *Court Call, 20.* Retrieved June 9, 2004, from http://www.astcweb.org/courtcall/story_display.lasso?pub_id=10000028& article_id=20000136.

Gillers, S. (2002, June 18). The flaw in the Andersen verdict. *New York Times,* p. A18.

Givens, D. P. (1981). Posture is power. *Barrister, 8,* 14–18.

Glaman, J. M., Jones, A. P., & Rozelle, R. M. (1996). The effects of co-worker similarity on the emergence of affect in work teams. *Group and Organization Management, 21,* 192–215.

Gold, V. (1987). Covert advocacy: Reflections on the use of psychological persuasion techniques in the courtroom. *North Carolina Law Review, 65,* 481–508.

Gordon, R. (1995, February 6). Setting parameters for trial science. *Legal Times,* p. A34.

Gordon, W. L., III. (1997). Reflections of a criminal defense lawyer on the O. J. Simpson trial. *Journal of Social Issues, 53,* 417–424.

Gorny, S. M. (2000). Getting into focus: Improving trial technique through focus groups. *Trial Lawyer, 23,* 111–117.

Graham, M. H. (1983). *Tightening the reins of justice in America: A comparative analysis of the criminal jury trial in England and the United States.* Westport, CT: Greenwood.

Grant, B. C. (1993). Focus groups versus mock trials: Which should you use? *Trial Diplomacy Journal, 16,* 15–22.

Gray, L. N. (1997). Direct, cross and redirect examination (one man's opinion). *New York State Bar Journal, 69,* 46–52.

Greenbaum, T. L. (1998). *The handbook for focus group research* (2d ed.). Thousand Oaks, CA: Sage.

Greene, E. (1989). On juries and damage awards: The process of decision making. *Law and Contemporary Problems, 52,* 225–246.

Greene, E., & Bornstein, B. H. (2003). *Determining damages: The psychology of jury awards.* Washington, DC: American Psychological Association.

Greene, E., & Wrightsman, L. S. (2003). Decision making by juries and judges: International perspectives. In D. Carson and R. Bull (Eds.), *Handbook of psychology in legal contexts* (2d ed., pp. 401–422). West Sussex, UK: Wiley.

Grisham, J. (1996). *The runaway jury.* New York: Dell.

Grisham, J. (1999). *The testament.* New York: Doubleday.

Hamer v. United States, 259 F.2d (9th Cir.), cert. denied, 359 U.S. 916 (1958).

Haney, C. (1997). Commonsense justice and capital punishment: Problematizing the "will of the people." *Psychology, Public Policy, and Law, 3,* 303–337.

Hannaford, P. L., Hans, V. P., Mott, N. L., & Munsterman, G. T. (2000). The timing of opinion formation by jurors in civil cases: An empirical examination. *Tennessee Law Review, 67,* 627–652.

Hans, V. P. (1982). Jury selection in two countries: A psychological perspective. *Current Psychological Reviews, 2,* 283–300.

Hans, V. P. (1990). Attitudes toward corporate responsibility: A psycholegal perspective. *Nebraska Law Review, 69,* 158–189.

Hans, V. P, & Lofquist, W. (1992). Jurors' judgments of business liability in tort cases: Implications for the litigation explosion debate. *Law and Society Review, 26,* 85–115.

Hans, V. P., & Sweigart, K. (1993). Jurors' views of civil lawyers: Implications for courtroom communication. *Indiana Law Journal, 68,* 1297–1332.

Hans, V. P., & Vidmar, N. (1982). Jury selection. In N. Kerr & R. Bray (Eds.), *The psychology of the courtroom* (pp. 39–82). Orlando, FL: Academic.

Hans, V. P., & Vidmar, N. (1986). *Judging the jury.* New York: Plenum.

Hart, L. (2002, June 16). "Smoking gun" memo unraveled jury deadlock. *Lawrence Journal-World,* p. 8A.

Hastie, R. (1991). Is attorney-conducted voir dire an effective procedure for the selection of impartial jurors? *American University Law Review, 40,* 703–726.

Hastie, R., Penrod, S. D., & Pennington, N. (1983). *Inside the jury.* Cambridge, MA: Harvard University Press.

Hawkins, C. (1960). *Interaction and coalition realignments in consensus-seeking groups: A study of experimental jury deliberation.* Unpublished doctoral dissertation, University of Chicago.

Hawkins, C. (1962). Interaction rates of jurors aligned in factions. *American Sociological Review, 27,* 689–691.

Heath, W. P., Grannemann, B. D., & Peacock, M. A. (2004). How the defendant's emotion level affects mock jurors' decisions when presentation mode and evidence strength are varied. *Journal of Applied Social Psychology, 34,* 624–664.

Herbert, J. D. (Ed.). (2003). Empirically supported treatments [Special issue]. *Behavior Modification, 27*(3).

Herbsleb, J. D., Sales, B. D., & Berman, J. J. (1979). When psychologists aid in the voir dire: Legal and ethical considerations. In L. E. Abt & I. R. Stuart (Eds.), *Social psychology and discretionary law* (pp. 197–217). New York: Van Nostrand Reinhold.

Heuer, L., & Penrod, S. (1989). Instructing jurors: A field experiment with written and preliminary instructions. *Law and Human Behavior, 13,* 409–430.

Hilgard, E. R. (1975). Hypnosis. *Annual Review of Psychology, 26,* 19–44.

Hinsz, V. B., & Indahl, K. E. (1995). Assimilation to anchors for damage awards in a mock civil trial. *Journal of Applied Social Psychology, 25,* 991–1026.

Hocking, J. E., Miller, G. R., & Fontes, N. E. (1978, April). Videotape in the courtroom: Witness deception. *Trial, 14*(4), 52–55.

Hoeflich, M. (2002, June 19). Andersen verdict sets tone. *Lawrence Journal-World,* p. 7B.

Hoeschen, B. L. F. (2001, June). The e-alternative: Online mock juries offer cheap and fast opinions. *ABA Journal, 87,* 26.

Holland v. Illinois, 493 U.S. 474 (1990).

Hollander, E. P. (1985). Leadership and power. In G. Lindzey & E. Aronson (Eds.), *Handbook of social psychology, Vol. 2* (3d ed., pp. 485–537). New York: McGraw-Hill.

Holmes, R. (1999). *Attorney trial advantage: Jury consultants using handwriting in & out of the courtroom.* Retrieved September 29, 2004, from http://www.pentec.net/JuryTrial/JuryTrial.html.

Holmes, R., & Holmes, S. (2003). Handwriting examiners as jury and trial consultants. *Forensic Examiner, 12,* 42–45.

Horowitz, I. A. (1980). Juror selection: A comparison of two methods in several criminal cases. *Journal of Applied Social Psychology, 10,* 86–99.

Horowitz, I. A. (1997). Reasonable doubt instructions: Commonsense justice and standard of proof. *Psychology, Public Policy, and Law, 3,* 285–302.

Horowitz, I. A., & Kirkpatrick, L. C. (1996). A concept in search of a definition: The effects of reasonable doubt instructions on certainty of guilt standards and jury verdicts. *Law and Human Behavior, 20,* 655–670.

Hovland, C. I., & Mandell, W. (1952). An experimental comparison of conclusion drawing by the communicator and by the audience. *Journal of Abnormal and Social Psychology, 47,* 581–588.

Hsieh, S. (2001, February 5). Trial lawyers are cutting cost of focus groups via the Internet. *Lawyers Weekly USA.* Retrieved August 5, 2003, from http://www.lawyersweeklyusa.com.

Huber, P. (1988). *Liability: The legal revolution and its consequences.* New York: Basic.

Huntley, J. E., & Costanzo, M. (2002, June). *Sexual harassment stories: Testing a story mediated model of juror decision-making in civil litigation.* Paper presented at the meeting of the American Society of Trial Consultants, Westminster, CO.

Imrich, D., Mullin, C., & Linz, D. (1995). Measuring the extent of pretrial publicity in major American newspapers: A content analysis. *Journal of Communication, 45,* 94–117.

Irvin v. Dowd, 366 U.S. 717 (1961).

Irvin v. State, 66 S. 2d 288 (Fla. 1953).

Jackson, J. D., Quinn, K., & O'Malley, T. (1999). The jury system in contemporary Ireland: In the shadow of a troubled past. *Law and Contemporary Problems, 62,* 203–232.

Jacobson v. United States, 112 S.Ct. 1535 (1992).

James, K. (2002, Spring). The making of *What Can Lawyers Learn from Actors*: The journey from live workshop to video tape. *Court Call, 18,* 8–10.

James, K., & Blumenfeld, A. (n.d.). Who we are. Retrieved July 13, 2002, from http://www.actofcommunication.com.

Janis, I. L. (1982). *Groupthink* (2d ed.). Boston: Houghton Mifflin.

Jardine, J. (2004, January 11). Survey inflicts poll-ax damage. Retrieved January 13, 2004, from http://www.modbee.com/columnists/jardine/v-print/story/7993392p-8861748c.html.

Jeans, J. W. (1975). *Trial advocacy.* St. Paul, MN: West.

J.E.B. v. Alabama ex rel. T.B., 114 S.Ct. 1419 (1994).

Johnson v. California, U.S. Supreme Court, No. 03–6539 (2004).

Johnson v. Louisiana, 406 U.S. 356 (1972).

Johnson, C., & Haney, C. (1994). Felony voir dire: An explanatory study of its content and effect. *Law and Human Behavior, 18,* 487–506.

Johnson, C., & Vinson, L. (1987). Damned if you do, damned if you don't: Status, powerful speech, and evaluations of female witnesses. *Women's Studies in Communication, 10,* 31–44.

Jurow, G. L. (1971). New data on the effect of a "death qualified" jury on the guilt determination process. *Harvard Law Review, 84,* 567–611.

Kagehiro, D. K., & Stanton, W. C. (1985). Legal vs. quantified definitions of standards of proof. *Law and Human Behavior, 9,* 159–178.

Kalven, H. (1958). The jury, the law, and the personal injury damage award. *Ohio State Law Journal, 19,* 159–178.

Kalven, H., & Zeisel, H. (1966). *The American jury.* Boston: Little, Brown.

Kaplan, M. F. (1999). Verdict-driven and evidence-driven juries. In W. F. Abbott & J. Batt (Eds.), *A handbook of jury research* (pp. 22-1–22-4). Philadelphia: American Law Institute/American Bar Association.

Kaplan, S. M. (1985, July). Death so say we all. *Psychology Today,* pp. 48–53.

Kassin, S. M., & Juhnke, R. (1983). Juror experience and decision making. *Journal of Personality and Social Psychology, 44,* 1182–1191.

Kassin, S., Meissner, C., & Norwick, R. (2003, July). *The post-interrogation safety net: "I'd know a false confession if I saw one."* Paper presented to the Psychology and Law International Interdisciplinary Conference, Edinburgh, UK.

Kassin, S. M., Smith, V. L., & Tulloch, W. F. (1990). The dynamite charge: Effects on the perception and deliberation behaviors of mock jurors. *Law and Human Behavior, 14,* 537–550.

Kassin, S. M., Williams, L. N., & Saunders, C. L. (1990). Dirty tricks of cross examination: The influence of conjectural evidence on the jury. *Law and Human Behavior, 14,* 373–384.

Kassin, S. M., & Wrightsman, L. S. (1979). On the requirements of proof: The timing of judicial instruction and mock juror verdicts. *Journal of Personality and Social Psychology, 37,* 1877–1887.

Kassin, S. M., & Wrightsman, L. S. (1983). The construction and validation of a juror bias scale. *Journal of Research in Personality, 17,* 423–442.

Kassin, S. M., & Wrightsman, L. S. (1988). *The American jury on trial: Psychological perspectives.* New York: Hemisphere.

Kebbell, M. R., & Johnson, S. D. (2000). Lawyers' questioning: The effect of confusing questions on witness confidence and accuracy. *Law and Human Behavior, 24,* 629–641.

Kelly v. United States, 250 F.947 (9th Cir., 1918).

Kelman, H. C., & Hovland, C. I. (1953). "Reinstatement" of the communicator in delayed measurement of opinion change. *Journal of Abnormal and Social Psychology, 48,* 327–335.

Kennebeck, E. (1973). *Juror number four.* New York: Norton.

Kennedy, T., Kennedy, J., & Abrahamson, A. (1995). *Mistrial of the century: A private diary of the jury system on trial.* Beverly Hills, CA: Dove.

Kerr, N. L. (1981). Effects of prior jury experience on juror behavior. *Basic and Applied Social Psychology, 2,* 175–193.

Kerr, N. L., Harmon, D. L., & Graves, J. K. (1982). Independence of multiple verdicts by jurors and juries. *Journal of Applied Social Psychology, 12,* 12–29.

Kerr, N. L., Kramer, G. P., Carroll, J. S., & Alfini, J. J. (1991). On the effectiveness of voir dire in criminal cases with prejudicial pretrial publicity: An empirical study. *American University Law Review, 40,* 665–701.

Kidd, P. S., & Parshall, M. B. (2000). Getting the focus and the group: Enhancing analytical rigor in focus group research. *Qualitative Health Research, 10,* 293–308.

Kinch, J. W. (1991). The jury survey: Improved social science input in change of venue decisions. *Glendale Law Review, 10,* 69–91.

Klein, R. B. (1993). Winning cases with body language. *Trial, 29,* 56–60.

Klein, S. R., & Kochman, R. W. (1998). How to prepare for and conduct an effective direct examination. *New Jersey Lawyer, 194,* 24–27.

Kline, F. G., & Jess, P. H. (1966). Prejudicial publicity: Its effect on law school mock juries. *Journalism Quarterly, 43,* 113–116.

Knodel, J. (1993). The design and analysis of focus group studies: A practical approach. In D. L. Morgan (Ed.), *Successful focus groups: Advancing the state of the art* (pp. 35–50). Newbury Park, CA: Sage.

Knox, M., & Walker, M. (1995). *The private diary of an O. J. juror.* Beverly Hills, CA: Dove.

Koch, C. S. (2001). Improving the odds: Using mock trials to hone strategies. *Trial Lawyer, 24,* 116–122.

Kohlberg, L. (1976). Moral stages and moralization: The cognitive-developmental approach. In T. Lickona (Ed.), *Moral development and behavior* (pp. 31–53). New York: Holt, Rinehart, & Winston.

Kramer, G. P., Kerr, N. L., & Carroll, J. S. (1990). Pretrial publicity, judicial remedies, and jury bias. *Law and Human Behavior, 14,* 409–438.

Krauss, E., & Bonora, B. (Eds.). (1983). *Jurywork: Systematic techniques* (2d ed.). St. Paul, MN: West.

Kravitz, D. A., Cutler, B. L., & Brock, P. (1993). Reliability and validity of the original and revised Legal Attitudes Questionnaire. *Law and Human Behavior, 17,* 661–677.

Kressel, N. J., & Kressel, D. F. (2002). *Stack and sway: The new science of jury consulting.* Boulder, CO: Westview.

Krueger, R. A. (1993). Control in focus group research. In D. L. Morgan (Ed.), *Successful focus groups: Advancing the state of the art* (pp. 65–85). Newbury Park, CA: Sage.

Krueger, R. A. (1998). *Analyzing and reporting focus group results.* Thousand Oaks, CA: Sage.

Kunstler, W. M., with Isenberg, S. (1994). *My life as a radical lawyer.* New York: Birch Lane Press.

Lambert, W. (1994, February 4). Trial consultants lose mystique as firms tighten their belts. *Wall Street Journal,* p. B7.

Langer, E. J., & Abelson, R. P. (1974). A patient by any other name . . . : Clinical group differences in labeling bias. *Journal of Consulting and Clinical Psychology, 42,* 4–9.

Larrabee, J. (1991, March 20). Deadly love affair has nation enthralled. *USA Today,* p. 3A.

Lassiter, C. (1996). TV or not TV—That is the question. *Journal of Criminal Law and Criminology, 86,* 928–1018.

Lawry, R. P. (1996). Cross-examining the truthful witness: The ideal within the central moral tradition of lawyering. *Dickinson Law Review, 100,* 563–586.

Lawson, S. (1994, March 28). Jury is still out on trial consultants, but many small firms find them valuable. *Lawyers Weekly USA,* p. B14.

Leathers, D. G. (1997). *Successful nonverbal communication* (3d ed.). Boston: Allyn & Bacon.

Lecci, L., & Myers, B. (1996, August). *Validating the factor structure of the Juror Bias Scale.* Paper presented at the meetings of the American Psychological Association, Toronto.

Lempert, R. (1991). Telling tales in court: Trial procedure and the story model. *Cardozo Law Review, 13,* 559–573.

Lesly, M., & Shuttleworth, C. (1988). *Subway gunman: A juror's account of the Bernhard Goetz trial.* Latham, NY: British American Library.

Levenson, L. L. (2003, November 3). The dynamite charge. *National Law Journal,* p. 15.

Levine, J. P. (1996). The impact of sequestration on juries. *Judicature, 79,* 266–272.

Lieberman, J., & Sales, B. (1997). What social science teaches us about the jury instruction process. *Psychology, Public Policy, and Law, 3,* 589–644.

Lingle, J. H., & Ostrom, T. M. (1981). Principles of memory and cognition in attitude formation. In R. E. Petty, T. M. Ostrom, & T. C. Brock (Eds.), *Cognitive responses in persuasion* (pp. 399–420). Hillsdale, NJ: Erlbaum.

Linz, D. G., & Penrod, S. (1984). Increasing attorney persuasiveness in the courtroom. *Law and Psychology Review, 8,* 1–47.

Linz, D., & Penrod, S. (1992). Exploring the First and Sixth amendments: Pretrial publicity and jury decision making. In D. Kagehiro & W. S. Laufer (Eds.), *Handbook of psychology and law* (pp. 1–20). New York: Springer.

Linz, D., Penrod, S., & McDonald, E. (1986). Attorney communication and impression making in the courtroom: Views from the bench. *Law and Human Behavior, 10,* 281–302.

Lisko, K. O. (1992). *Juror perceptions of witness credibility as a function of linguistic and nonverbal power.* Unpublished doctoral dissertation, Department of Communication Studies, University of Kansas, Lawrence.

Lisko, K., & Barker, S. (2004, Spring). To certify: Increasing trial consultant competency and enhancing professional credibility. *Court Call, 20.* Retrieved June 9, 2004, from http://www.astcweb.org/courtcall/story_display.lasso? pub_id=10000028&article_id=20000134.

Litigation Sciences. (1983). Brochure. Los Angeles, CA: Author.

Litigation Sciences. (1988). *Litigation Sciences: The leader in jury research.* Rolling Hills Estates, CA: Author.

Lloyd-Bostock, S., & Thomas, C. (1999). Decline of the "little parliament": Juries and jury reform in England and Wales. *Law and Contemporary Problems, 62,* 7–40.

Lockhart v. McCree, 106 S.Ct. 1758 (1986).

Loeterman, B. (Producer). (1997). *What Jennifer saw* [Television broadcast]. Boston: WGBH/Frontline.

Loftus, E. F., & Palmer, J. C. (1974). Reconstruction of automobile destruction: An example of interaction between language and memory. *Journal of Verbal Learning and Verbal Behavior, 13,* 585–589.

Loftus, E. F., & Zanni, G. (1975). Eyewitness testimony: The influence of the wording of a question. *Bulletin of the Psychonomic Society, 5,* 86–88.

Lord, C. G., Lepper, M. R., & Preston, E. (1984). Considering the opposite: A corrective strategy for social judgment. *Journal of Personality and Social Psychology, 47,* 1231–1243.

Lowenfield v. Phelps, 108 S.Ct. 546 (1988).

Lupfer, M., Cohen, R., Bernard, J. L., Smalley, D., & Schippmann, J. (1985). An attributional analysis of jurors' judgments in civil cases. *Journal of Social Psychology, 125,* 743–751.

Lupfer, M. B., Cohen, R., Bernard, J. L., & Brown, C. M. (1987). The influence of level of moral reasoning on the decisions of jurors. *Journal of Social Psychology, 127,* 653–667.

Lykken, D. T. (1998). *Tremor in the blood: Uses and abuses of the lie detector.* New York: Plenum.

Maass, A., & Clark, R. D., III. (1984). Hidden impact of minorities: Fifteen years of minority influence research. *Psychological Bulletin, 95,* 428–450.

MacCoun, R., & Kerr, N. L. (1988). Asymmetric influence in mock jury deliberations: Jurors' bias for leniency. *Journal of Personality and Social Psychology, 54,* 21–33.

Mackie, D. M., Worth, L. T., & Asuncion, A. G. (1990). Processing of persuasive in-group messages. *Journal of Personality and Social Psychology, 58,* 812–822.

Mahoney, A. R. (1982). American jury voir dire and the ideal of equal justice. *Journal of Applied Behavioral Science, 18,* 481–494.

Malouff, J., & Schutte, N. S. (1989). Shaping juror attitudes: Effects of requesting different damage amounts in personal injury trials. *Journal of Social Psychology, 129,* 491–497.

Marcus, P. (1978). The *Allen* instruction in criminal cases: Is the dynamite charge about to be permanently defused? *Missouri Law Review, 43,* 613–641.

Marshall, R. T. (1973). The telling opening statement. *Practical Lawyer, 19,* 27–35.

Marti, M. W., & Wissler, R. L. (2000). Be careful what you ask for: The effect of anchors on personal injury damage awards. *Journal of Experimental Psychology: Applied, 6,* 91–103.

Massengill, R. (1994). *Portrait of a racist: The man who killed Medgar Evers?* New York: St. Martin's.

Matheo, L., & DeCaro, L. L. (2001). 11 ways to improve courtroom performance. *Brief, 31,* 58–66.

Matlon, R. J. (1988). *Communication in the legal process.* New York: Holt, Rinehart, & Winston.

Matlon, R. J. (1991, October). *Opening statements and closing arguments: A research review.* Paper presented at the meeting of the American Society of Trial Consultants, San Francisco, CA.

Matlon, R. J. (1998, Winter). The history of the American Society of Trial Consultants: A personal look. *Court Call, 14*(1), 1–4.

Mauet, T. A. (1996). *Trial techniques* (4th ed.). Boston: Little, Brown.

Mauro, T. (2004, January 21). Judges wrongly close court to protect jurors. *USA Today,* p. 15A.

McArthur, L. Z. (1981). What grabs you? The role of attention in impression formation and causal attribution. In E. T. Higgins, C. P. Herman, & M. P. Zanna (Eds.), *Social cognition: The Ontario symposium, Vol. 1* (pp. 201–246). Hillsdale, NJ: Erlbaum.

McCabe, S., & Purves, R. (1972). *The jury at work.* Oxford: Oxford University Penal Research Unit.

McCullough, G. W. (1994, March). *Juror decisions as a function of linguistic structure of the opening statement and closing argument.* Paper presented at the meeting of the American Psychology-Law Society, Santa Fe, NM.

McElhaney, J. W. (1987). Horse-shedding the witness: Techniques for witness preparation. *Trial, 10,* 80–84.

McElhaney, J. W. (2000, October). From start to finish. *ABA Journal,* 50–56.

McGuire, W. J. (1969). The nature of attitudes and attitude change. In G. Lindzey & E. Aronson (Eds.), *The handbook of social psychology, Vol. 3* (2d ed., pp. 136–314). Reading, MA: Addison-Wesley.

Menon, J. W. (1995). Adversarial medical and scientific testimony and lay jurors: A proposal for medical malpractice reform. *American Journal of Law and Medicine, 21,* 281–300.

Merritt, D. J., & Barry, K. A. (1999). Is the tort system in crisis? New empirical evidence. *Ohio State Law Journal, 60,* 315–398.

Metos, G. F. (1990). Cross-examination: Methods and preparations. *Utah Bar Journal, 3,* 11–15.

Millward, L. J. (2000). Focus groups. In G. M. Breakwell, S. Hammond, & C. Fife-Shaw (Eds.), *Research methods in psychology* (2^d ed., pp. 303–324). London: Sage.

Minow, N. N., & Cate, F. H. (1991). Who is an impartial juror in an age of mass media? *American University Law Review, 40,* 631–664.

Mize, G. (1999). On better jury selection: Spotting unfavorable jurors before they enter the jury room. *Court Review, 36,* 10–15.

Moller, E. (1996). *Trends in civil jury verdicts since 1985.* Santa Monica, CA: RAND Institute for Civil Justice.

Moran, G. (2001). Trial consultation: Why licensure is not necessary. *Journal of Forensic Psychology Practice, 1*(4), 69–76.

Moran, G., & Comfort, J. C. (1982). Scientific juror selection: Sex as a moderator of demographic and personality predictors of impaneled felony juror behavior. *Journal of Personality and Social Psychology, 43,* 1052–1063.

Moran, G., & Cutler, B. L. (1989, August). Dispositional predictors of criminal case verdicts. In B. L. Cutler (Chair), Contemporary psychological and legal perspectives on jury selection. Symposium conducted at the meeting of the American Psychological Association, New Orleans, LA.

Moran, G., & Cutler, B. L. (1991). The prejudicial impact of pretrial publicity. *Journal of Applied Social Psychology, 21,* 345–367.

Moran, G., Cutler, B. L., & DeLisa, A. (1994). Attitudes toward tort reform, scientific jury selection, and juror bias: Verdict inclination in criminal and civil trials. *Law and Psychology Review, 18,* 309–328.

Morgan, F. W. (1990). Judicial standards for survey research: An update and guidelines. *Journal of Marketing, 54,* 59–70.

Morris, W. (1998). *The ghosts of Medgar Evers: A tale of race, murder, Mississippi, and Hollywood.* New York: Random House.

Moscovici, S. (1985). Social influence and conformity. In G. Lindzey & E. Aronson (Eds.), *Handbook of social psychology: Vol. 2* (3d ed., pp. 347–412). New York: McGraw-Hill.

Moscovici, S., & Zavalloni, M. (1969). The group as a polarizer of attitudes. *Journal of Personality and Social Psychology, 12,* 125–135.

Mossman, K. (1973, May). Jury selection: An expert's view. *Psychology Today,* pp. 78–79.

Mullins, S. D. (2000). Focus groups for small cases. *Trial Lawyer, 23,* 433–436.

Mu'Min v. Virginia, 111 S.Ct. 1899 (1991).

Myers, B., & Lecci, L. (1998). Revising the factor structure of the Juror Bias Scale: A method for the empirical validation of theoretical constructs. *Law and Human Behavior, 22,* 239–256.

Myers, D. G., & Kaplan, M. F. (1976). Group-induced polarization in simulated juries. *Personality and Social Psychology Bulletin, 2,* 63–66.

Myers, D. G., & Lamm, H. (1976). The group polarization phenomenon. *Psychological Bulletin, 83,* 602–627.

Narby, D. J., Cutler, B. L., & Moran, G. (1993). A meta-analysis of the association between authoritarianism and jurors' perceptions of defendant culpability. *Journal of Applied Psychology, 78,* 34–42.

Nelson, J., & Ostrow, R. J. (1972). *The FBI and the Berrigans: The making of a conspiracy.* New York: Coward, McCann & Geoghegan.

Nemeth, C., Endicott, J., & Wachtler, J. (1976). From the '50s to the '70s: Women in jury deliberations. *Sociometry, 39,* 293–304.

Nietzel, M. T., & Dillehay, R. C. (1983). Psychologists as consultants for changes of venue: The use of public opinion surveys. *Law and Human Behavior, 7,* 309–335.

Nietzel, M. T., & Dillehay, R. C. (1986). *Psychological consultation in the courtroom.* New York: Pergamon.

Nietzel, M. T., McCarthy, D. M., & Kern, M. J. (1999). Juries: The current state of the empirical literature. In R. Roesch, S. D. Hart, & J. R. P. Ogloff (Eds.), *Psychology and law: The state of the discipline* (pp. 23–52). New York: Kluwer Academic/Plenum.

Nizer, L. (1961). *My life in court.* New York: Pyramid.

Notes and Comments. (1968). On instructing deadlocked juries. *Yale Law Journal, 78,* 100–142.

O'Barr, W. M. (1982). *Linguistic evidence: Language, power, and strategy in the courtroom.* San Diego, CA: Academic.

O'Connor, S. D. (2003). *The majesty of the law: Reflections of a Supreme Court justice.* New York: Random House.

Ogle, J. (1999, November 3). Survey to determine if prejudice exists in murder case. *Hays Daily News,* p. 1.

Olczak, P. V., Kaplan, M. F., & Penrod, S. (1991). Attorneys' lay psychology and its effectiveness in selecting jurors: Three empirical studies. *Journal of Social Behavior and Personality, 6,* 431–452.

Oliver, E. (1998). Testing, testing. *Trial Diplomacy Journal, 21,* 399–409.

Olsen-Fulero, L., & Fulero, S. (1997). Commonsense rape judgments: An empathy-complexity theory of rape juror story making. *Psychology, Public Policy, and Law, 3,* 402–427.

Olson, W. K. (1991). *The litigation explosion: What happened when America unleashed the lawsuit.* New York: Dutton.

Opening statements: Setting the stage for victory. (1998). *Trial, 34,* 66–77.

Patton v. Yount, 467 U.S. 1025 (1984).

Patton, G. W. R., & Kaericher, C. E. (1980). Effect of characteristics of the candidate on voter's preference. *Psychological Reports, 47,* 171–180.

Pennington, N., & Hastie, R. (1981). Juror decision-making models: The generalization gap. *Psychological Bulletin, 89,* 246–287.

Pennington, N., & Hastie, R. (1988). Explanation-based decision making: Effects of memory structure on judgment. *Journal of Experimental Psychology: Learning, Memory, and Cognition, 14,* 521–533.

Pennington, N., & Hastie, R. (1992). Explaining the evidence: Tests of the story model for juror decision making. *Journal of Personality and Social Psychology, 62,* 189–206.

Pennington, N., & Hastie, R. (1994) The story model for juror decision making. In R. Hastie (Ed.), *Inside the juror* (pp. 192–224). New York: Cambridge University Press.

Penrod, S. D. (1979). *Study of attorney and "scientific" jury selection models.* Unpublished doctoral dissertation, Harvard University.

People v. Gainer, 19 Cal. 3d 835 (1977).

People v. Randall, 9 N.Y. 2d 413 (1961).

Perlman, P. (1994). The compelling opening statement: Two-minute markers. *Trial, 30,* 64–68.

Perry, N. W., & Wrightsman, L. S. (1991). *The child witness: Legal issues and dilemmas.* Newbury Park, CA: Sage.

Peskin, S. H. (1980). Nonverbal communication in the courtroom. *Trial Diplomacy Journal, 3,* 4–5.

Petty, R. E., & Cacioppo, J. T. (1979). Issue involvement can increase or decrease persuasion by enhancing message-relevant cognitive responses. *Journal of Personality and Social Psychology, 37,* 1915–1926.

Piorkowski, J. D., Jr. (1987). Professional conduct and the preparation of witnesses for trial: Defining the acceptable limitations of "coaching." *Georgetown Journal of Legal Ethics, 1,* 389–410.

Pitera, M. J. (1995, April). *Jury selection: Two perspectives.* Unpublished manuscript, Department of Psychology, University of Kansas, Lawrence.

Pollock, A. (1977). The use of public opinion polls to obtain changes of venue and continuances in criminal trials. *Criminal Justice Journal, 1,* 269–288.

Posey, A. J. (2002, March). *Appellate decisions in change of venue cases: No luck the second time around.* Poster session presented at the biennial meeting of the American Psychology-Law Society, Austin, TX.

Posey, A. J., & Dahl, L. M. (2002). Beyond pretrial publicity: Legal and ethical issues associated with change of venue surveys. *Law and Human Behavior, 26,* 107–125.

Pratkanis, A. R., Greenwald, A. G., Leippe, M. R., & Baumgardner, M. H. (1988). In search of reliable persuasion effects: III. The sleeper effect is dead: Long live the sleeper effect. *Journal of Personality and Social Psychology, 54,* 203–218.

Pyszczynski, T. A., Greenberg, J., Mack, D., & Wrightsman, L. S. (1981). Opening statements in a jury trial: The effect of promising more than the evidence can show. *Journal of Applied Social Psychology, 11,* 434–444.

Pyszczynski, T. A., & Wrightsman, L. S. (1981). The effects of opening statements on mock jurors' verdicts in a simulated criminal trial. *Journal of Applied Social Psychology, 11,* 301–313.

Qualitative Research Consultants Association. (2003, April). *Professional competencies of qualitative research consultants.* Retrieved August 1, 2003, from http://www.qrca.org.

Raitz, A., Greene, E., Goodman, J., & Loftus, E. F. (1990). Determining damages: The influence of expert testimony on jurors' decision making. *Law and Human Behavior, 14,* 385–395.

Reed, J. P. (1965). Jury deliberations, voting, and verdict trends. *Southwest Social Science Quarterly, 45,* 361–370.

Reilly, R. (1991, September 23). Somebody, please, postpone the fight: One man's opinion. *Sports Illustrated, 75*(13), 36–39.

Reskin, B. F., & Visher, C. A. (1986). The impacts of evidence and extralegal factors in jurors' decisions. *Law and Society Review, 20,* 423–438.

Rideau v. Louisiana, 373 U.S. 663 (1963).

Rieke, R. D. (1971). *The role of argument in the trial at law.* Paper presented at the meeting of the Speech Communication Association, San Francisco, CA.

Rieke, R. D., & Stutman, R. K. (1990). *Communication in legal advocacy.* Columbia: University of South Carolina Press.

Robbennolt, J. K. (2002). Punitive damage decision making: The decisions of citizens and court judges. *Law and Human Behavior, 26,* 315–341.

Robbennolt, J. K., & Studebaker, C. A. (1999). Anchoring in the courtroom: The effects of caps on punitive damages. *Law and Human Behavior, 23,* 353–373.

Robbennolt, J. K., & Studebaker, C. A. (2003). News media reporting on civil litigation and its influence on civil justice decision making. *Law and Human Behavior, 27,* 5–27.

Robinette, P. R. (1999). *Differential treatment of corporate defendants as a form of actor identity and evaluator expectations.* Unpublished doctoral dissertation, Department of Communication Studies, University of Kansas, Lawrence.

Rose, M. R. (1999). The peremptory challenge accused of race or gender discrimination? Some data from one county. *Law and Human Behavior, 23,* 695–702.

Roth, M. P. (1986). *The juror and the general.* New York: Morrow.

Rothwax, H. J. (1996). *The collapse of criminal justice.* New York: Random House.

Rozen, M., & Jeffries, B. S. (2002, July 3). Twelve frustrated jurors. *Texas Lawyer, 21,* 1.

"Rule 32.03," 1 Missouri Court Rules: State Courts, 187 (2003).

Ryan, H. (2004, January 9). *Judge rules to move Scott Peterson's trial from Modesto.* Retrieved January 13, 2004, from http://courttv.com/trials/peterson/010704_venue_ctv.html.

Saks, M. (1976a). The limits of scientific jury selection: Ethical and empirical. *Jurimetrics Journal, 17,* 3–22.

Saks, M. J. (1976b, January). Social scientists can't rig juries. *Psychology Today,* pp. 48–50, 55–57.

Saks, M. J. (1977). *Jury verdicts: The role of group size and social decision rule.* Lexington, MA: Lexington Books.

Salmi, L. R. (1999). Don't walk the line: Ethical considerations in preparing witnesses for deposition and trial. *Review of Litigation, 18,* 135–179.

Saltzburg, S. A., Martin, M. M., & Capra, D. J. (1998a). *Federal rules of evidence manual: Vol. 3* (7th ed.). Charlottesville, VA: Lexis.

Saltzburg, S. A., Martin, M. M., & Capra, D. J. (1998b). *Federal rules of evidence manual: Vol. 2* (7th ed.). Charlottesville, VA: Lexis.

Santivasci, M. (1993). Change of venue in criminal trials: Should trial courts be required to consider demographic factors when choosing a new location for a criminal trial? *Dickinson Law Review, 98,* 107–132.

Schachter, S. (1951). Deviation, rejection, and communication. *Journal of Abnormal and Social Psychology, 46,* 190–207.

Scheflin, A. W. (1977). Book review [Ginger, *Jury Selection in Criminal Trials,* and Timothy, *Jury Woman*]. *Santa Clara University Law Review, 17,* 247–265.

Scheflin, A. W. (1995). Legal commentary on the diary. In H. Thornton, *Hung jury: The diary of a Menendez juror* (pp. 131–164). Philadelphia: Temple University Press.

Schlenker, B. R. (1980). *Impression management: The self-concept, social identity and interpersonal relations.* Monterey, CA: Brooks/Cole.

Schuetz, J., & Snedaker, K. H. (1988). *Communication and litigation: Case studies of famous trials.* Carbondale: Southern Illinois University Press.

Schuller, R. A., & Hastings, P. A. (1996). Trials of battered women who kill: The impact of alternative forms of expert evidence. *Law and Human Behavior, 20,* 167–187.

Schulman, J., Shaver, P., Colman, R., Emrich, B., & Christie, R. (1973, May). Recipe for a jury. *Psychology Today,* pp. 37–44, 77–84.

Schulman, J., Shaver, P., Colman, R., Emrich, B., & Christie, R. (1987). Recipe for a jury. In L. S. Wrightsman, S. M. Kassin, & C. Willis (Eds.), *In the jury box: Controversies in the courtroom* (pp. 13–47). Newbury Park, CA: Sage.

Schütz, A. (1998). Audience perceptions of politicians' self-presentational behaviors concerning their own abilities. *Journal of Social Psychology, 138,* 173–188.

Seibert, F. S. (1970). Trial judges' opinions on prejudicial publicity. In C. R. Bush (Ed.), *Free press and fair trial: Some dimensions of the problem* (pp. 1–35). Athens: University of Georgia Press.

Seltzer, R., Venuti, M., & Lopes, G. (1991). Juror honesty during the voir dire. *Journal of Criminal Justice, 19,* 451–462.

Severance, L. J., & Loftus, E. F. (1982). Improving the ability of jurors to comprehend and apply criminal jury instructions. *Law and Society Review, 17,* 153–197.

Sheldon, A. (2004, Winter). Give it away! *Court Call, 20.* Retrieved June 13, 2004, from http://www.astcweb.org/courtcall/print_story.lasso?article_id=20000111.

Sheldon, A. M. (2000, Fall). Standards make a profession. *Court Call, 1–2,* 3.

Sheppard v. Maxwell, 384 U.S. 333 (1966).

Sherif, M., & Hovland, C. (1961). *Social judgment.* New Haven, CT: Yale University Press.

Simon, R. J., & Mahan, L. (1971). Quantifying burdens of proof: A view from the bench, the jury, and the classroom. *Law and Society Review, 5,* 319–330.

Sinclair v. United States, 279 U.S. 749 (1929).

Singer, A. (1996a, April). Selecting jurors: What to do about bias. *Trial, 21,* 28.

Singer, A. (1996b). Focusing on jury focus groups. *Trial Diplomacy Journal, 19,* 321–330.

Small, D. I. (1998). *Preparing witnesses: A practical guide for lawyers and their clients.* Chicago: American Bar Association.

Smith, J. D. (1991). The advocate's use of social science research into verbal and nonverbal communication: Zealous advocacy or unethical conduct? *Military Law Review, 134,* 173–193.

Smith, L. (1981). *The art of advocacy.* New York: Bender.

Smith, V. L. (1991). Impact of pretrial instruction on jurors' information processing and decision making. *Journal of Applied Psychology, 76,* 220–226.

Smith, V. L., & Kassin, S. M. (1993). Effects of the dynamite charge on the deliberations of deadlocked mock jurors. *Law and Human Behavior, 17,* 625–643.

Smothers, R. (1994, February 1). Jurors are told of racial views in Evers killing. *New York Times,* p. A12.

Sommer, R., & Sommer, B. (2002). *A practical guide to behavioral research: Tools and techniques* (5th ed.). New York: Oxford University Press.

Spanos, N. P., Quigley, C. A., Gwynn, M. I., Glatt, R. I., & Perlini, A. H. (1991). Hypnotic interrogation, pretrial preparation, and witness testimony during direct and cross-examination. *Law and Human Behavior, 15,* 639–653.

Spiecker, S. C., & Worthington, D. L. (2003). The influence of opening statement/ closing argument organizational strategy on juror verdict and damage awards. *Law and Human Behavior, 27,* 437–456.

Stallard, M. J., & Worthington, D. L. (1998). Reducing the hindsight bias utilizing attorney closing arguments. *Law and Human Behavior, 22,* 671–683.

Stanford v. Kentucky, 492 U.S. 361 (1989).

Stans, M. H. (1978). *The terrors of justice: The untold side of Watergate.* New York: Everest House.

Stapley, G. (2004, January 15). *Pollster told to be in court.* Retrieved January 21, 2004, from http://www.modbee.com/reports/peterson/prelim/v-print/story/8011973p8876559c.html.

Stapley, G., & Cote, J. (2004, January 9). *Allegations arise in Peterson trial survey.* Retrieved January 13, 2004, from http://www.modbee.com/local/story/7981057p-8852389c.html.

Starr, V. H. (1983). From the communication profession: Communication strategies and research needs on opening statements and closing arguments. In R. J. Matlon & R. J. Crawford (Eds.), *Communication strategies in the practice of lawyering* (pp. 424–448). Annandale, VA: Speech Communication Association.

Stasser, G., Kerr, N. L., & Bray, R. M. (1982). The social psychology of jury deliberations: Structure, process, and product. In N. L. Kerr & R. Bray (Eds.), *The psychology of the courtroom* (pp. 221–256). Orlando, FL: Academic.

State v. Smart (N.H. 1991/1993), aff'd. 622A. 2d 1197 (N.H. 1993).

State Farm Mutual v. Campbell, 123 S.Ct. 1965 (2003).

Steblay, N. M., Besirevic, J., Fulero, S. M., & Jimenez-Lorente, B. (1999). The effects of pretrial publicity on juror verdicts: A meta-analytic review. *Law and Human Behavior, 23,* 219–235.

Stephan, F., & Mishler, E. (1952). The distribution of participation in small groups: An exponential approximation. *American Sociological Review, 17,* 598–608.

Stewart, J. B. (1998, March 30). The bench. *New Yorker,* p. 43.

Stolle, D. P., Robbennolt, J. K, & Wiener, R. (1996). The perceived fairness of the psychologist trial consultant: An empirical investigation. *Law and Psychology Review, 20,* 139–173.

Storms, M. D. (1973). Videotape and the attribution process: Reversing actors' and observers' points of view. *Journal of Personality and Social Psychology, 27,* 165–175.

Strier, F. (1998, March). *The future of trial consulting: Issues and projections.* Paper presented at the meetings of the American Psychology-Law Society, Redondo Beach, CA.

Strier, F. (1999). Whither trial consulting: Issues and projections. *Law and Human Behavior, 23,* 93–115.

Strier, F. (2001). Why trial consultants should be licensed. *Journal of Forensic Psychology Practice, 1*(4), 77–85.

Strodtbeck, F., & Mann, R. (1956). Sex role differentiation in jury deliberations. *Sociometry, 19,* 3–11.

Studebaker, C. A., & Penrod, S. D. (1997). Pretrial publicity: The media, the law, and common sense. *Psychology, Public Policy, and Law, 3,* 428–460.

Sue, S., Smith, R. E., & Pedroza, G. (1975). Authoritarianism, pretrial publicity and awareness of bias in simulated jurors. *Psychological Reports, 37,* 1299–1302.

Sunstein, C. R., Hastie, R., Payne, J. W., Schkade, D. A., & Viscusi, W. K. P. (2002). *Punitive damages: How juries decide.* Chicago: University of Chicago Press.

Swain v. Alabama, 380 U.S. 202 (1965).

Sweet, C. (2000, Fall). Anatomy of an online focus group. *Court Call, 1–2,* 4–5.

Tanford, S., & Cox, M. (1988). The effects of impeachment evidence and limiting instructions on individual and group decision making. *Law and Human Behavior, 12,* 477–497.

Taylor, S. E., & Crocker, J. (1981). Schematic bases of social information processing. In E. T. Higgins, C. P. Herman, & M. P. Zanna (Eds.), *Social cognition: The Ontario symposium: Vol. 1* (pp. 89–134). Hillsdale, NJ: Erlbaum.

Thistlethwaite, D. L., De Hann, H., & Kamenetzky, J. (1955). The effects of "directive" and "nondirective" communication procedures on attitudes. *Journal of Abnormal and Social Psychology, 51,* 107–113.

Thomas, E. (1991). *The man to see: Edward Bennett Williams, ultimate insider, legendary trial lawyer.* New York: Simon and Schuster.

Thornton, H. (1995). *Hung jury: The diary of a Menendez juror.* Philadelphia: Temple University Press.

Timothy, M. (1974). *Jury woman.* Palo Alto, CA: Emty.

Title 45, Code of Federal Regulations, Department of Health and Human Services, Part 46, Protection of human subjects (45 CFR 46), Section 46.116 (1991).

Toobin, J. (1994, October 31). Juries on trial. *New Yorker,* pp. 42–47.

Toobin, J. (1996). *The run of his life.* New York: Simon & Schuster.

Torry, S. (1994, November 14). Their job is ensuring jury isn't twelve angry people. *Washington Business,* p. 34.

Traver, R. (1958). *Anatomy of a murder.* New York: St. Martin's.

Trillin, C. (1995, May 29). State secrets. *New Yorker,* pp. 54–64.

Turner, M. (2004, September 10). *Stan State professor who oversaw juror bias survey is put on paid leave.* Retrieved September 29, 2004, from http://www.modbee.com/local/v-print/story/9121583p-10021578c.html.

Tversky, A., & Kahneman, D. (1974). Judgment under uncertainty: Heuristics and biases. *Science, 185,* 1124–1131.

Twiggs, H. F. (1994, September). Do-it-yourself focus groups: Big benefits, modest cost. *Trial, 30,* 42–47.

Underwood, B. J. (1957). Interference and forgetting. *Psychological Review, 64,* 49–60.

United States v. Brown, 2d Cir., No. 02–1135 (2003).

United States v. Costello, 255 F.2d 876 (2d Cir.), cert. denied, 357 U.S. 937 (1958).

United States v. DeJesus, 347 F.3d 500 (2003).

United States v. Dorsey, 865 F.2d 1275 (1989).

United States v. Kenner, 354 F.2d 780 (1965).

United States v. McVeigh and Nichols, 918 F. Supp. 1467 (1996).

United States v. Smith, 857 F.2d 682 (1988).

Universal Camera Corp. v. N.L.R.B., 340 U.S. 474 (1951).

Van Voris, B. (1997, October 13). Client memo embarrasses Dallas firm. *National Law Journal, 19,* pp. A1, A30.

Vidmar, N. (1995). *Medical malpractice and the American jury: Confronting the myths about jury incompetence, deep pockets, and outrageous damage awards.* Ann Arbor: University of Michigan Press.

Vidmar, N. (1999a). The Canadian criminal jury: Searching for a middle ground. *Law and Contemporary Problems, 62,* 141–172.

Vidmar, N. (1999b). Foreword. *Law and Contemporary Problems, 62,* 1–5.

Vidmar, N. (2002). Case studies of pre- and midtrial prejudice in criminal and civil litigation. *Law and Human Behavior, 26,* 73–105.

Villasenor, V. (1977). *Jury: The people versus Juan Corona.* Boston: Little, Brown.

Vinson, D. E. (1986). *Jury trials: The psychology of winning strategy.* Charlottesville, VA: Michie.

Vinson, D. E., & Davis, D. S. (1996). *Jury persuasion: Psychological strategies and trial techniques.* Little Falls, NJ: Glasser Legalworks.

Visher, C. A. (1987). Juror decision making: The importance of evidence. *Law and Human Behavior, 11,* 1–18.

Walker, G. (1995, October 22). Lawyers must show restraint if our jury system is to survive. *Boston Herald,* p. 34.

Weiser, A., & Latiolais-Hargrave, J. (2000). *Judge the jury.* Dubuque, IA: Kendall/ Hunt.

Weiss, W., & Steenbock, S. (1965). The influence on communication effectiveness of explicitly urging action and policy consequences. *Journal of Experimental Social Psychology, 1,* 396–406.

Weld, H. P., & Danzig, E. R. (1940). A study of the way in which a verdict is reached by a jury. *American Journal of Psychology, 53,* 518–536.

Wells, G. L., Ferguson, T. J., & Lindsay, R. C. L. (1981). The tractability of witness confidence and its implications for triers of fact. *Journal of Applied Psychology, 66,* 688–696.

Wells, G. L., Miene, P. K., & Wrightsman, L. S. (1985). The timing of the defense opening statement: Don't wait until the evidence is in. *Journal of Applied Social Psychology, 15,* 758–772.

Wenner, D. A. (1998, January). Preparing for trial, an uncommon approach: The trial lawyer can use focus groups to flag potential juror reactions and prepare effective arguments for trial. *Trial, 34,* 62–70.

Werner, C. M., Strube, M. J., Cole, A. M., & Kagehiro, D. K. (1985). The impact of case characteristics and prior jury experience on jury verdicts. *Journal of Applied Social Psychology, 15,* 409–427.

Whellan, M. (1990). What's happened to due process among the states? Pretrial publicity and motions for change of venue in criminal proceedings. *American Journal of Criminal Law, 17,* 175–193.

Whitcomb, D. (2003, July 24). *Judge issues partial gag order in Kobe Bryant case.* Retrieved September 12, 2003, from http://ca.sports.yahoo.com/030725/5/ ul96.html.

Wiggins, E., & Breckler, S. (1990). Special verdicts as guides to decision making. *Law and Psychology Review, 14,* 1–41.

Williams, K. D., Bourgeois, M. J., & Croyle, R. T. (1993). The effects of stealing thunder in criminal and civil trials. *Law and Human Behavior, 17,* 597–609.

Winthrop, Stimson, Putnam, & Roberts (law firm). (1990). *Witness preparation guidelines.* New York: Author.

Wissler, R. L., Hart, A. J., & Saks, M. J. (1999). Decision-making about general damages: A comparison of jurors, judges, and lawyers. *Michigan Law Review, 98,* 751–826.

Woodward, J. (1952). A scientific attempt to provide evidence for a decision on change of venue. *American Sociological Review, 17,* 447–452.

Wrightsman, L. S. (2001). *Forensic psychology.* Belmont, CA: Wadsworth.

Wrightsman, L. S., & Heili, A. (1992, September). *Working paper: Measuring bias in civil trials.* Unpublished paper, Department of Psychology, University of Kansas, Lawrence.

Wrightsman, L. S., & Posey, A. J. (1995). Psychological commentary on the diary. In H. Thornton, *Hung jury: The diary of a Menendez juror* (pp. 99–130). Philadelphia: Temple University Press.

Wydick, R. C. (1995). The ethics of witness coaching. *Cardozo Law Review, 17,* 1–52.

Younger, I. (1976). *The art of cross-examination.* Chicago: American Bar Association.

Zander, M. (1974). Are too many professional criminals avoiding conviction? A study of Britain's two busiest courts. *Modern Law Review, 37,* 28–61.

Zaragoza, M. S., & Lane, S. M. (1994). Source misattributions and the suggestibility of eyewitness memory. *Journal of Experimental Psychology: Learning, Memory, and Cognition, 20,* 934–945.

Zeisel, H., & Diamond, S. S. (1976). The jury selection in the Mitchell-Stans conspiracy trial. *American Bar Foundation Research Journal, 1976*(1), 151–174.

Zeisel, H., & Diamond, S. S. (1978). The effect of peremptory challenges on jury and verdict: An experiment in a federal district court. *Stanford Law Review, 30,* 491–529.

Zimbardo, P. G., & Lieppe, M. R. (1991). *The psychology of attitude change and social influence.* New York: McGraw-Hill.

Zuckerman, M., DePaulo, B. M., & Rosenthal, R. (1981). Verbal and nonverbal communication of deception. *Advances in Experimental Social Psychology, 14,* 1–59.

Author Index

Subject Index

Advocate versus researcher, 70–71
Allen charge, 146–149
Allen v. United States, 144
Alterman, Kate, 48
American Association of Public Opinion
    Research, 74, 88
American Bar Association
    on hung juries, 148–149
    standards on cross-examination, 112
American Society of Trial Consultants (ASTC)
    on change-of-venue surveys, 68–69, 222–223
    on coaching witnesses, 49
    criminal versus civil cases and, 6–7, 53
    formation of, 7
    Grievance Committee of, 231
    journal of, 7
    licensing and certification by, 23, 68, 232–233
    membership of, 5, 6
    optimism in, 4
    Pro Bono Committee of, 228
    purposes of, 7
    Research Committee of, 229
    set of ethical principles by, 22–23, 49, 69, 207
    standards and guidelines for, 19, 23, 49, 68–69,
        75, 79, 87–89, 94, 207, 224–225, 229–230,
        231, 233
    survey of members, 6–7, 79
    Web site of, 7, 231
Anatomy of a Murder, 37–38
Anchoring and adjustment heuristic,
    136–137, 142
Antiauthoritarianism, 161, 162
Anti-plaintiff bias, 170–171

Arthur Andersen trial, 197–198
Asbestos-injury lawsuits, 34
Ashland Oil case, 93–94
Assimilation versus contrast, 137
Attitudes
    toward business regulation, 171
    about civil litigation, 171
    toward corporations, 171–172
    toward death penalty, 204
    toward the "litigation explosion," 170
    about personal responsibility,
        170–171
    as predictors of verdicts, 159, 162, 163, 165,
        166, 168, 169, 177, 201, 203–204
    toward risk taking, 170
    about standard of care, 170
Attitudes toward Corporations Scale, 171–172
Attorney work product, 210
Attorneys. *See* Lawyers
Authoritarianism
    in jurors, 158, 159, 160, 162
    and verdicts, 162–163, 165

Bailey, F. Lee, 199
Baron and Budd law firm, 34, 35
Batson v. Kentucky, 220
Beckwith, Byron. *See* de la Beckwith, Byron
Belli, Melvin, 199
Bennett, William, 28
Berrigan brothers, 174, 175, 176, 177, 181, 182
Bias
    antiplaintiff, 159, 170
    in civil trials, 159, 169–170